Sustaining the Future

Activities for Environmental Education in U. S. History

Jeffrey L. Brown
Editor

Global Learning, Inc.
1018 Stuyvesant Avenue, Union NJ 07083, (908) 964-1114
1995

ISBN 0-928630-03-X

Credits

Cover artwork adapted from Trina Paulus original

Printing courtesy of **PSE&G** Public Service Electric and Gas Company

Printed on recycled paper in the United States of America

Contents

Global Learning, Inc.

Global Learning, Inc.

Foreword

From world history and cultures to US History, Global Learning has been helping teachers incorporate the global concept of *sustainable development* within social studies and history courses since 1988. The US History and Sustainable Development Project began in early 1993 when we recruited a team of classroom teachers, social studies supervisors, and college professors to help conceptualize and write high school lessons on sustainability for US History. Several of these team members also helped to field test the lessons, along with additional teachers in their schools, in the 1993-94 school year. A number of the piloting teachers then helped draft new lessons.

During field testing, the piloting teachers worked with an external evaluation consultant, Dr. Michael Knight of Kean College of New Jersey, to develop an alternative assessment design, which is described in the last chapter. The design was then implemented in the 1994-95 school year by the participating teachers in the Freehold Regional High School District, and with the active support of James Jannarone, the Administrative Assistant for Curriculum and Instruction. The results of the post tests were not available prior to publication of this volume.

The Geraldine R. Dodge Foundation of Morristown provided generous support over the three year span of this project. We are most grateful for their encouragement and investment in this resource and teacher development. We are also grateful to the Victoria Foundation of Montclair for their assistance in launching this project.

I would like to thank each and every person who made this project possible. The wonderful institution of the Union Public Library provided a meeting room for early meetings of the project team, assistance from their research librarians over numerous questions of detail, and their useful collection of publications. In addition to the aforementioned contributors, lesson authors are appreciatively noted in the table of contents. Two persons particularly helpful with research for two lessons and not noted elsewhere are Martin L. Calhoun, Senior Research Analyst at the Center for Defense Information, and Patrick J. Owens, ARDEC Historian at Picatinny Arsenal. Joy Williams, Global Learning's former secretary, continued to provide word processing from a distance in Indiana. For the third time, Bucky Schnarr skillfully and generously crafted layout and design from his desktop publishing perch. Special thanks to Paula Gotsch, an

essential part of the creative synergy that is Global Learning.
Thank you very much!

US History and Sustainable Development Project Team

Jeffrey Brown, Project Director
Executive Director of Global Learning

Paula Gotsch, Associate Project Director
Associate Director of Global Learning

Fred Cotterell, Social Studies Supervisor
Paramus High School

Thomas Crop, Social Studies Supervisor
Bridgewater-Raritan School District

Richard W. LoPinto, Professor of Biological Sciences
Fairleigh Dickinson University

Joseph T. Moore, Professor of History & Social Studies Education
Montclair State University

Linda Whalen Murchio, Teacher
Freehold Township High School

John Opie, Chair, Social Science and Policy Studies Department
New Jersey Institute of Technology

Piloting Teachers and Schools

Freehold Regional High School District: James Jannarone,
Administrative Assistant for Curriculum and Instruction

Freehold Borough HS	Freehold Township HS
Stanley Koba	Peter Krais
Ellyn Lyons	Linda Whalen Murchio
	Nancy Wallace
Howell Township HS	
Dawn Petry	
Marlboro High School	Manalapan High School
John Murray	Thomas Reinhart
Robert Sylvestri	

Bridgewater-Raritan HS	Paramus High School
Thomas Crop	Fred Cotterell
Sara Eisenberg	Patricia Crompton
Daniel Mahony	
Jack Ruhl	Vineland High School
	Drusilla Lafferty

Three teachers in the Freehold Regional High School District—
Donna Evangelista, Bernard Olsen and Robin Reilly—
collaborated with the project by serving as "control" teachers
during the assessment phase. They administered a pre- and a
post-test, but did not teach any of the lessons to their classes.

Jeffrey L. Brown
Project Director

Introduction to Sustainability

What's the life expectancy of Uncle Sam? Will he live forever? Has he reached middle age yet? Does he have any symptoms of terminal illnesses? Is he robust and healthy and of good genetic stock? Has he squandered his resources and befouled his nest beyond repair?

Such is the question of sustainability addressed to the United States. As a culture, we are known for our presentism, our lack of historical perspective. Perhaps we have taught history for so long as if it doesn't matter that we have concluded it doesn't. Or perhaps our traditional skepticism has been reinforced by having so many so-called lessons of history backfire on our political leaders.

But there is a mood and movement afoot in this country today to reassert the importance of learning from our past. These are often coupled with a call to recognize how, in a tightly woven, ultimately sensitive global context, we are also creating the future—whether by our actions or our inaction. This mood and movement challenge us not only to clarify, but to assert our positive values, to identify and to solve our problems, and in the best tradition of our belief in progress, to grow into our responsible fullness as a diverse society.

Secondary students—full adults in many traditional societies— can have their motivation activated and their minds engaged by the question of sustainability. Teachers who have piloted these and other lessons on sustainable development report that students don't want to stop discussing the issues. Students actively engage in role playing, complete their research, argue their perspectives, organize extracurricular activities to make a difference.

The subtitle of this book is *Activities for Environmental Education in US History*—but the environment is viewed within the context of the relatively new concept of sustainable development. First given widespread attention in *Our Common Future,* the 1987 report of the United Nations Commission on Environment and Development to the General Assembly, and then boosted by the Earth Summit, the UN Conference on Environment and Development in Rio de Janeiro in 1992, sustainable development has been defined as "development that meets the needs of the present without compromising the ability of future generations to meet their needs."

Sustainable development contains within it three major elements—the **environment**, **development** and **equity**. What may enable Uncle Sam—and the world's people—to meet broad-based needs in a sustainable way over the coming generations is increased understanding of how these three elements are not isolated from one another, but are interconnected. As the World Commission on Environment and Development has noted:

> Through our deliberations and the testimony of people at the public hearings we held on five continents, all the commissioners came to focus on one central theme: many present development trends leave increasing numbers of people poor and vulnerable, while at the same time degrading the environment. How can such development serve next century's world of twice as many people relying on the same environment? This realization broadened our view of development. **We came to see it not in its restricted context of economic growth in developing countries. We came to see that a new development path was required, one that sustained human progress not just in a few places for a few years, but for the entire planet into the distant future. Thus "sustainable development" becomes a goal not just for the "developing" nations, but for industrial ones as well.**
>
> (Our Common Future, p.4—emphasis added)

Three lessons emerge from the interrelationships of the environment, development and equity. *First,* **the traditional relationship between the environment and the economy in industrialized societies like the United States is being reversed.** Instead of pursuing economic activities of production and distribution as primary and looking at the consumption of natural resources and the impacts on the environment as incidental, we humans are beginning to realize *we must put the environment first*. This means committing ourselves to conserving resources even as we use them. It also means including the environmental "costs" of an economic activity as integral to the overall costs of that activity, not treating them as a "by-product" or an afterthought to be cleaned up. "Thus economics and ecology must be completely integrated in decision-making and lawmaking processes not just to protect the environment, but also to protect and promote development." (OCF, p.37) If we do not do these things, we will deplete nonrenewable resources like petroleum or the biological diversity of the rainforests so that future generations will be deprived of

Global Learning, Inc.

their benefits. We could also alter the biosphere so as to threaten the continuation of human—and other—life itself.

A *second* lesson has emerged as well. **The processes by which people meet their needs can be called *development*.** Thus examination of a country's "development" includes not just **economic** processes and institutions, but also **cultural**, **social** and **political processes**. These processes and their institutions have evolved historically, are all interrelated, and are all nested in global systems.

Third, **the concept of equity refers in general to achieving social justice.** Within the context of sustainable development, equity refers to **the goal of eliminating poverty in the world**, and particularly eliminating the gap between rich and poor countries that has been growing wider for decades, if not for centuries. "A world in which poverty and inequity are endemic will always be prone to ecological and other crises." (OCF, p.44) Thus sustainable development affirms that the primary goal of the broad processes of development should be the elimination of poverty.

There are at least three reasons why the rich should not be getting richer while the poor get poorer. First, reducing the amount of human suffering in the world requires the end of abject poverty. Second, poverty creates conflict and instability, which can lead to social unrest, repression and violence. Social and political systems cannot be sustained in the long run if they rest on such unstable foundations. "...relationships that are unequal and based on dominance of one kind or another are not a sound and durable basis for interdependence." (OCF, p.67) Third, poverty also adds tremendous stress to the already beleaguered environment as poor people use resources and pollute their surroundings despite the long term consequences because their immediate needs are so severe. There is no consensus in the world community on how to achieve this goal of eliminating poverty in the world. However, within the framework of sustainable development, present and proposed actions should be evaluated, in part, on how they will contribute to, or detract from, this goal of equity, as well as for their total impact on the environment.

The activities in this book apply this trifocal lens of sustainability to the history of the United States. This of course is not a comprehensive history of the country, but rather a modest collection of supplemental resources. Historical events and topics frequently "covered" by classroom teachers have been selected to help the teachers to decide to utilize the activities. Often connections with contemporary concerns have been made explicit to engage students in the challenging task of applying lessons of history today. Effort has been made to limit the initial number of class periods for any lesson, with extension activities also included so greater attention can be paid to the topics if time does permit.

What's Uncle Sam's prognosis? If today's students raise, research, discuss, debate, explore, and act upon the question of sustainability, we believe future generations will have a go at the question, too!

Reference

World Commission on Environment and Development. *Our Common Future.* New York: Oxford University Press, 1987.

Recommended Supplementary Resources

Earth and the American Dream is a video broadcast by HBO in 1994 to tell "the story of the American Dream and the price the environment paid for that dream." Ten ten-minute segments provide excellent discussion starters across the breadth of US History. The video is available from Direct Cinema, P.O. Box 10003, Santa Monica, CA 90410; 800-525-0000. Call HBO to see if it will be rebroadcast, too.

Carolyn Merchant's *Major Problems in American Environmental History* (Lexington, MA: D.C. Heath & Co., 1993) is an excellent source of original source materials and background essays.

The 1994 Information Please Environmental Almanac is compiled by World Resources Institute and is published by Houghton Mifflin Company (Boston and New York, 1994).

World Resources: A Guide to the Global Environment is published biennially by World Resources Institute through Oxford University Press (New York).

Worldwatch Institute publishes *State of the World* annually through W.W. Norton & Co. (New York).

Global Learning, Inc.

Lesson 1

Problem Solving
A Generic Model

One of the main goals of these lessons on sustainable development is to teach students how to become more effective problem solvers. While this goal is often stated in social studies materials, rarely is problem solving addressed explicitly. In historical materials, more often than not, the presentation of dates, places and disembodied events undermines this very goal by making students feel history is an impersonal steamroller.

Throughout these lessons there are many opportunities for students to take the roles of problem solvers, whether in role plays, in analyzing historical problems, in developing a possible solution to a contemporary problem, or in developing an actual plan of action that the students themselves undertake on a local problem. Thus we are providing two versions of a simple six step problem solving process that students, whether individually or in various groupings, can use—one model for historical problems and one for contemporary issues.

It is our goal that students will use this process frequently enough to internalize it as a useful tool for solving problems in any number of settings. Of course, there are times when the teacher may want to focus on only one problem solving skill in a particular lesson, e.g., defining the problem, or generating alternative solutions, rather than using the entire process each lesson.

The six steps involve:

1. defining the problem,
2. generating proposed solutions,
3. evaluating the proposed solutions,
4. choosing from among the alternative solutions,
5. acting on the proposed solution, and
6. evaluating the results.

In the historical model, the steps have been telescoped into four, but all six elements are still there.

Step 1   Defining the problem.

It is often said that a problem well-defined is half-solved. Complex problems such as those involved in sustainable development may be highly controverted and may be based on a combination of data, scientific conjecture, opinions and even hunches. It is important for students to know if statements are based on facts or on opinions, as well as to be able to identify those that follow from various sets of assumptions and differing worldviews. Facts alone will not adequately define or resolve highly complex problems. Thus there is an opportunity for students to learn a variety of approaches for testing truth claims and weighing competing authorities on unprovable subjects.

In addition, in our culture problems are often posed as if there must be a win/lose outcome. If people, however, focus on meeting their various needs and interests instead of achieving a fixed position, win/win solutions are often possible. Thus this model suggests that the problem be defined so as to include all parties' needs and interests.

Step 2   Generating alternative solutions.

Brainstorming is a process that encourages a group to generate a large number of possible alternatives. The rules for brainstorming are designed to encourage full participation by everyone, as well as creativity and divergent thinking. Only after the brainstorming is finished should the group go back over the list and begin to evaluate the ideas that have been generated. This model suggests students work with more than two alternatives at any one time so as to overcome any inclination toward either/or thinking.

Step 3   Evaluating proposed solutions.

We judge possible solutions according to how effective we think they will be in solving the problem in both the short term and the long term. The key questions are, "Will it work, and how will we know if it does work?" We also judge proposed solutions as to whether or not they are consistent with our values. At times the teacher will want the students to generate the criteria by which solutions will be judged and at times the criteria provided will probably suffice. These value criteria have been adapted from *Latin America and the Caribbean from a Global Perspective*, Miami: Florida International University, 1991.

Step 4   Choosing a solution from among the alternatives.

After weighing up the relative strengths and weaknesses of the options, students should decide which alternative to pursue.

Step 5   Implementation.

Students may develop a plan of action that they would like to see someone else implement, e.g., the U.S. Congress, their local planning board, a corporation or an environmental group. Thus their planning would be mostly theoretical and the benefit of the process would primarily be in learning how to go about analyzing a problem and developing an appropriate response to it.

On the other hand, students can use this same problem solving process to develop a plan of action that they themselves undertake. For example, many students concerned about the state of the environment have developed plans to change specific practices in their own school, like eliminating the use of styrofoam in the cafeteria, or their own community, like educating their community about non-point sources of pollution. In this case, the implementation step would include the students' carrying out the actions they have planned.

Step 6   Evaluation.

If the implementation step of this problem solving process has as its learning objective the creation of a theoretical solution that no one actually implements, students, of course, will not be able to evaluate the successes and failures of their plan. However, if the plan is one that gets acted upon, either directly through a student project, or indirectly, for example, by a letter writing campaign to an elected official, students may be able to evaluate their results in the "real" world.

The evaluation step contains several assumptions. One is that problem solving in the real world is a dynamic, not a static, process. Thus, the nature of the problem and the criteria by which one judges the outcomes may change even as one is working on them. Secondly, we view the world as a dynamic system. Within systems—and especially the highly complex ecosystem—things ramify and often have unanticipated consequences. Thus one problem's solutions may well turn into new problems that need to be solved. Problem solving thus is not a cut and dried affair, but an ongoing process.

Whether or not the evaluation step can be applied in the problem solving activities of the students, the teacher will want to bring closure to the classroom use of this process. One way to do so would be to have students write a personal essay on what they liked or disliked in the various proposed plans of action developed by the class. Another activity would be for students to say how they could help see that their plan is implemented.

Problem Solving Model: Historical Period

To analyze historical problems and ways people approached their solution.

1. **Define the problem**
   a. State the problem.
   b. Who were the *parties* involved? What were their *needs* and *interests*?
   c. What *impacts* did the problem have?
   d. What were the *causes* of the problem?
   e. Identify the *facts* regarding the problem.
   f. Identify statements that were *opinions* or *projections* regarding the problem.
   g. What *values* and *assumptions* were involved in this problem?

2. **What solution, if any, was implemented?**
   a. *Who* carried out the solution?
   b. *Where* was it carried out?
   c. *When* was it carried out and how long did it take?
   d. *What resources* were needed and used?
   e. *What obstacles* needed to be overcome?
   f. *How* was the action taken to accomplish the solution?
   g. To what extent did it solve the original problem?
   h. *What consequences*—positive or negative—did the solution have on such areas as:
      • the area's natural resources,
      • the environment (i.e., the biosphere),
      • various groups and classes of people,
      • the political system,
      • the economy?
   i. Which of these consequences were not anticipated ahead of time? What, if anything, was learned from these *unanticipated consequences?*
   j. *What new problems,* if any, did the solution lead to?

3. **Criteria for judging solutions**
   a. Effectiveness
      • How was the impact on the problem measured or felt?
      • To what extent did the solution actually solve the problem?
   b. Values
      The following criteria reflect a democratic, global perspective committed to a sustainable future. They can be answered by statements or by placement on a continuum.

Global Learning, Inc.

Involvement—Those who were directly affected by and involved in the problem were part of the solution.

Not At All 1	2	Somewhat 3	4	Very Much 5

Supporting Evidence:

Equity—The legitimate claims and interests of all parties involved were addressed to their satisfaction.

Not At All 1	2	Somewhat 3	4	Very Much 5

Supporting Evidence:

Focus—Both the short-term consequences and the long-term consequences of the problem were addressed.

Not At All 1	2	Somewhat 3	4	Very Much 5

Supporting Evidence:

Acceptability—The proposed solution took into account any differences in political, economic and cultural values; it was acceptable to those who made the decisions and to those who must live by the decisions.

Not At All 1	2	Somewhat 3	4	Very Much 5

Supporting Evidence:

Affordability—Given the economic and the environmental conditions and capabilities of the times, the solution was realistically affordable.

Not At All 1	2	Somewhat 3	4	Very Much 5

Supporting Evidence:

Other Criteria—

Supporting Evidence:

Global Learning, Inc.

4. What were other possible solutions to this problem?

  a. Brainstorm alternative solutions to the problem. Rules for brainstorming:
- Push for quantity, don't worry about quality.
- All ideas are accepted—everything gets written down.
- No comments, positively or negatively, on anyone else's ideas.
- Say anything that comes to mind, even if it seems silly.
- Think about what others have suggested and use those ideas to get your brain moving along new lines.

  b. Do a preliminary sorting and evaluation of your list. Eliminate any that were not available at this historic period of time due to levels of technology, knowledge etc. Select from 3 to 10 of the best alternative solutions for a more thorough evaluation according to the criteria.

  c. For each of these alternative solutions, what might have been the consequences—positive or negative—on such areas as:
- the area's natural resources,
- the environment (i.e., the biosphere),
- various groups and classes of people,
- the political system,
- the economy?

Problem Solving Model: Contemporary Period

To generate possible solutions to current problems.

1. **Define the problem**
   a. State the problem.
   b. Who are the *parties* involved? What are their *needs* and *interests?*
   c. What *impacts* does the problem have?
   d. What are the *causes* of the problem?
   e. Identify the *facts* regarding the problem.
   f. Identify statements that are *opinions* or *projections* regarding the problem.
   g. What *values* and *assumptions* are involved in this problem?

2. **What are possible solutions?**
   a. Brainstorm alternative solutions to the problem. Rules for brainstorming:
      • Push for quantity, don't worry about quality.
      • All ideas are accepted—everything gets written down.
      • No comments, positively or negatively, on anyone else's ideas.
      • Say anything that comes to mind, even if it seems silly.
      • Think about what others have suggested and use those ideas to get your brain moving along new lines.
   b. Do a preliminary sorting and evaluation of your list. Select no more than your best 10 for a more thorough evaluation according to the criteria.

3. **Criteria for judging solutions**
   a. Effectiveness
      Will the proposed solution solve the problem? How will the impact on the problem be measured or felt?
   b. Values
      The following criteria reflect a democratic, global perspective committed to a sustainable future. They can be answered by statements or by placement on a continuum.

Global Learning, Inc.

Involvement—Those who are directly affected by and involved in the problem were part of the solution.

Not At All 1	2	Somewhat 3	4	Very Much 5

Supporting Evidence:

Equity—The legitimate claims and interests of all parties involved are addressed to their satisfaction.

Not At All 1	2	Somewhat 3	4	Very Much 5

Supporting Evidence:

Focus—Both the short-term consequences and the long-term consequences of the problem are addressed.

Not At All 1	2	Somewhat 3	4	Very Much 5

Supporting Evidence:

Acceptability—The proposed solution took into account any differences in political, economic and cultural values; it is acceptable to those who must make the decisions and to those who must live by the decisions.

Not At All 1	2	Somewhat 3	4	Very Much 5

Supporting Evidence:

Affordability—Given the current economic and environmental conditions and capabilities, the solution is realistically affordable.

Not At All 1	2	Somewhat 3	4	Very Much 5

Supporting Evidence:

Other Criteria—

Supporting Evidence:

Global Learning, Inc.

4. Choose a preferred solution

5. Implementation

Develop a written plan of action (or a public policy position) that answers all of the following questions:

a. *Who* will carry out the solution?

b. *Where* will it be it carried out?

c. *When* will it be it carried out?

d. *What resources* will be needed?

e. *What obstacles* will need to be overcome?

f. *How* will the action be taken to accomplish the solution?

g. What *consequences*—positive and negative—might you expect from the implementation of this plan on such areas as:

- the area's natural resources,
- the environment (i.e., the biosphere),
- various groups and classes of people,
- the political system, the economy?

h. If appropriate, do it.

6. Evaluation

If the plan of action or the policy gets implemented in the "real" world, evaluate its consequences according to the original criteria and any new criteria that have emerged.

a. To what extent did it solve the original problem?

b. What *consequences*—positive or negative—did the solution have on such areas as:

- the area's natural resources,
- the environment (i.e., the biosphere),
- various groups and classes of people,
- the political system,
- the economy ?

c. Which of these consequences were not anticipated ahead of time? What, if anything, was learned from these *unanticipated consequences?*

d. What new problems, if any, did the solution lead to?

Six Step Problem Solving

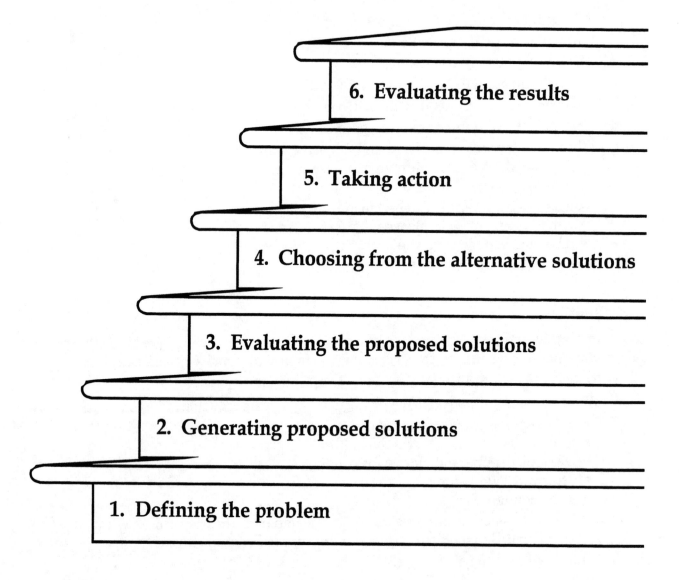

6. Evaluating the results

5. Taking action

4. Choosing from the alternative solutions

3. Evaluating the proposed solutions

2. Generating proposed solutions

1. Defining the problem

Lesson 2

What is Sustainable Development?

The Chair

Historical Period	Any
Sustainable Development Concept	Defining sustainable development
Purpose	To illustrate the definition of sustainable development through the life cycle of a chair.
Objectives	Students will be able to:

1. Define sustainable development.
2. Illustrate the relationships among the three main concepts of the environment, economic development, and equity.

Time Required	1 to 2 class periods
Materials Needed	Handout 1: *A Chair*

Handout 2: *Sustainable Development*

Foils 1 and 2: *Sustainable Development*

For Option B: large sheets of newsprint, multicolored markers, pictures of chairs, reference books or fact sheets

Teacher Background Sustainable development contains within it three major elements—the environment, development and equity. This activity is designed to give a concrete example to the students of the complex relationships among these three elements.

Procedure OPTION A: Whole Class.

1. Place a chair on the teacher's desk or table, or put a large picture of a chair in the middle of the chalkboard.
2. Ask students what materials are needed to make this chair. Write the heading, *Materials needed:*, on the chalkboard and

list students' responses. Include everything from wood to glue to screws or nails, paint or varnish or urethane.

3. To the right of the *Materials needed:* heading, write another heading, *Natural resources:* and ask students, *From what natural resources are these materials made?* List the responses.

4. Next ask, *Which of these natural resources are renewable resources?* <u>Underline the renewable resources with one line.</u>

5. Ask: *Which of these natural resources are recyclable?* <u>Underline the recyclable resources with two lines.</u>

6. Ask: *When this chair is no longer useable or useful, how is it disposed of?* Write responses under the heading of *Disposal.* *What impact does this disposal practice have on the environment?*

7. Discussion questions:

   a. *At what point is it no problem for the environment to make chairs?* (relatively few, using nontoxic materials, have access to renewable resources...)

   b. *At what point can it become a problem for the environment?*

   c. *The environment has been called both* **the source** *and* **the sink.** *What does that expression mean in terms of our chair?* (It's the source of all resources and the place where everything winds up, i.e., the biosphere must absorb all natural and human-made impacts.)

   d. *How would you describe the relationship between the environment and the human activity of making chairs* (i.e., manufacturing or economic development activities)? *What's good for the relationship? What's harmful?*

   e. *How do chairs sometime illustrate differences in wealth, security, access to resources and power?*

   f. *What* **equity** *issues might arise from these differences? i.e., When are these differences equitable or fair, and when are they inequitable?*

8. Distribute **Handout 2: *Sustainable Development*** to each student. Conclude the lesson by displaying the graphic on **Foils 1 and 2** and having the students copy the information onto **Handout 2.**

Procedure   OPTION B: Small Groups.

1. Using magazines or catalogues, cut out pictures of a variety of chairs that represent different costs, social status, and materials, e.g., a wooden kitchen chair, a metal frame chair with foam padding and vinyl covering, a wood and tubular steel student chair with writing surface, a leather covered, padded chair with teakwood frame, a resin chair etc. Or you

can just write descriptions of different chairs on the top of **Handout 1** and have the students draw the chair on their newsprint.

2. Glue each picture onto the center of a large piece of newsprint or butcher paper, 24x36 inches. You will need one sheet per small group.

3. Divide the class into small groups, from 3 to 5 students each. Provide each group with several different colored markers.

4. Give *each student* page 1 of **Handout 1** and *each group of students* one copy of page 2, the suggested layout. Depending on the amount of time available for this activity, let students know they should address at least questions 1, 2, 3, 11, and 12. You may also want to reduce the number of questions on this list.

5. To get the full learning potential from this activity, have some fact sheets or reference books available that answer the questions regarding natural resources, countries of origin, tools and machinery, etc. Another option would be to let some of the group members go to the library to research the unanswered questions and report back to their respective groups.

6. Have each group present its results to the class. Then, using the discussion questions above, conduct a general discussion that clarifies the definition of sustainable development and the interrelationship of **the environment, development,** and **equity.**

7. Distribute **Handout 2** to each student. Conclude the lesson by displaying the graphic on **Foils 1 and 2** and having the students copy the information onto **Handout 2**.

Student Assessment   Students can analyze the cradle to the grave process that the class did with a chair using another object like a pen or a plastic container. Students can also write a short essay on how the concept of sustainable development is different from the stereotype of manufacturers and environmentalists always being antagonistic to each other.

A Chair

Description or picture of this group's chair:

DIRECTIONS:

On your large sheet of newsprint or butcher paper, answer the following questions.

If time is limited, answer as many as you can from your general knowledge, but especially questions 1, 2, 3, 11 and 12. If time and background resources permit, have different members of your group look up answers to some of the questions that you don't already know.

1. What *materials* are needed to make this chair, including its finish?

2. From what *natural resources* are these materials made?

3. If these resources are *renewable,* underline them once. If they are *recyclable,* put parentheses ( ) around them.

4. What are some representative *countries of origin* of these resources?

5. What forms of *transportation* are used to get these materials to the manufacturer and to get the finished products to stores?

6. What *impacts on the environment* do these forms of transportation have?

7. What *tools or machines* are needed to make the chair?

8. What *natural resources* are needed to make these tools and machines?

9. What *energy sources* are used to run these machines?

10. What *impacts* do these energy sources have *on the environment?*

11. When this chair is no longer useable or useful, how is it *disposed* of?

12. What *impact* does this disposal have *on the environment?*

Organize your answers on the large newsprint generally according to the layout on the following page.

If possible, use different color markers to distinguish between headings and answers.

Suggested Layout for Answers

Materials Needed **	Natural Resources **	Countries of Origin

Tools or Machines	Natural Resources for Tools or Machines	
		picture of chair
Energy Sources for Machines	Forms of Transportation used in Manufacturing and Sale of Chair	Disposal of used Chairs **
Impact of Energy Sources on Environment	Impact of Transportation on Environment	Impact of Disposal on Environment **

*** if time is limited, answer these*

Sustainable Development

_____

_____

_____

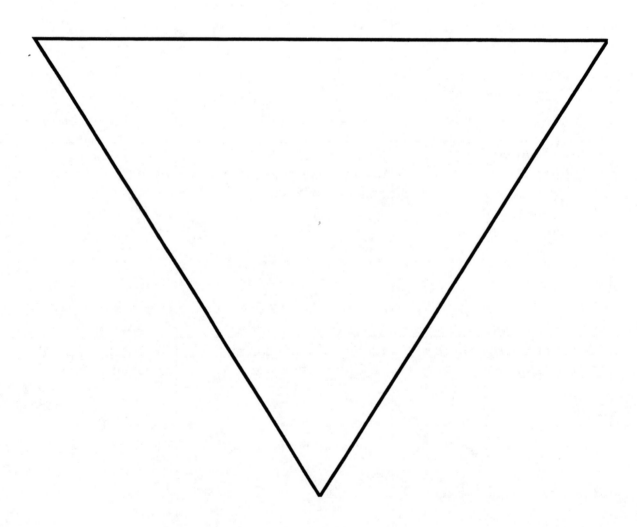

Global Learning, Inc.

Sustainable Development

... meets the needs of the present

without compromising the ability of

future generations to meet their own needs.

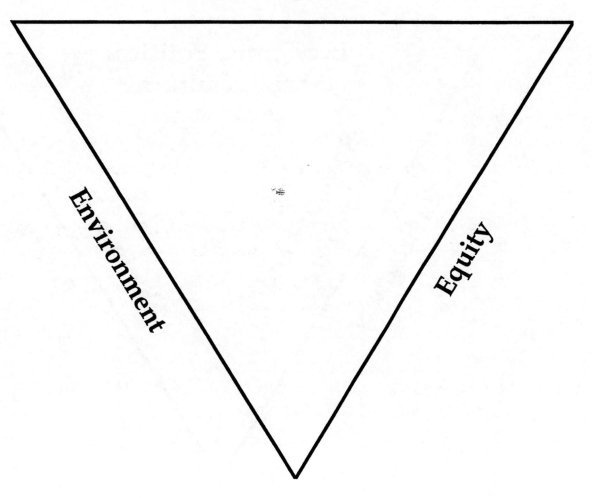

Sustainable Development

... meets the needs of the present

without compromising the ability of

future generations to meet their own needs.

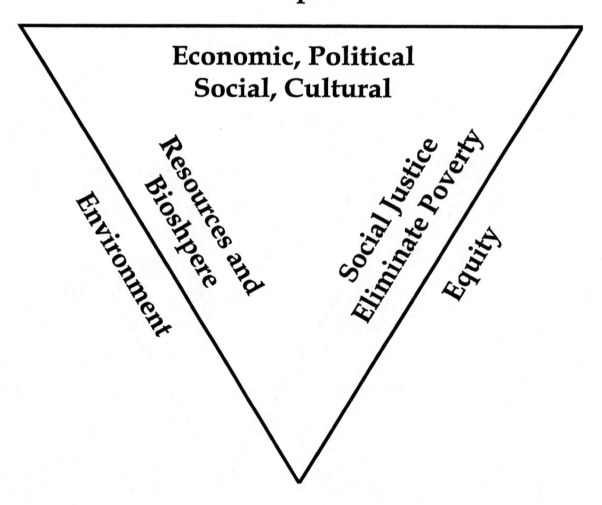

Development

Economic, Political
Social, Cultural

Resources and Bioshpere

Environment

Social Justice
Eliminate Poverty

Equity

Global Learning, Inc.

Lesson 3

How is Sustainable Development Like a Seed?

Historical Period	Recent U.S. (1975-present)
Sustainable Development Topic	Defining sustainable development
Purpose	The purpose of this lesson is to develop a deeper understanding of the concept of sustainable development by changing the perspective from which it is approached. This lesson is recommended as a concluding summary of the topic of sustainable development.
Objectives	Students will be able to:

1. See connections between previously understood and seemingly unrelated concepts and the concept of sustainable development.
2. Use those connections to acquire a deeper understanding of sustainable development.

Time required	One class period
Procedure	

1. Have each student individually generate a list of words which come to mind when she/he thinks about the concept of sustainable development.
2. Have each student share her/his individual list with a partner in an attempt to extend both lists.
3. Write the following analogy on the chalkboard: *How is sustainable development like a seed?*
4. Focus discussion on the concept of a *seed*. Elicit from the students ideas which come to mind when they think of the word seed (seeds are a source of life, each generation of seeds provides a life-link to the past, seeds must be nurtured to

survive, each generation of seeds makes it possible for the next to exist.)

5. Have the students refer back to the lists of words dealing with sustainable development generated at the start of this activity. Discuss with the class how sustainable development is similar to and different from a seed.

6. Record results in columns on the board labeled *Similar* and *Different*.

7. Encourage students to empathize with the concept. Ask students questions to have them feel they are what they are describing: *What would they need if they were a seed? What concerns would they have? What could they accomplish? How would they feel?*

8. Elicit responses and record key words on the board. Select two which are opposites or which seem to be contradictory (like nurture-needy and life-sustaining). Explore the apparent contradiction and establish a bridge to the original topic that allows insight into the essence of the concept.

9. Have students pick out other conflicting words from the board and explain how both are accurate descriptions of the concept.

10. Have students volunteer their own direct analogies and explain the comparison. (How is sustainable development like a diamond? A gift? An inheritance? etc.)

Evaluation Using their new perspectives on sustainable development, students could write poems or essays about the concept, create collages, or otherwise illustrate a conflicting pair of descriptive attributes with a written explanation of the attributes' validity below the illustration.

Global Learning, Inc.

Lesson 4

Early Encounters
Inevitable Conflict Between English Settlers and Native Americans?

Historical Period   Contact and Exchange in the Atlantic World (to 1607)

Sustainable Development Topics   Environment, development, equity

Purpose

1. To examine the interaction between Eastern Woodland Native Americans and Europeans in North America.
2. To assess the impact of that encounter upon each group and ultimately upon the environment.
3. To think critically about the relationship between humans and their environment.

Objectives   Students will be able to:

1. Identify Native American groups and European explorers who might have encountered each other.
2. Describe specific contacts between European explorers and Native Americans.
3. Recognize why trading contacts may have been generally peaceful.
4. Identify differences between "harmony" and "control" attitudes toward the environment.
5. Explain European agricultural technology which reinforced their desire to control their environment.
6. Understand why conflict between English settlers and Native Americans continued.
7. Recognize that the European need to control their environment became the prevailing attitude of the United States regarding use of the land.

Time Required   2 or 3 class periods

Materials Needed	Textbook map on Early European Exploration Routes to North America
	Textbook map on Native American Groups
	Textbook sections on Exploration; Native American Life and Culture
	Additional resource material from library or teacher-selected books
	Handout 1: *How Do Different Cultures Relate To and Interact With the Environment?*
	Handout 2: *What Is a Savage?*
	Handout 3: *Puritan View of Land Ownership*
	Handout 4: *Prophecy of Kate Luckie*

Teacher Background

Too often history textbooks ignore the important fact that there was much contact between Europeans and Eastern Woodland Native Americans for a hundred years. Thus, the lesson for the first day relates to those encounters among explorers, traders and Native American groups. For the most part those relations were peaceful because each side had something the other side wanted or desired, e.g., furs, metal. The lesson for the second day examines the differences in attitudes between the Native Americans and the English settlers concerning use of the land. Indeed, this difference may help explain the resultant conflict between these two groups.

Procedure

Day 1

1. Divide the class into groups representing the regions of New England, Mid-Atlantic and Great Lakes.
2. Using the two maps listed under *Materials Needed,* have each group match individual explorers with Native American groups they might have encountered.
3. Students select several explorers, and by using textbook or other sources, write a one- paragraph description of each explorer's physical contact with one or several of the native groups. If the sources provide adequate information, encourage the students to write a second paragraph about the encounter from the perspective of the native groups.
4. Each group reports on its research.
5. After initial contact and before English settlement, Europeans engaged in trade with Native Americans. Students should speculate on the nature of that encounter between European traders and Native Americans: *Why might such contact have actually been friendly and relatively non-threatening for both groups? What items might have been desired and traded?*
6. English settlers arrived in North America by the early 1600s and built permanent settlements. *Why might these colonists*

who brought their families and built villages come into more conflict with Native Americans than the European traders?

7. Distribute **Handouts 1** and **2** for homework.

Procedure   Day 2

1. Have students re-read the two quotations from **Handout 1**. *What is each saying about the environment?*

2. Using the chalkboard, make a chart with two column headings: *Harmony* and *Control*. Have students list examples from the readings for the two columns.

3. Divide the class into groups of three, and give each the following questions:

   a. *Explain the differences between the harmony and the control views of agriculture and the environment.*

   b. *Which type might be more destructive to the environment? Why? Give some examples.*

   c. *What effect did European farming technology have on the land?*

   d. *Why might there be continuing conflicts between Native Americans and English settlers?*

4. Students engage in a discussion of their answers.

5. Distribute **Handout 3**.

   a. *How does this account further help to explain inevitable conflict between the two groups?*

   b. *How does this conflict relate to land use?*

6. Students should discuss which attitude toward land use (harmony or control) became the attitude of the United States as it expanded westward. They should illustrate their opinions with examples.

Procedure   Day 3—Lesson Extensions

1. A writing sample might discuss the following:
   Was the attitude of the Native Americans towards the environment better than was the Europeans'? What is the basis for this judgment of better or worse?

2. Distribute **Handout 4** and discuss the questions.

3. For a contemporary extension, lead a class discussion on current environmental problems and how they might relate to this lesson.

Sources   Chief Sagoyewatha: Milton Finkelstein et al. *Minorities: USA.* New York: Globe Books, 1971.

John Winthrop, Handout 1: George F. Wilson. *European Settlers: Saints and Strangers.* New York: Raynel & Hitchcock, 1945.

John Winthrop, Handout 3: Charles M. Segal et al. *Puritans, Indians and Manifest Destiny*. New York: G.P. Putnam's Sons, 1977.

Kate Luckie: Cara Dubois. *Wintu Ethnography*. Berkeley, CA: University of California Press, 1935.

Global Learning, Inc.

How Do Different Cultures Relate To and Interact With the Environment?

Native Americans

Native Americans such as the Iroquois, Algonquin, and Huron in the northeast of what is today the United States, and those tribes who met settlers at Roanoke, are generally portrayed as being more connected with and in tune with mother earth than the settlers. The Native Americans are pictured as seeing themselves as part of nature's balance, as believing that the land belonged to everyone without borders or fences, and as worshiping the gifts of the earth, such as the animals they used for food. This harmony was related by Chief Sagoyewatha of the Senecas when he explained his way of life:

> *The Great Spirit had made it (land) for the use of Indians. He had created the buffalo, the deer, and other animals for food. He had made the bear and the beaver. Their skins served us for clothing. He had scattered them over the country and taught us how to take them. He had caused the earth to produce corn for bread. All this he had done for his red children because he loved them.*

Some Native Americans were nomadic, often using different camps in summer and in winter. For example, some northeastern Native Americans camped near the ocean in summer and moved inland in winter. Their hunting parties tracked and killed animals for food, for their skins, and for their bones, which, among other uses, were splintered and sharpened and used as sewing needles. They gathered wild fruits, vegetables and roots to use as food, medicine, and for a wide variety of other purposes.

European Settlers

Europeans are pictured as having a need to overcome and conquer the earth, to dominate and force it to serve their needs. Europeans dealt with their new American environment in ways consistent with their own traditional European methods of planting crops and maintaining farm animals for food. This attitude was expressed by John Winthrop, who led 700 Puritan colonists to Massachusetts Bay colony in 1630:

> *The whole earth is the Lord's garden, and He has given it to the sons of men, so that they will increase and multiply and replenish the earth and subdue it. Why then should we stand here (England) competing for land when a whole continent lies waste without any improvement?*

What Is a Savage?

English settlers thought of Native Americans as savages just as the Romans thought of the English forebearers as savages 1,500 years earlier. The Latin root for savage, *silvaticus,* means belonging to a forest, i.e., wild. To the Romans, who were not only great builders of cities but also successful farmers who lived and farmed on land cleared of forests, those who did not control the environment to produce food, those who lived in the forests and swamps, were savages. Such people lacked a high level of civilization permitted by the abundant production of food which the Roman agricultural practices permitted. Following Rome's "civilizing" of England, the conquered peoples, the English, adopted Roman ways and thus viewed people who had less control over the environment as savages.

Farming Techniques: Differences Between European Settlers and Native Americans

The words savage and civilized thus originated in the way environmental resources were used. Europeans exerted great control over the environment, subjugating it for the purpose of agriculture to produce the food that would support human life. Farming was for many Europeans far more efficient than it was for any northeastern Native Americans. Farming was less important for Native Americans than was hunting animals and gathering the edible vegetation of field and forest. Native American farming consisted of plantings in scattered forest areas where enough sunlight penetrated through the trees to support the growth of crops. The Iroquois used small planting sticks to make a hole in the ground into which corn or bean seeds were placed. For all agriculture, digging into hard packed soil so that it can receive seeds is essential, because if seeds were simply scattered on hard ground, they would dry up and die. Buried in the moist soil, the seeds have a chance to germinate into adult plants. They are also protected from foraging birds and other animals.

This one-hole-at-a-time digging stick method of farming contrasts markedly with food growing practices of the Europeans. Instead of digging one hole at a time so as to bury seeds, they used a plow to dig up acres of hardened soils. They then scattered and buried into this overturned soil massive numbers of seeds. Because of the plow, Europeans could produce a greater quantity of food than the Native Americans and thus support a larger population.

European settlers were more productive farmers also because they had the help of domesticated animals like oxen and horses that could pull a plow through hard soils far more effectively than could a person. These work animals, which were introduced to North America by European colonists, also contributed manure to the soil which served as fertilizer. Native Americans in the northeast did not have available to them animals capable of being domesticated. They depended for meat upon wild animals which they hunted. The Native Americans did try however to improve the habitat for these animals, such as deer and turkey. The Native Americans would deliberately burn areas of the forest to create grasslands to support greater populations of these animals.

Europeans had other more efficient technologies for farming. Metal was unknown to Native Americans, whose way of life was essentially stone age. Metal could be used to fashion effective and more efficient knives, axes, saws, and plows. The Iroquois had only sharpened rocks and animal bones to make implements needed for cutting trees and planting crops. These differences in available technologies may help to explain why Native Americans depended more on utilizing the environment as they found it rather than fashioning it to their needs as the Europeans did.

Global Learning, Inc.

Puritan View of Land Ownership

As early as 1632, the Native Americans and the Puritans began to "...quarrel about the bounds of their lands...." The Puritans maintained the right of the Native Americans to such soil as they could occupy and improve. In 1633 this principle was made to assume the shape of law. It was held that all land not occupied by the Native Americans as agriculturalists "lay open to any that could or would improve it."

John Winthrop responded to objections raised concerning this law.

> This savage people ruleth over many lands without title or property; for they enclose no ground, neither have they cattle to maintain it, but remove their dwellings as they have occasion, or as they can prevail against their neighbors. And why may not Christians have liberty to go and dwell amongst them in their wastelands and woods (leaving them such places as they have manured for their corn)....For God has given to the sons of men a twofold right to the earth; there is a natural right and a civil right. The first right was natural when men held the earth in common, every man sowing and feeding where he pleased: then, as men and cattle increased, they appropriated some parcels of ground by enclosing and peculiar manurance, and this in time got them a civil right.

1. According to the Puritans, how are humans to use the land?

2. According to the Puritans, why are they better suited to control the land than the Native Americans?

3. What is the purpose of fencing in the land?

4. Can you think of any modern examples of ways that people show they claim or own land?

Prophecy of Kate Luckie, a Native American Woman 1925

People talk a lot about the world ending. Maybe this child [pointing to her eldest child] will see something, but this world will stay as long as Indians live. When the Indians all die, then God will let the water come down from the north. Everyone will drown. That is because the white people never cared for land or deer or bear. When we Indians kill meat, we eat it all up. When we dig roots, we make little holes. When we build houses, we make little holes. When we burn grass for grasshoppers, we don't ruin things. We shake down acorns and pine nuts. We don't chop down the trees. We only use dead wood. But the white people plow up the ground, pull up the trees, kill everything. The trees say, "Don't. I am sore. Don't hurt me." But they chop it down and cut it up. The spirit of the land hates them. They blast out trees and stir it up to its depths. They saw up the trees. That hurts them. The Indians never hurt anything, but the white people destroy all. They blast rocks and scatter them on the earth. The rock says, "Don't! You are hurting me." But the white people pay no attention. When the Indians use rocks, they take little round ones for their cooking. The white people dig deep long tunnels. They make roads. They dig as much as they wish. They don't care how much the ground cries out. How can the spirit of the earth like the white man? That is why God will upset the world—because it is sore all over. Everywhere the white man has touched it, it is sore. It looks sick. So it gets even by killing him when he blasts. But eventually the water will come.

This water, it can't be hurt. The white people go to the river and turn it into dry land. The water says: "I don't care. I am water. You can use me all you wish. I am always the same. I can't be used up. Use me. I am water. You can't hurt me." The white people use the water of sacred springs in their houses. The water says: "That is all right. You can use me, but you can't overcome me." All that is water says this. "Wherever you put me, I'll be in my home. I am awfully smart. Lead me out of my springs, lead me from my rivers, but I came from the ocean and I shall go back into the ocean. You can dig a ditch and put me in it, but I go only so far and I am out of sight. I am awfully smart. When I am out of sight, I am on my way home."

Consider what you have learned about the differing views on the environment held by the Native Americans and the English settlers.

1. *Why would these words have had great meaning for those early Native Americans?*

2. *Why would they have had little meaning for the English settlers?*

3. *To what extend, if at all, do these words have meaning for most Americans today?*

Lesson 5

Belief in Self-sufficiency

Living Off the Environment

Historical Period	Colonization and Settlement (1585-1763)
Sustainable Development Concept	Carrying capacity
Purpose	

1. To demonstrate how people in early colonial America lived in a relatively *self-sufficient* manner in terms of their relationships with Europe and the different colonial regions, and yet they were still totally *dependent* on their physical environment.
2. To identify how the early colonists' belief in their own self-sufficiency may still influence some contemporary attitudes regarding the natural environment today.

Objectives

Students will be able to:

1. Define the concepts of *self-sufficiency* and *carrying capacity*.
2. Identify resources the colonists found in the new world that enabled them to live relatively self-sufficiently from Europe.
3. Evaluate the impact of the use of these resources on the environment.
4. Compare the factors that influenced the carrying capacity of colonial America to those that influence carrying capacity today.

Time Required   3 class periods

Materials Needed   Textbook section on Colonial Life

Large sheets of paper and markers

Paper clips and small cup or tumbler

Teacher Background   Carrying Capacity.

1. The students should have read their textbook section on life in colonial America.

2. *Webster's New World Dictionary* defines self-sufficiency as "having the necessary resources to get along without help, independent."

3. Many students will feel that early settlers lived in the wilderness of the new world without any impact on the environment. On the surface, this may seem to be true. However, the longer range issue is how the attitudes and values brought to, and developed in, this "new" continent by European colonists shaped future generations' attitudes and approaches to the natural environment so that they began to tax the *carrying capacity* of the land.

4. *Carrying capacity is the maximum number (population) of a given organism a given ecosystem can support.* What this implies for humans is the extent to which the land can support the people without significant degradation to the land. The concept of carrying capacity was well illustrated by Congressman Morris K. Udall of Arizona in 1970 when he stated: "You know that if you put 10 cows on 1000 acres you can have 10 cows forever. The grass will grow. The trees will be green and bright and produce oxygen. The brooks will babble. But if you exceed the carrying capacity of that land— 15, 20, 30 cows, whatever it is—sooner or later you won't have any grass or any trees or any cows."

5. In the discussion near the end of the second day of this activity, be certain to point out that the concept of self-sufficiency was very important to the myth of independence and to the individualism of American people. Give some examples from history or folklore, like Daniel Boone or Paul Bunyon.

Procedure   Day 1

1. Have each member of the class write down a definition for the term *self-sufficiency* on a 4x6 card or a sheet of paper. Collect the definitions, shuffle them and hand them back out. Ask people to read aloud their definitions and have the class discuss the meanings and nuances.

2. Write the dictionary definition of self-sufficiency on the chalkboard and discuss their definitions in light of the dictionary definition. Conclude this introductory activity by noting that the early colonists came to think of themselves as very self-sufficient, especially from their European countries of origin and from other colonies on the continent. They were, however, totally *dependent* on the natural resources of their local environments.

    Global Learning, Inc.

3. Divide the class into three groups representing New England, Middle, and Southern Colonies. Have each group select a member to be the *facilitator* to keep the group on task and a *recorder* to write down the answers from the brainstorming activity.

4. Post or remind the class of the general rules of brainstorming:

   a. The purpose of brainstorming is to generate as many ideas as possible in a short period of time; we are not worried about *quality* in brainstorming, but *quanitity*.

   b. We want each person to say what comes to her or his mind.

   c. When we brainstorm, we do not allow any comments, positive or negative, because that will inhibit people from saying what comes to mind.

   d. All ideas are accepted and written down.

5. Have each group "brainstorm" a list of resources that the early colonists would find upon arrival in that section of North America, i.e. trees, soil condition, available water (rivers, lakes, ocean), wildlife and even climatic conditions. Tell each group to include specific features that would make their region different from the other two. They can use their textbooks for this activity. Have the recorder in each group write the information on a large sheet of paper.

6. After the groups have finished brainstorming, tell them to discuss any items about which they have questions or disagreements. This is the time to be critical with what has been brainstormed.

7. Give **Handout 1: *Some Cultural Universals*** to each student. Have the three groups each divide the items in Handout 1 among themselves so one or two students are answering one to three items for the entire group. After the individual work is completed, have the students share their answers within their groups. Encourage additional responses from group members to develop a full set of answers. Tell the students that they are responsible to know the entire list of answers, not just the two or three they have individually completed. Also tell them they will describe to the full class in the next class period their region, its natural resources, and how the17th Century colonists in that region made use of those resources .

Procedure Day 2

1. Have the students divide two sheets of paper in half vertically. Label the left column *similar* and the right column *different*. As each group reports to the entire class on their

region, have the rest of the class note items that are similar to and different from their own region.

2. Conduct a general discussion about similarities and differences after all three groups have reported. Especially focus on items that made people in the three regions feel more or less self- sufficient in the 1600's.

3. Ask the group to consider at what point one ceases to be self-sufficient. *In what ways do we depend on others today? Are there any ways in which we are self-sufficient today? To what extent do we still depend on the natural resources within our geographic region?*

Procedure   Day 3

1. To introduce the concept of *carrying capacity* to the class, show the class an upside down cup or tumbler and a box of paper clips. Ask the students how many paper clips they think you can balance on the top of the upside down cup. Proceed to place the clips on the cup until they start falling off. That number is the cup's *carrying capacity.*

2. *Carrying capacity is the maximum number (population) of a given organism a given ecosystem can support.*

3. Tell the class that you want them to look at the three colonial regions that they've been working with as ecosystems and you want them to begin to evaluate the various regions' carrying capacities.

4. *How do we know when a regional ecosystem gets in trouble? What are the indicators that the region's carrying capacity has been exceeded?* E.g., unsafe water supply, unhealthy air quality, can't produce enough food for the number of people living there, traffic jams, soil is depleted and won't grow sufficient crops for food or clothing, high crime rate etc.

5. Have the students divide a sheet of paper in half vertically and label the left column *positive* and the right column *negative.* The two columns stand for a positive impact on the environment and a negative impact on the environment. Have each student list ten items from their original region's answers to the Cultural Universals worksheet in each column. Take one or two examples from at least half the class, covering all three regions. *Do any of the negative impacts suggest that the region was pushing the limits of its carrying capacity? Are there any items that eventually exceeded that region's carrying capacity (e.g., exhaustion of southern soil due to cotton monocropping)?*

Lesson Extension   *What are some of the things being proposed or done today out of a concern for maintaining our region's or country's carrying capacity?* List answers on the board. Compare them with **Handout 2: *Carrying Capacity Checkup and Connections*,** or with a more recent example from the Carrying Capacity Network.

Sources   Alice Ann Cleaveland et al. *Universals of Culture*. New York: Global Perspectives in Education, 1979.

Clearinghouse Bulletin, June 1992. Carrying Capacity Network, 1325 G Street, NW, Suite 1003, Washington, DC 20005; 800-466-4866.

Some Cultural Universals

1. *How were the natural resources of your region used to meet the following needs or activities?*

2. *What other resources did your region still need to obtain from someplace else to meet these needs or to conduct these activities?*

I. Material Culture

    A. Food

    B. Clothing and adornment of the body

    C. Tools and weapons

    D. Housing and shelter

    E. Transportation

    F. Household articles, furniture, cooking utensils

II. The Arts, Play and Recreation

    A. Forms of the arts, play and recreation

    B. Folk arts and fine arts

III. Economic Organization

    A. Systems of trade and exchange

    B. Producing and manufacturing

    C. Property

Global Learning, Inc.

Carrying Capacity Checkup & Connections

Atmosphere—Approximately forty percent of air pollution in the U.S. is attributable to motor vehicles. (Peter Paris, American Lung Association, 1740 Broadway, New York, NY 10019, 212-315-8700)

Energy—If the rate of growth of natural gas consumption continues at 3.5% per year, that means that every 20 years an amount of new gas must be produced that is equal to all the previous discoveries in history. (Albert Bartlett, University of Colorado Department of Physics as appeared in Beyond the Limits, 74)

Immigration— "Two-thirds of all births in Los Angeles County's public hospitals last year were to illegal immigrant mothers—at a cost to the county of $30 million." (Rep. Anthony Beilenson (D-CA) in the Los Angeles Times 4/02/92)

Water— "Groundwater is being removed faster than it is replenished in 35 states, including the rapidly- growing states of California, Arizona, and Florida." ("Growing Population Threatens U.S. Water Supplies" Population-Environment Balance, 1325 G Street, NW #1003, Washington, D.C. 20005, 202- 879-3000)

Population— "The addition of 2.5 million people per year to the United States requires careful analysis as to how we will provide for additional people in a country where 53% of its current residents live in areas which fail to meet Clean Air Act standards, and one-third of its land is desertified." ("The Carrying Capacity Approach: Environmental Restoration and Economic Stability," by Karen Kalla, Sierra Club Population Program, 408 C St., NE, Washington, D.C. 20002, 202-675-7901)

Consumption— "The number of U.S. shopping malls reached 32,563 in 1987, more than the number of high schools." (The Christian Science Monitor 4/30/92)

Land— "Each year, between 1.2 and 1.5 million acres of rural land are converted to development and urban use, according to estimates from the American Farmland Trust and American Demographics Magazine. That translates into the loss of more than 5 1/2 square miles of rural land per day." (Development, Summer 1991, National Growth Management Leadership Project, 915 15th St. NW #600, Washington, D.C. 20005, 202-628-1270)

Biota—The first U.S. Endangered Species list compiled in 1967 had 67 entries. As of May 8, 1992, 700 domestic species were listed, slightly more than half of which are plants and invertebrates. (Division of Endangered Species, U.S. Fish and Wildlife Service, Washington, D.C. 20240, 703-358-2171)

Quality of Life—For the first 50 years of our country's existence, each member of Congress represented about 30,000 people. Because of our population growth, now each Member represents about 570,000 people, 19 times higher. (World Population Balance, POB 23472, Minneapolis, MN 55423, 612-869-1640)

Let us know what's happening in your county, state, or bioregion!
Contact us with recent victories you would like to celebrate with other Bulletin readers, local developments you think might have nation-wide implications or interest, or just general information on your group or individual activities. Call us toll- free, 1-800-466-4866, or send any printed matter to 1325 G Street, NW, Suite 1003, Washington, D.C. 20005.

CCN Speakers'/Writers' Bureau
CCN maintains a list of individuals and groups who are available to speak publicly or prepare articles on various carrying capacity issues. Have something to say? Sign up as a speaker or writer. Need a speaker? Get a referral through the Bureau. We want to hear from you! Call us toll-free, 1-800-466-4866, and speak with CCN staffer Julie Bomengen for details.

Source: Carrying Capacity Network, *Clearinghouse Bulletin*, June 1992.

Lesson 6

Choices for Development
Hamilton versus Jefferson

Historical Period   The Revolution and the New Nation (1754-1815)

Sustainable
Development Topic   Economic development

Purpose   The purpose of this lesson is to highlight one area of the conflict between the Federalist and the Republican parties: options for economic development. This historic example will illustrate the recurring themes of development and the importance of sustainable choices. Using primary source material, students will be able to identify the arguments for and against, the costs and benefits of, and the values implicit in both options. This lesson can be extended by having students evaluate a contemporary industrializing nation and the importance of sustainable development.

Objectives   Students will be able to:

1. Evaluate economic development options for costs and benefits.
2. Identify arguments for and against development options.
3. Compare the effects of these options on physical quality of life and the environment.
4. Evaluate values about economic development.
5. Apply standards of sustainable development when considering development options.

Time Required   The lesson requires one homework assignment and three class periods. The lesson extension requires two to three class periods including one period in the library for research.

Materials Needed   Handout 1: *Thomas Jefferson: Notes on the State of Virginia*
Handout 2: *Alexander Hamilton: Report on Manufactures*
Handout 3: *Role Assignment Sheet for Advocacy Groups*
Handout 4: *Role Assignment Sheet for Congressional Committee*

Global Learning, Inc.

Handout 5: *Format of Hearing*
Student text for reference to historic time period

Teacher Background

This lesson will work into your discussion about the conflict between the Federalists and Republican parties and more specifically, the clash between Hamilton and Jefferson. Prior to this lesson, students should have read text background regarding the differing views of America's future and how it should be achieved. Students should have a knowledge of the Federalist plan for a national bank, taxes on distillers, tariffs on imports, and the goal of creating an independent commercial economy. Likewise, they should have a knowledge of the Republican opposition to the bank plan and preference for a small government and the agrarian ideal.

The readings to be used for this lesson highlight the philosophic as well as practical differences between Hamilton and Jefferson. Hamilton's "Report on Manufactures" was a speech presented to the House of Representatives on December 5, 1791. The Bank of the United States had been instituted and Congress was asking for guidance on how the country's new wealth should be invested for future national growth. Jefferson's "Notes on the State of Virginia" was written in 1787 and clearly explained his views of Americans as noble citizen-farmers who were best qualified to implement the tenets of democracy because of their love for and dependence on their land.

Procedure

Homework

Divide class in half and distribute **Handout 1: *Thomas Jefferson: Notes on the State of Virginia*** to one half and **Handout 2: *Alexander Hamilton: The Report on Manufactures*** to the other half. Both readings have the same set of five questions which should be completed with the reading. It is recommended that this part of the lesson be given as a homework assignment to save time. It may be helpful for students to rewrite or summarize the paragraphs in modern English.

Procedure

Day 1

1. Students will spend the day preparing to testify or to hear testimony regarding the best path for economic development. Inform students that they will be divided into three groups: **Republicans, Federalists**, and a **Congressional Committee**. Their goal today is to prepare for presentation and defense of arguments which support their party's position on the issue of industrial versus agrarian development.

2. Separate the class into their respective reading groups. Choose four or more students from the two reading groups to act as members of the Congressional Committee who will hear the testimony of the two parties, question witnesses,

and ultimately decide a path for development. Committee members should represent different regions of the United States, including the North, South, and territories.

3. Students remaining in reading groups will now be labeled as the **Republican Advocacy Group** (read Jefferson) and the **Federalist Advocacy Group** (read Hamilton). At this point you should have a Committee group of 4 or more students, a Republican advocacy group of 8 or more students, and a Federalist advocacy group of 8 or more students.

   Note to Teacher: If you have a large class, you can alter the role assignments by doubling up on roles, adding more witnesses, or adding to your congressional committee. If you have a small class, you may eliminate the witness roles or any of the support roles in the advocacy groups. Once students have moved to their groups, they should review homework reading and questions together. Members of the congressional committee will have the benefit of reviewing both arguments.

4. Distribute **Handout 3:** *Role Assignment Sheet for Advocacy Groups,* **Handout 4:** *Role Assignment Sheet for Congressional Committee,* and **Handout 5:** *Format of Hearing.* Students may select, or you may assign, the roles in the advocacy groups and the congressional committee group. Once students have reviewed their assigned roles, they should begin to work cooperatively to prepare for their group's presentation. In your directions to the students, be sure to stress that each member of the group plays an important part in creating a successful presentation of their argument. Outlines for the primary speeches, secondary speeches, and witness testimony should be prepared by the advocacy groups. The Congressional Committee should prepare questions for the advocacy groups. Outlines and questions should be turned in at the end of the class period. (See "Student Assessment.") Instruct students that the rebuttal phase of the hearing is a less formal opportunity for defense and clarification of a plan following speeches. The scribes and assistants should be prepared to assist the primary speaker with their rebuttal during the hearing.

Procedure   Day 2

Today students will formally present their plans for economic development. See "Hearing Agenda" for specific agenda. Congressional Committee members should be seated in front of the room facing the two advocacy groups who are seated in clusters. Proceed with the agenda.

Procedure   Day 3

This day should be used for debriefing the hearing and its results. The goal of this class meeting is to encourage students to think critically about their choices and the social, political, and economic development values they used in the decision making process. The following questions may be used to guide that discussion.

Debriefing   **Questions**

1. What were the strengths and weaknesses of each plan?
2. What values and objectives were considered by the Congressional Committee in their decision?
3. According to *Our Common Future,* the 1987 report of the UN Commision on Environment and Development, development which is sustainable includes the following:

   - a **political system** that secures effective citizen participation in decision making;
   - an **economic system** that is able to generate surpluses and technical knowledge on a self- reliant and sustained basis;
   - a **social system** that provides for solutions for the tensions arising from disharmonious development;
   - a **productive system** that respects the obligation to preserve the ecological base for development;
   - a **technological system** that can search continuously for new solutions;
   - an **international system** that fosters sustainable patterns of trade and finance;
   - an **administrative system** that is flexible and has the capacity for self-correction.

   To what extent were these two plans for development sustainable according to each of these criteria? Were the values and objectives of the Congressional Committee sustainable?

4. Obviously we are not a nation of farmers as Jefferson would have liked it. Ultimately, the United States followed the Hamilton vision for development. This was not a result of a conscious decision on the part of the House of Representatives, but rather the result of circumstances resulting from the War of 1812, technological innovation, improved transportation, and migration to the United States. Ask students to brainstorm how each of these circumstances fostered implementation of Hamilton's plan.
5. Ask students to imagine the United States of today if Jefferson's plan had become a reality. What would our lifestyle be? How would the American landscape be different?

What would our level of industrialization be? What would our relationships with other nations be? What was it about Hamilton's plan that made it the chosen course of development? How could it have been improved so that the environmental consequences of industrialization could have been anticipated and perhaps avoided?

6. Is there evidence that Hamilton and Jefferson considered the environmental impact of their respective plans? How has our view of the environment changed since the founding of this nation? Make an argument for considering the environment in future development plans for this country.

Lesson Extension Contemporary industrializing nations are facing many of the same dilemmas the United States faced in its early years while simultaneously being confronted with the problems of modernity. Ask students to suggest a list of nations that have recently appeared in the news and a brief description of the problem that nation is facing. You might want to prompt students with a suggestion of your own, such as Brazil and rainforest destruction or Somalia and social disintegration and starvation. Once your list is compiled on the chalkboard, break students into small groups and assign each group to research a nation and problem. Ask students to relate the problem being faced to the issues of sustainable development by assigning each student within the groups one of the following questions:

1. To what extent does the political system of this country provide for citizen participation?
2. To what extent does the economic system provide for its people and foster self-reliance?
3. To what extent does the social system encourage human dignity and fair treatment of all?
4. To what extent does the production system provide for preservation and careful use of resources and environmental integrity?
5. To what extent does this nation encourage technological or practical research and development for solutions to problems?
6. To what extent does this nation participate in balanced international trade and finance?
7. To what extent is the government of this country flexible in providing a system of checks and balances?

Prior to assigning the questions, you should establish a scale or standard that will be used when evaluating the countries and their problems. (For example, on a 1 to 7 scale, 1 = to a great extent, 3 = to a significant extent, 5 = not very much, and 7 = not at all.) Once students have worked together to answer these questions, they should reconvene in their groups to discuss their results and the relationship of each of these components of sustainable development to the solution of that nation's problem. Ultimately, all groups should report back to the class on the results of their research and discussion. The goal of the activity and ensuing discussion is to enable students to find the linkages between recurring development issues and historic as well as contemporary problems. Ask students to compare and contrast issues of present day development with the issues of development in the 18th century.

Student Assessment Students who were members of Advocacy Groups will be evaluated using the following point structure. You will notice that some of the 100 points are determined individually and some are part of a group assessment. This format can be changed to meet your needs.

	Content	Organization	Presentation
Group Outlines (primary, secondary, witness)	5	5	—
Primary Speech	5	5	5
Secondary Speech	5	5	5
Witness Testimony	5	5	5
Rebuttal	5	5	5
Responses to Questions	5	5	5

Individual participation will determine the remaining 15 points. The overall participation in the group experience should be considered. Did the students fulfill their roles in the hearing? Did they respond to debriefing questions?

Assessment for the Congressional Committee members will be on an individual basis and will follow the following scheme:

	Content	Organization	Presentation
Preparation of Questions	5	5	—
—quality of questions	5	5	5
—propriety of questions	5	5	5
—adherence to role	5	5	5
—coordination with group questions	5	5	5
Comment Period	5	5	5

Committee Participation overall will determine the remaining 15 points. Did the Committee encourage a clear analysis of the plans for development? Did the committee represent the concerns of their constituents?

Global Learning, Inc.

Thomas Jefferson: Notes on the State of Virginia (excerpt), 1787

We never had an interior trade of any importance. Our exterior commerce has suffered very much from the beginning of the present contest. During this time we have manufactured within our families the most necessary articles of clothing. Those of cotton will bear some comparison with the same kinds of manufacture in Europe; but those of wool, flax and hemp are very coarse, unsightly, and unpleasant: and such is our attachment to agriculture, and such our preference for foreign manufactures, that be it wise or unwise, our people will certainly return as soon as they can, to the raising raw materials, and exchanging them for finer manufactures than they are able to execute.

The political economists of Europe have established it as a principal that every state should endeavor to manufacture for itself: and this principle, like many others, we transfer to America, without calculating the difference or circumstance which should often produce a difference of result. In Europe the lands are either cultivated, or locked up against the cultivator. Manufacture must therefore be resorted to of necessity not of choice, to support the surplus of their people. But we have an immensity of land courting the industry of the husbandman [i.e., farmer]. Is the best then that all of our citizens should be employed in its improvement, or that one half should be called off from that to exercise manufactures and handicraft arts for the other? Those who labour in the earth are the chosen people of God, if ever he had a chosen people, whose breasts he has made his peculiar deposit for substantial and genuine virtue. It is the mark set on those, who not looking up to heaven, to their own soil and industry, as does the husbandman, for their subsistence, depend for it on the casualties and caprice of customers. Dependence begets subservience and venality, suffocates the gem of virtue, and prepares fit tools for the designs of ambition. This, the natural progress and consequence of the arts, has sometimes perhaps been retarded by accidental circumstances: but, generally speaking, the proportion which the aggregate of the other classes of citizens bears in any state to that of its husbandmen, is the proportion of its unsound to its healthy parts, and is a good-enough barometer whereby to measure degree of corruption. While we have land to labour then, let us never wish to see our citizens occupied at work-bench, or twirling a distaff. Carpenters, masons, smiths, are wanting in husbandry: but, for the general operations of manufacture, let our work-shops remain in Europe. It is better to carry provisions and materials to workmen there, than bring them to the provisions and materials, and with them their manners and principals. This loss by the transportation of commodities across the Atlantic will be made up in happiness and permanence of government. The mobs of great cities add just so much to the support of pure government, as sores do to the strength of the human body. It is the manners and the spirit of a people which preserve a republic in vigour. A degeneracy in these is a canker which soon eats to the heart of its laws and constitution.

Questions

1. According to the reading, what direction should American development take?

2. What are the arguments the author uses to support this plan?

3. What is the ultimate goal of this development plan?

4. How would this plan provide for the immediate needs of the people? How would it provide for the needs of people in the long term?

5. What is the relationship of the environment and resources to this plan?

6. What are the weaknesses of this plan? Are the arguments for its implementation consistent with the goals of the new government?

Global Learning, Inc.

Alexander Hamilton: Report on Manufactures (excerpts)

The Secretary of the Treasury, [i.e., Hamilton] in obedience to the order of the House of Representatives, of the 15th day of January, 1790, has applied his attention, at as early a period as his other duties would permit, to the subject of manufactures; and particularly to the means of promoting such as will tend to render the United States independent of foreign nations for military and other essential supplies; and he thereupon respectfully submits the following report....

1. **As To The Division Of Labor**

    It has justly been observed that there is scarcely anything of greater moment in the economy of a nation than the proper division of labor. The separation of occupations causes each to be carried to a much greater perfection than it could possibly acquire if they were blended...the mere separation of the occupation of the cultivator from that of the artificer [i.e., a skilled maker of things] has the effect of augmenting the productive powers of labor and, with them, the total mass of the produce or revenue of a country.

2. **As To An Extension Of The Use Of Machinery; A Point Which, Though Partly Anticipated, Requires To Be Placed In One Or Two Additional Lights**

    The employment of machinery forms an item of great importance in the general mass of national industry. It is an artificial force brought in aid of the natural force of man; and, to all the purposes of labor, is an increase of hands--an accession of strength, unencumbered, too, by the expense of maintaining the laborer. May it not, therefore, be fairly inferred that those occupations which give greatest scope to the use of this auxiliary contribute most to the general stock of industrious effort and, in consequence, to the general product of industry?

3. **As To The Additional Employment Of Classes Of The Community Not Originally Engaged In The Particular Business**

    This is not among the least valuable of the means by which manufacturing institutions contribute to augment the stock of industry and production. In places where those institutions prevail, besides the persons regularly engaged in them, they afford occasional and extra employment to industrious individuals and families who are willing to devote leisure resulting from the intermissions of their ordinary pursuits to collateral labors, as a resource for multiplying their acquisitions or enjoyments. The husbandman [i.e., farmer] himself experiences a new source of profit and support from increased industry of his wife and daughters, invited and stimulated by the demands of neighboring manufactories.

    Besides this advantage of occasional employment to classes having different occupations, there is another, of a nature allied to it, and of similar tendency. This is the employment of persons who would otherwise be idle, and in many cases, a burden on the community, either from bias of temper, habit, infirmity of body, or some other cause indisposing or disqualifying them for the toils of the country. It is worthy of particular remark that, in general, women and children are rendered more useful, by manufacturing establishments, than they would otherwise be....

4. **As To The Promoting Of Emigration From Foreign Countries**

    ...Manufacturers who, listening to the powerful invitations of a better price for their fabrics or their labor; of greater cheapness of provisions and raw materials; of an exertion from the chief part of the taxes, burdens and restraints which they endure in the Old World; of greater personal independence and consequence under the operation of a more equal government; and of what is far more precious than mere religious toleration--a perfect equality of religious privileges--would probably flock from Europe to the United States to pursue their own trades or professions if they were once made sensible of the advantages they would enjoy, and were inspired with an assurance of encouragement and employment, will, with difficulty, be induced to transplant themselves with a view to becoming cultivators of land.

If it be true, then, that it is the interest of the United States to open every possible avenue to emigration from abroad, it affords a weighty argument for the encouragement of manufactures; which, for the reasons just assigned will have the strongest tendency to multiply inducements to it.

5. **As To The Furnishing Greater Scope For The Diversity Of Talents And The Dispositions Which Discriminate Men From Each Other**

This is a much more powerful means of augmenting the fund of national industry than may at first sight appear. It is a just observation that minds of the strongest and most active powers for their proper objects fall below mediocrity and labor without effect if confined to uncongenial pursuits; and it is thence to be inferred that the results of human exertion may be immensely increased by diversifying its objects. When all the different kinds of industry obtain in a community, each individual can find his proper element and can call into activity the whole vigor of his nature; and the community is benefited by the services of its respective members in a manner in which each can serve it with most effect.

6. **As To The Affording A More Ample And Various Field For Enterprise**

...To cherish and stimulate the activity of the human mind by multiplying the objects of enterprise is not among the least considerable of the expedients by which the wealth of a nation may be promoted. It must be less in a nation of cultivators than in a nation of cultivators and merchants; less in a nation of cultivators and merchants than in a nation of cultivators, artificers, and merchants.

7. **As To The Creating, In Some Instances, A New, And Securing, In All, A More Certain And Steady Demand For The Surplus Produce Of The Soil**

This is among the most important of the circumstances which have been indicated. It is a principal means by which the establishment of manufactures contributes to an augmentation of the produce or revenue of a country and has immediate and direct relation to the prosperity of agriculture....a domestic market is greatly to be preferred to a foreign one; because it is, in the nature of things, far more to be relied upon.

It is a primary object of the policy of nations to supply themselves with subsistence from their own soils; and manufacturing nations, as far as circumstances permit, endeavor to procure from the same sources the raw materials necessary for their own fabrics. This disposition, urged by the spirit of monopoly, is sometimes even carried to injudicious extreme.

The foregoing considerations seem sufficient to establish, as general propositions, that it is the interest of nations to diversify the industrious pursuits of the individuals who compose them; that the establishment of manufacture is calculated not only to increase the general stock of useful and productive labor but even to improve the state of agriculture in particular; certainly to advance the interest of those who are engaged in it...

Questions

1. According to the reading, what direction should American development take?

2. What are the arguments the author uses to support this plan?

3. What is the ultimate goal of this development plan?

4. How would this plan provide for the immediate needs of the people? How would it provide for the needs of people in the long term?

5. What is the relationship of the environment and resources to this plan?

6. What are the weaknesses of this plan? Are the arguments of its implementation consistent with the goals of the new government?

Role Assignment Sheet for Advocacy Groups

Primary Speaker	Will present the plan for development in light of the arguments which were presented in the reading. The emphasis in this speech should be on the strengths of the plan in terms of its provision for the well being of the people, constructive use of resources, and the ultimate goal of sustainable economic development. Will work with Secondary Speaker during rebuttal.
Secondary Speaker	This student will highlight the weaknesses in the opponent's plan with special attention to the costs to the wellbeing of the people, environment, and economic growth. Will work with the Primary Speaker during the rebuttal.
Assistant to the Primary Speaker	Will act as an aid to the Primary Speaker in formulating the speech and will be available to assist the Primary Speaker during the question and answer period.
Scribe to the Primary Speaker	Will take notes during the brainstorming phase of the speech writing process and during presentation of speeches for the purpose of assisting in the rebuttal and question period.
Scribe to the Secondary Speaker	Will take notes during the brainstorming phase of the speech writing process and during presentation of speeches for the purpose of assisting in the rebuttal and question period.
Witness A	Will role play an interested party in favor of the argument during the testimony phase of the debate.
Witness B	Will role play an interested party in favor of the argument during the testimony phase of the debate.

Role Assignment Sheet for Congressional Committee

Committee Chairperson Will run the hearing according to the established agenda format. The chairperson will allocate time to fellow committee members during the questioning period and the comment period. The chairperson will handle any problems that arise during the hearing and will have the final word as to the disposition.

Committee Time Keeper Will assist the chairperson by keeping accurate time during the hearing. The time keeper will inform speakers and witnesses when their time is up.

Members of the Committee All committee members, including the time keeper and chairperson, will be required to role play representatives from different regions of the early United States including the North, South, and territories. As such, they should prepare questions in advance that reflect the concerns of the people they represent and present those questions to the appropriate witnesses and speakers during the hearing.

Format of Hearing

Republican Primary Speaker—4 minutes

Federalist Primary Speaker—4 minutes

Republican Secondary Speaker—3 minutes

Federalist Secondary Speaker—3 minutes

Federalist Rebuttal—2 minutes

Republican Rebuttal—2 minutes

Federalist Witness A—2 minutes

Republican Witness A—2 minutes

Federalist Witness B—2 minutes

Republican Witness B—2 minutes

Questions from Congressional Committee to speakers or witnesses—10 minutes

Comments from the members of the Congressional Committee—5 minutes

Vote

Global Learning, Inc.

Lesson 7

The Hudson River and the Erie Canal

Historical Period   Expansion and Reform (1801-1861)

Sustainable Development Topics   Interconnectedness of economics, the environmental resource base and equity

Purpose   To look at life in the Hudson Valley in the 1800s and analyze how the region's economic and social/cultural development was changed by the building of the Erie Canal from Albany to Buffalo and how the environmental resource base fueled development and western expansion.

Objectives   Students will be able to:

1. Trace the Erie Canal system and the areas of production and development in the Hudson River Valley using outline maps.
2. List the effects of economic development in the Hudson Valley region and the regions opened to trade by the building of the Erie Canal.
3. Differentiate among these effects in terms of short term and long term effects, positive and negative effects, and social and environmental effects.

Time Required   Homework assignments and 2 class periods

Prerequisite   *What is Sustainable Development? The Chair*

Materials Needed   Handout 1: *Building of the Erie Canal*
Handout 2: *Life in the Hudson River Valley in the 1800s*
Handout 3: *What Really Happened?*

Teacher Background   The Hudson River, in the early 1800s, was one of the most commercially utilized routes in the nation. Ocean-going vessels could go as far as the Albany-Troy area because of a river bed below sea level. In 1825 the Erie Canal was completed and provided a direct connection through the MohawkValley to

Buffalo on Lake Erie. Thus the Hudson and Mohawk Valleys became the only navigable route through the Appalachian Mountains for that time.

Note: The Erie Canal was so economically successful that over four thousand miles of canals were built throughout the northeast by the year 1840. The Grand Canal, stretching from Philadelphia to Pittsburgh was a major effort to replicate the economic success of the Erie. But the Grand Canal and other smaller canals built in this period were not as economically successful and disappeared with the building of the railroads. The Erie Canal is still in existence today, serving as the longest section of the New York State barge canal system.

Students may be familiar with the folk song from the Canal era.

> I've got a mule and her name is Sal,
> Fifteen miles on the Erie Canal.
> She's a good worker and a good old pal,
> Fifteen miles on the Erie Canal.
> We've hauled some barges in our day,
> Filled with lumber, coal, and hay,
> And we know every inch of the way
> From Albany to Buffalo.

> (Author unknown)

In this same time period (1825-1870s), the Hudson River School of Landscape Painting was a major influence in the art world, attracting painters from Europe to the Hudson's shores. (See Handout 2.) It is probable that the students' U.S. History textbook has reproductions of paintings from the Hudson River School era.

The history of the area provides a backdrop to look at the interconnections between the environment, economic and social development, and equity, as well as the short term and long term consequences of the region's development path—both positive and negative.

Answers to questions 2 and 3 on Handout 1: average speed (363 miles divided by 7 or 10 days) = 2.2 or 1.5 mph; and farmers paid one tenth as much to ship their flour after the canal was built. For question 5, see Handout 4: *Prophecy of Kate Luckie* in Lesson 4: *Early Encounters*.

Procedure   Homework

Have students read **Handout 1:** *Building of the Erie Canal* and **Handout 2:** *Life in the Hudson River Valley* for homework. Tell them to answer the questions at the end of Handout 1 and to list 5 changes in the natural environment of the region that resulted from the rapid economic development in the area, especially after the completion of the Erie Canal in 1825.

Procedure   Day 1

1. Begin the discussion by asking students for one of their observations about environmental changes in the Hudson Valley region. List them on the board and discuss them.

2. Ask: *What is the connection between these environmental changes in the Hudson River Valley and the building of the Erie Canal?*

3. Working in pairs, have students locate and mark on the map in Handout 2 the places where environmental problems developed in the Hudson Valley area, e.g., deforestation in Rensselaer County, pollution of streams in the Catskill Mountains etc.

4. Discuss:

   a. Which negative effects on the environment at the time were reversed fairly easily and in a relatively short time? List. How were they reversed?

   b. Which negative effects on the environment have been more difficult to reverse? List.

   c. Why might it be more difficult to reverse negative effects on the environment today? List reasons and discuss, e.g., long life of some modern toxins, bureaucratic hassles, slowness of legal proceedings, etc.

   d. What were some of the negative social effects of rapid expansion? What were some positive social effects of rapid expansion?, e.g., jobs for immigrants.

   e. Sum up by pointing out that economic development involves *trade-offs*. People concerned with *sustainable* development look at how the trade-offs in a given development decision will affect future generations as well as our own. Sustainable development asks: In the *long term,* what will be the best decisions? What decisions will be equitable for all, not just part of, the population?

5. Tell students that tomorrow they are going to go back in time to take part in a regional town meeting. The meeting has been called by the **American Scenic and Historic Preservation Society** (a society that actually existed in the 1800s), to consider designating a large tract of land along the Hudson River's western banks as a public park area, free from economic development.

6. Divide the class into 5 groups.

   Group 1: local artists and tourists from Europe
   Group 2: immigrant laborers (and families) from NY City
   Group 3: industrialists and bankers
   Group 4: boat captains and canal workers
   Group 5: state government representatives

7. For homework, tell students to review Handout 1: *Life in the Hudson Valley* to consider how their group might view the park proposal in order to serve as an informed representative at the regional town meeting.

Procedure   Day 2

1. Tell students to sit with their assigned groups. Give them 15-20 minutes to discuss their group's position on the park proposal. They need to reach an agreement in their group on whether to vote Yea! or Nay! on the proposal. Each group has to list at least 3 reasons for their choice. *Emphasize they should be voting from the point of view of the people they are representing, not their present-day, personal preferences.*

2. Convene the class as a regional town meeting and serve as chairperson. Also record on the chalkboard the votes and the reasons for each group's vote. After each group has voted and given the reasons for their decision, ask if any group wants to change their vote. Allow discussion time. Announce the formal results of the vote.

3. Distribute **Handout 3: *What Really Happened?*** Allow reading time.
   a. Were there any surprises?
   b. Did the outcome in the historical account match the way your group voted?
   c. Was there enough information for you to figure out how your group might have voted on the conservation proposal?

4. End the class discussion by formally closing the regional town meeting.

Student Assessment   Students can be evaluated on the basis of their initial homework listing 5 changes in the Hudson Valley and Erie Canal regions, their participation in group work, and their participation in class discussion, especially their ability to support positions with statements of fact or value perspectives.

Lesson Extension   Ask students to find an article in the newspaper about an environmental problem that has the possibility of a short term solution, and an article about an environmental problem that will need a long range solution; or an article about a problem where both short and long term solutions will be needed.

Sources   Heiman, Michael, "Production Confronts Consumption: Landscape Perception and Social Conflict in the Hudson Valley," *Environmental and Planning D:* Society and Space 7, 1989.

Stein, R. Conrad. *The Story of the Erie Canal.* Chicago: Childrens Press, 1985.

Building of the Erie Canal

What were three impacts that the building of the Erie Canal had on the environment?

It was nearly impossible for settlers from European countries to cross the Appalachian Mountains two hundred years ago. The Appalachian Mountain chain was a veritable wall which ran from what was to become Canada to what is now Alabama. Only a few scattered settlers crossed this jagged wall of mountains using trails made by the Native Americans of the area.

As time passed the area east of the mountains became more and more industrialized while west of the mountains, farmers toiled growing food. Some people felt that these two territories would become isolated countries because the passages through the mountains were so difficult. It was the persistence of then Governor of New York, DeWitt Clinton, that led to the raising of the enormous funds needed to build a canal to connect the manufacturing east with the farmers in the west.

It was the newly arriving Irish immigrants, fleeing from famine, who became the work force for building the canal. Workers toiled for 14 grueling hours a day on the canal which would run through New York, from the Hudson River to Lake Erie (a distance of 363 miles.)

At first crews cut down trees along the route but this left large stumps and long roots to be removed. An "unsung" inventive worker designed a large stump pulling device. It was a huge two-wheeled, one-axle machine that was positioned over a stump. With the aid of a chain and pulley, the stump was pulled out of the ground. Later another device was invented which pulled the trees out of the ground, roots and all.

At least a thousand of these workers became ill with malaria and many died while pushing their way through a swamp as part of the canal route. Native Americans–the Cayuga who lived in the area–had warned the builders not to enter the swamp but were not heeded. People at the time didn't know that mosquitoes carried malaria.

Eighty-four locks, each ninety feet long and fifteen feet wide, were needed to lift boats over the Appalachians through the Erie Canal. **Locks are water-filled chambers with huge doors on either end**. They are usually built in a series up the face of a hill or mountain. The doors of the lock are closed and water is pumped into the chamber. This way a boat can be lifted, lock by lock, over a mountain and down the other side. The builders had no previous experience to guide them for such an undertaking. Experts of the time estimated it would take the builders three years or more to complete the lock system. The builders completed the work of building the locks in three months.

An amazing feat for the builders took place at, what became, the town of Lockport. There the canal had to rise sixty-six feet up a cliff of solid rock. Using explosives, the workers blasted five sets of double locks out of the face of the cliff, creating a set of watery stepping-stones for canal boats. The Erie Canal was a system of locks, bridges, aqueducts, and an elaborate system of gates and sluices which provided water for the canal and to operate the locks. A vast network of branch canals allowed local farmers to access the main canal.

Before the canal opened, western farmers paid a hundred dollars a ton to transport their sacks of flour by horseback to New York City. After the canal opened, the cost dropped to ten dollars a ton. Eastern farm families migrated via the new waterway to areas that later became the states of Ohio, Indiana, Illinois and Michigan.

It took seven to ten days for boats to go from the Hudson River to Buffalo, pulled by a team of two or three mules or horses. Buffalo grew from a small village to a booming city in less than a decade. A service industry grew up along the banks of the canal to accommodate the passengers and boat tenders. Grocery stores, hotels, supply outlets and saloons soon flourished along the path of the canal.

From its beginning the Erie Canal made money for the state of New York. In 1826, its first year of operation, tolls paid by boat owners brought in more than three quarters of a million dollars (a large amount of money at the time). In nine years, the canal completely paid off its building debt. The canal continued to profit until 1882, when tolls were abolished. By that time the Erie Canal had paid for itself thirty times over.

The Erie Canal thrived even into the railroad era. Over the years the State of New York had to widen the ditch and modernize the locks several times. Today the Erie Canal is the longest section of what is now the New York State Barge Canal System.

Questions:

1. What are locks in a canal system?
2. What was the average rate of speed in miles per hour for a trip on the Erie Canal from the Hudson River to Buffalo?
3. How much cheaper was it for western farmers to ship their flour to New York City using the Erie Canal?
4. What were three impacts that the building of the Erie Canal had on the environment?
5. This reading takes the view that westward expansion was a politically and economically desireable triumph. How might Native Americans who were living in the areas of expansion have viewed "Westward Expansion?"

Global Learning, Inc.

Erie Canal

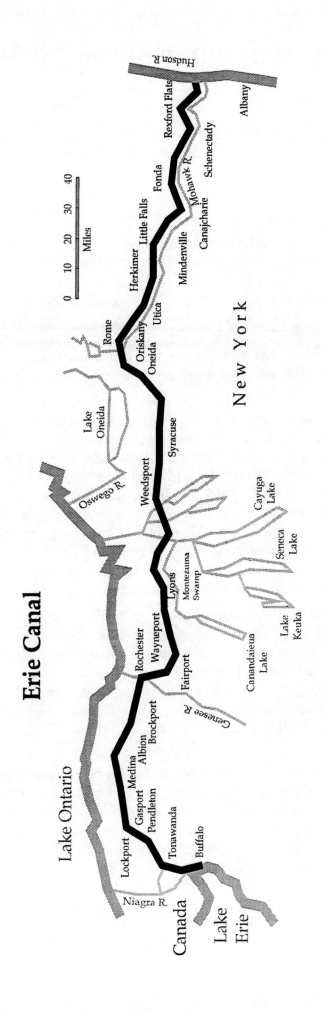

Life in the Hudson Valley in the 1800s

DIRECTIONS: After completing this reading, list five changes in the natural environment of the Hudson Valley region that resulted from the rapid economic development in the area after the completion of the Erie Canal.

Today, with the Valley's industries and cities oriented toward onshore transportation routes and away from the river, one can scarcely imagine that the calm waters of the majestic river 150 years ago supported one of the most intensively utilized commercial routes in the nation. With a bed lying below sea level, the broad lower half of the Hudson River could accommodate ocean-going vessels as far as the Albany-Troy area. Here, goods were exchanged for transport on the famous Erie Canal, completed in 1825 through the Mohawk Valley to Buffalo on Lake Erie. **Taken together, the Hudson-Mohawk valleys provided the only navigable break through the Appalachian Mountains in the United States.**

From the 1780s until the 1830s, travel on the river was dominated by the slow, broad-bottom Hudson River sailing sloop. Averaging 100 tons in capacity, the ships would take from a few days to a week to make the 150-mile run from Albany to New York City, depending upon wind and tides. Every Hudson village had its own fleet, and at the height of sloop use in the 1830s, over a hundred could be spotted from a single vantage on the River's broad Tappen Zee section. In 1807, however, Robert Fulton's *Clermont* made **the first steam voyage up the Hudson** from New York to Albany in just over 32 hours. Soon thereafter steam became the preferred mode of passenger travel, with the sloops reserved for bulk cargo. By 1840 over a hundred steamboats and several hundred sloops were active day and night on the river, and flotillas of up to 50 barges, fastened together and with a steamtug in the middle for propulsion, were beginning to appear....

...On the west bank, **the Catskill counties** were alive by the 1820s with lumbering, tanning, and mining activities. The mountainous terrain had been opened for commercial exploitation through an intricate system of canals and turnpikes. Between 1824 and 1850, the mountain valleys in the village of Catskill supported the largest tanning industry in the nation. Hides were brought in from as far away as Patagonia. Throughout the Catskills, thousands of acres of hemlock were cleared and stripped for the tannin in the bark, and once-pristine mountain streams now ran rancid with hair, grease, acids, and other tanning wastes.

...Downriver, the west bank areas around **Nyack, Haverstraw, and Kingston** were already leading quarrying and brick manufacturing centers by the 1820s, supplying much of the material used to pave and build New York City. With the completion of the Delaware and Hudson Canal in 1828, designed to bring in coal from the Pennsylvania fields, the Kingston (Rondout) terminus became a major shipping and manufacturing center. Kingston was also the center of the state's cement production following discovery of deposits through canal construction. Miles of shaft were sunk to quarry Rosendale Cement, world-famous for its capacity to harden under water. By mid-century, 30 miles north of New York City, Haverstraw's brick trade had expanded to cover several miles of waterfront with clay quarries, drying racks, kilns, and shipment wharves. Here labor militancy was a perennial

Global Learning, Inc.

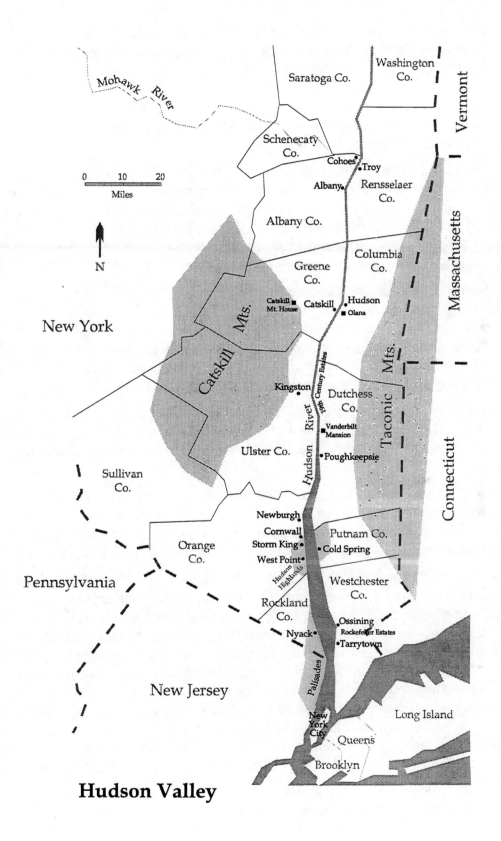

Hudson Valley

issue, with scabs commonly brought in from Quebec. At about the same time, nearby, at Rockland Lake on a ledge above the Hudson, several thousand people were employed at ice production just to serve the cooling requirements of the city downriver.

With its shallow slope, **the eastern bank of the river** supported most of the agriculture and even more settlement than the western shore. Here major iron foundries and forges were established at Troy, Hudson, Poughkeepsie, Cold Spring, and Peekskill. On the east bank, 30 miles south of Albany, Hudson was the fourth largest city in the state in 1820 and an international port of trade noted for woolen manufacturing, whaling, and quarrying. Poughkeepsie, 40 miles farther downriver, was also known for its textiles and as an important brewing and limestone center.

Founded by Yankees in the 1780s, **Troy** was the quintessential manufacturing boom town. In 1827 the wife of a cobbler, fed up with repeated washing of her husband's shirts just to clean the collar, cut off the soiled section and invented the detachable shirt collar. Lasting until the invention of the washing machine in the early twentieth century, the US shirt collar industry at its height employed 15,000 workers in over 20 factories spread throughout the city.

Back on the west bank, **Albany,** chartered in 1686, was already the state capital and an important brewing and lumber market by the time the Erie Canal opened. The city's 4,300-foot-long mooring basin was the principal transshipment center for canal traffic. Already by the mid-1830s, at the height of European fascination with the Valley's natural wonders, the city's dozen steamboats provided daily service to New York City, with 700,000 passengers arriving and departing yearly....

...The Hudson Valley also gave birth and inspiration to the young nation's first indigenous school of painting. Beginning in 1825 with Thomas Cole's arrival in New York City and his initial trip by steamboat up the Hudson, **the Hudson River School of Landscape Painting** lasted until the 1870s....

...At the peak of the school's influence in the 1830s and 1840s, the intensely settled Valley swarmed with Europeans on the Grand Tour of America's 'wild wonders.' Judging from their diaries as they steamed up the river, most appeared oblivious to intense shoreline resource extraction and to the squalid living conditions of adjoining tenant farmers....

...In their rush to fulfill the growing European and American demand for views of a romantic wilderness, Cole and his contemporaries, including Asher B. Durand, Frederick E. Church, and poet William Cullen Bryant, often overlooked or screened out with vegetation the burnt-over fields, stinking tanneries, polluted streams, clamorous sawmills, and other production intrusions....Cole avoided urban scenes because he considered urban social life as lacking in those wholesome qualities which allowed art to be a source of moral inspiration. When they did address human habitation in the valley, Cole and the other artists typically preferred Sunday scenes so as to avoid signs of work and the harsher realities of tenant farming....In a letter of 1836, he complained that the tanneries and a railroad then under construction along Catskill Creek above his studio were "cutting down all of the trees in the beautiful valley on which I have looked so often with a loving eye."...

...Most of the Catskill visitors came for the season to marvel at, and perhaps sketch or record in their diaries, the scenes made famous by the artists. They also came to escape the riots, congestion, heat, malaria, yellow fever, and other environmental and social discomforts of the valley lowlands and the crowded metropolis downriver. Clutching the ubiquitous guidebooks, visitors were advised of exact times and positions when best to view

God's creation so as to avoid the disagreeable facts of production owing to tanning, mining, logging, and subsistence farming....

...By 1830 most of the Valley's once-thick forest cover had been cut at least once, and usually several times, to supply the fuel and raw material for the numerous forges, steamboats, and tanneries active in the region. At the scenic Hudson Highlands, straddling the river at West Point 40 miles north of New York City, the forest cover upon Cole's first passage was already greater than it had been 20 years earlier, when the entire area had been cleared to fuel nearby iron foundries. To the north, deforestation was so severe in Rensselaer County that according to one observer the remaining "woodlands [were]...worth more than the same quality of land under tolerable cultivation, including buildings, fences, and every improvement...."

The Recreational Escape to Nature

Eagerly sought out by wealthy collectors in New York and London, the Hudson River artists enjoyed an unusual degree of success and exposure. In the Hudson Highlands and along the Catskill escarpment, luxurious mountaintop hotels were erected to provide a comfortable experience of the would-be wilderness traveler in search of the scenes made famous by the artists. Many river travelers on the Grand Tour sought out the Catskill Mountain House.

Established in 1823, this fabled resort was one of the nation's first major vacation destinations not tied to medicinal waters. Here, perched 2,250 feet above the Valley on the hotel's veranda, the wealthy guests could imagine an idealized rural landscape devoid of social struggle. According to a noted Catskill historian:

Pilgrims enroute to the Mountain House might hold their noses as tanner's wagons passed by or rub their eyes when the smoke of forest fires made the mountain air thick and biting, yet they could console themselves by reflecting that they were in the midst of what the best authorities certified to be a wilderness Garden of Eden into which only the famous Mountain House intruded....

What Really Happened?

Following the introduction of dynamite in the 1870s, the Hudson Valley experienced a major increase in rock quarrying and stone crushing. The disruption was particularly intense in the lower valley, where estate owners on the eastern bank were incensed by the reverberations and scenic destruction emanating from the opposing Palisades. Stretching some 25 miles from Fort Lee, New Jersey to Haverstraw, New York, the 100-500-foot-high cliffs were both an important scenic landmark and a major source of paving material for the metropolis. Taking a cue from the then-burgeoning **Conservation Movement**, the east-shore residents rallied behind park development as a way to forestall destruction.

Based in New York State, the **American Scenic and Historic Preservation Society** was established to argue for the historic and cultural significance of geological landmarks as justification for preservation. In the 1890s it joined forces with a Palisades Protection Association to prevent further quarrying. The latter association was organized by wealthy businessmen and financiers with homes on Westchester County's opposing shore. The alliance's narrow social origin was obvious, as editorials lamented the public's indifference to the desecration. During this period, J. Pierpont Morgan, then vice-president of the Society, led a campaign for private purchase and donation of land atop the Palisades for scenic preservation.

The philanthropy, although significant, was in itself insufficient to halt the profitable quarry industry, and appeals were made for more forceful public intervention. By December 1900 the preservation forces succeeded in having the New York and New Jersey legislatures establish a **Palisades Interstate Park Commission** with power to condemn and acquire land. The park commission soon got to work removing all signs of human labor and habitation, such as the then-numerous quarry and fishing shanties at the base of the cliffs. The resulting interstate park-system eventually spread to cover thousands of acres in over a dozen dispersed units, with an accumulated 40 miles of protected shoreline reaching to the Hudson Highlands at Storm King Mountain.

Although scenic preservation of privileged views was the initial impetus for intervention, the bi-state compact required a broader political base. Historically the Hudson Valley had never been an important consumption refuge for the working class. For them, Coney Island, Central Park, and other urban locales sufficed. By the 1890s, however, New York's farming population had already peaked, and the state was preeminent as the national leader in manufacturing. One response to the clamor by millions of laborers for better working conditions and benefits was the provision of fresh-air camps and of organized union outings to Catskill and Hudson Valley retreats that had previously been the private domain of the elite. With strong public support, the state governments joined in this effort, and an elaborate system of public parks, linked by inexpensive rail and boat lines, was established to provide a recreational refuge for the working class.

Global Learning, Inc.

Lesson 8

Slave Spirituals and the American Spirit

Historical Period	Civil War and Reconstruction (1850-1877) Plantation Life in the Antebellum South
Sustainable Development Topic	Values about the environment, belief systems
Purpose	To identify enduring beliefs about the environment and to evaluate their relevance for today.
Objectives	Students will be able to:

1. Identify the importance of slave spirituals in life on the plantation.
2. Analyze spirituals critically for themes related to belief systems and values of early African Americans.
3. Evaluate the impact of these values and beliefs on America's past, present, and future.
4. Identify personal values that affect environmental decision making and problem solving.

Time Required	One pre-class homework assignment and one period
Materials Needed	Handout 1: *Slave Spirituals and the American Spirit* Handout 2: *Three Spirituals* Handout 3: *On the Pulse of the Morning* Handout 4: *Student Worksheet* Handout 5: *Sense of Place Map* Text for background on the Southern plantation and slavery
Teacher Background	This lesson is designed to encourage students to make connections between the values expressed by slaves through their spirituals and those expressed in Maya Angelou's 1993 inaugural poem, *On the Pulse of the Morning*. Students will recognize the importance of values and beliefs in facing the challenges of slavery as well as the challenges of our time. Ms. Angelou was inspired by the three spirituals found in Handout 2.

By interpreting the symbolism of these spirituals, students will uncover the values indirectly expressed by the lyrics. In the second step of the lesson, students will interpret Ms. Angelou's poem and the metaphors of the rock, tree, and river. Finally, they will be asked to synthesize the message expressed in both the poem and spirituals to uncover implicit values and visions of the future.

The extension of this lesson focuses on personal environmental identity. The goal of this lesson is to facilitate student reflections about their personal environmental experiences and values about the environment.

In his course "Patterns of Environmentalism," Mitchell Thomashow of the New England Graduate School defines environmental identity as "an individual's developmental relationship with nature." (Opie, p.85) He explains that to build environmental commitment, students must first evaluate their experiences with the natural world and decipher how those experiences have affected their conception of the environment. If students feel detached, insulated, and independent of the natural world, commitment to "walk lightly on the earth" is improbable.

In the core lesson, students analyze the role of the natural world as the inspiration and the setting for triumph over adversity as illustrated in the spirituals and the inaugural poem. To personalize the lesson, students will be asked to create what Thomashow calls **"a sense of place map."** According to Thomashow, sense of place refers to our feelings about land and community.

> Through our appreciation of place, we develop a community niche. The habits of familiarity, the kindred species, the cultural nuances, the environmental landscapes; these are the qualities that mold and shape our environmental identity....Sense of place is fundamental to environmental identity. It is the domestic basis of environmentalism; it's the source of our deepest connection to the natural world....It is the inspiration behind the idea of sacred place; symbolic landscapes that contain and reflect the substance of ecological worship." (Opie, p.96)

The sense of place map is a symbolic document that students will use to identify their personal connection to the world of their past, their present, and their vision of the future. It can take any creative form including, but not limited to, a drawing, poem, song, or short story. Through its creation and presentation, students will ultimately gain an understanding of their place in the environment.

Global Learning, Inc.

Procedure	Homework
	Distribute **Handout 1:** *Slave Spirituals and the American Spirit*. This reading and questions should be completed as a homework assignment the evening prior to the lesson activity.

Procedure	Day 1
	1. Review the questions completed for homework.
	2. Divide students into small groups of about 3 or 4. Distribute **Handouts 2, 3, and 4.** Instruct students to read the spirituals first and to respond to question 1 and 2 individually on the worksheet (Handout 4). Students should read Maya Angelou's poem found on Handout 3 and complete the remaining questions with their group.
	3. Once the groups are finished responding to the questions and have recorded their answers, review their answers in plenary. Be sure to accept as many responses as possible and to encourage students to explain their answers completely, especially when disagreement arises.

Lesson Extension	Assign the *Sense of Place Map* found on **Handout 5.** You should give students at least a few days to complete these maps.

Procedure	Day 2
	1. When the maps are completed, ask students to bring them to class. At the start of class, ask students to respond individually to the following questions in writing:
	• How do you feel about each of the places on your map?
	• How do these places reflect your feelings about yourself, other people, the environment, your past, your present, your future?
	• Do you recognize any metaphors in your map?
	• Which of your values are expressed in your map?
	2. Once students have finished responding to these questions, ask them to choose a partner with whom they will share their maps. Direct them to take turns explaining their maps to their partner. Their responses to the questions can be used to help them in their explanation.
	3. As a conclusion to the lesson, ask students to volunteer to explain their partner's map. They can compare their feelings about themselves and their relationships to the environments and the community.
	4. A final option is to ask students to put their maps together to create a visual display entitled, "Our Place."

Student Assessment

If you do not intend to use the Extension Activity, you can assign an essay in which students identify and describe a place where they go to "recharge" or to seek solace and to compare the inspiration of their place to the inspiration of the rock, river, and tree in the poem and spirituals. Assessment of the Sense of Place Map can be loosely constructed or you might want to establish specific criteria for evaluation.

References Used for this Lesson

"Conversations With Oprah: Maya Angelou," *The Oprah Winfrey Show,* July 13, 1993. Harpo Productions, Inc., Chicago

Johnson, James and J. Rosamond. *The Book of American Negro Spirituals.* New York: Viking Press, 1969.

Krehbiel, Henry Edward. *A Study in Racial and National Music: Afro-American Folk-Songs.* New York: Fredrick Ungar Publishing Co., 1962.

Lovell, John, Jr. *Black Song: The Forge and the Flame.* New York: Macmillan, 1972.

Opie, John (ed.). "Patterns of Environmentalism: The Reflective Environmentalist," *Environmental History Review.* Spring, 1992, vol. 16, pp.83-98.

Slave Spirituals and the American Spirit

The nature of American slavery and its effects on African Americans are issues which have prompted debate as old as this nation. Many scholars point to the richness of culture shared by enslaved African Americans as evidence that this community was successful in developing and preserving a cultural identity separate from that of their white masters despite slavery. As a community, African Americans retained their own traditions, social system, and religion. We can see evidence of the enduring effects of this culture today when we take a moment to look back in time to a way of life that has influenced what it is to be American.

In the May 30, 1867 issue of *The Nation,* a writer described this eyewitness account of a "shout":

> ...the true 'shout' takes place on Sundays, or on 'praise' nights through the week, and either in the praise house or in some cabin in which a religious meeting has been held. Very likely more than half the population of a plantation is gathered together. Let it be the evening, and a light wood fire burns red before the door of the house and on the hearth. For some time one can hear, though at a good distance, the vociferous exhortation or prayer of the presiding elder or of the brother who has a gift that way and is not 'on the back seat'—a phrase interpretation which is under the censure of church authorities for bad behavior—at all regular intervals 'deaconing' a hymnbook hymn, which is sung two lines at a time and whose wailing cadences, borne on the night air, are indescribably melancholy.

> But the benches are pushed back to the wall when the formal meeting is over, and old and young, men and women, sprucely dressed young men, grotesquely half-clad field hands—the women generally with gay head handkerchiefs twisted about their heads and with short skirts—boys with tattered shirts and men's trousers, young girls barefooted, all stand up in the middle of the floor, and when the 'sperichil' is struck up begin first walking and by and by shuffling around, one after the other, in a ring. The foot is hardly taken from the floor, and the progression mainly is due to a jerking hitching motion which agitates the entire shouter and soon brings out streams of perspiration. Sometimes they dance silently, sometimes as they shuffle they sing the chorus of the spiritual, and sometimes the song itself is also sung by the dancers. But more frequently a band, composed of some of the best singers and of tired shouters, stand at the side of the room to 'base' the others, singing the body of the song and clapping their hands together or on their knees. Song and dance are alike extremely energetic, and often, when the shout lasts into the middle of the night, the monotonous thud, thud of the feet prevents sleep within half a mile of the praise house. (Krehbiel, p.33)

As you can tell from this description by an awed onlooker, the slave shouts were emotional, spiritual, and social gatherings of slaves on a plantation. The songs that were sung during these gatherings have been handed down to us as an important part of our American heritage. They have been borrowed and adapted by Americans over the past two centuries for worship hymns, folk songs, rock and roll lyrics, camp songs, and poetry. Their unique contribution to American culture extended beyond these shores to influence music globally.

For example, in 1895, Dr. Antonin Dvorak, a Czech composer of classical music, studied spirituals when he visited the United States. He remarked:

> It is a proper question to ask, What songs, then, belong to the American and appeal more strikingly to him than any others? What melody would stop him on the street if he were in a strange land, and make the home feeling well up in him, no matter how hardened he might be, or how wretchedly the tune were played? Their number, to be sure, seems to be limited. The most potent, as well as the most beautiful among them, according to my estimation, are certain of the so-called plantation melodies and slave songs, all of which are distinguished by unusual and subtle harmonies....(Krehbiel p.153)

Dr. Dvorak drew inspiration for his Symphony No 9 in E minor, op. 93 *From the New World* from "Negro spirituals." When you listen to this symphony, there are places where you can almost hear the singing chorus and clapping hands of a shout.

What are the origins of these beautiful songs? Many scholars have debated the origin of the music. Some have argued that they were inspired by the hymns of the white masters. Separate slave religion was not permitted on the plantation, and black churches were banned by law. Nevertheless, slaves developed their own interpretation of Christianity, adapting that which they were taught by the white ministers to their own African traditions. Slave communities held their own services, often in secret, and developed their own form of worship including shouts. Consequently, most scholars have concluded that spirituals are in fact original expressions of these enslaved people and not adaptations of the slave owner's music. When evaluating these songs for their original qualities, scholars point to the following characteristics: they are emotional and spontaneous; they reflect the life and aspirations of slaves; and they are clearly the collective work of a specific group of people, slaves, and not a specific artist. They are, therefore, true *folk songs* and the bequest of African American slaves.

Early African American music is typically broken into two categories, secular songs, commonly referred to as "corn songs," and spirituals or "shout songs." Corn songs were sung in the fields or when slaves were hard at work. They ranged from motivational to lamenting and focused on the task at hand. Shouts however were songs of religious faith and hope. These songs reflected their endurance and the strength of their spirit in the face of slavery.

The black community was just that--a community of slaves who shared a common condition and common future. Their ability to survive the adversity of their enslavement was greatly dependent on their commitment to a cause greater than themselves. In his book *Black song: The Forge and the Flame,* John Lovell, Jr. comments: "Perhaps the lessons that he cruelly learned from slavery taught him to subordinate minor details to major considerations." (Lovell, p.385) Spirituals express this common cause for slaves, but surprisingly, slavery is not the major theme. Booker T. Washington described spirituals this way: "The Negro folk-song has for the Negro race the same value that the folk-song of any other people has for that people. It reminds the race of the 'rock whence it was hewn,' it fosters race pride, and in the days of slavery it furnished an outlet for the anguish of smitten hearts." (Krehbiel, p.30) Spiritual singers used their voices to affirm their collective faith in their future salvation and liberation from slavery.

Just who the individual composers of these songs were will never be known. How they were created is a little clearer thanks to historical accounts like the following reported in 1862. An interviewer asked a slave how spirituals were composed. He replied:

Global Learning, Inc.

I'll tell you, it's this way: My master called me up and ordered me a short peck of corn and a hundred lashes. My friends saw it and was sorry for me. When they came to the praise meeting that night they sang about it. Some were very good singers and knew how; and they worked it in, worked it in, you know, till they got it right: and that's the way. (Krehbiel, p.24)

What is the value of the spiritual today? As you read the following spirituals you will notice that they go beyond being simply a piece of Americana. They affirm the African American experience of slavery and they reflect the resilience of that community. However they also speak to all of us about the human condition and our collective hopes for a better tomorrow. Freedom, justice, and the beauty of the earth are timeless themes for the songs of struggle and redemption. They are major themes in the lives of all people. Perhaps this is their legacy.

Questions

1. Review the observer's account of the shout in the first part of the reading. How might an African American have described the scene? How do you explain the differences between the two views of the same scene?

2. What are the theories about the origin of these songs? What evidence has been used to substantiate these theories?

3. What is the difference between a "corn song" and a "shout song?"

4. What are the major themes of spirituals?

5. How were spirituals created?

6. List songs that you are familiar with that may be related to spirituals.

Three Spirituals

There's No Hiding Place Down There

There's no hiding place down there,
There's no hiding place down there,
Oh I went to the rock to hide my face,
The rock cried out "No hiding place,
   there's no hiding place down there."

Oh the rock cried out,
"I'm burning too."
Oh the rock cried out "I'm burning too
I want to go to heaven as well as you,
   there's no hiding place down there."

Oh the sinner man he gambled and fell,
Oh the sinner man he gambled, and fell
Oh the sinner man gambled,
He gambled and fell;
He wanted to go to heaven,
   but he had to go to hell.

Down by the Riverside

Goin' to lay down my burden,
Down by the riverside,
Down by the riverside,
Down by the riverside.
Goin' to lay down my burden,
Down by the riverside,
Down by the riverside.

I ain't gonna study war no more—
Ain't gonna study war no more—
   study war no more.
I ain't gonna study war no more—
   study war no more.

I Shall Not Be Moved

I shall not, I shall not be moved,
I shall not, I shall not be moved,
Like a tree that's planted by the waters,
I shall not be moved.

Global Learning, Inc.

On The Pulse Of The Morning

by Maya Angelou

A Rock, A River, A Tree
Hosts to species long since departed,
Marked the mastodon,
The dinosaur, who left dried tokens
Of their sojourn here
On our planet floor,
Any broad alarm of their hastening doom
Is lost in the gloom of dust and ages.

But today, the Rock cries out to us, clearly,
    forcefully,
Come, you may stand upon my
Back and face your distant destiny,
But seek no haven in my shadow,
I will give you no hiding place down here.

You, created only a little lower than
The angels, have crouched too long in the bruising darkness
Have lain too long
Facedown in ignorance,
Your mouths spilling words

Armed for the slaughter.
The Rock cries out to us today,
You may stand upon me;
But do not hide your face.

Across the wall of the world,
A river sings a beautiful song. It says,
Come, rest here by my side.

Each of you, a bordered country,
Delicate and strangely made proud,
Yet thrusting perpetually under siege.
Your armed struggles for profit
Have left collars of waste upon
My shore, currents of debris upon my breast.
Yet today I call you to my riverside,
If you will study war no more.

Come, clad in peace,
And I will sing the songs
The Creator gave to me when I and the
Tree and the Rock were one.
Before cynicism was a bloody sear across your brow
And when you yet knew you still knew nothing.
The River sang and sings on.

There is a true yearning to respond to
The singing River and the wise Rock.
So say the Asian, the Hispanic, the Jew,
The African, the Native American, the Sioux,
The Catholic, the Muslim, the French, the Greek,

The Irish, the Rabbi, the Priest, the Sheik,
The Gay, the Straight, the Preacher,
The privileged, the homeless, the Teacher.
They hear. They all hear
The speaking of the Tree.

They hear the first and last of every Tree
Speak to humankind today.
Come to me, Here beside the River.
Plant yourself by the River.

Each of you, descendent of some passed-
On traveler, has paid for.

You who gave me my first name, you,

Pawnee, Apache, Seneca, you
Cherokee Nation who rested with me. Then
Forced on bloody feet.
Left me to the employment of
Other seekers—desperate for gain,
Starving for gold.

You, the Turk, the Arab, the Swede,
The German, the Eskimo, the Scot,
The Italian, the Hungarian, the Pole,
You the Ashanti, the Yoruba, the Kru, bought
Sold, stolen, arriving on a nightmare
Praying for a dream.

Here, root yourselves beside me.
I am that Tree planted by the river,
Which will not be moved.

Global Learning, Inc.

I am yours—your passages have been paid.
Lift up your faces, you have a piercing need
For this bright morning dawning for you.
History, despite its wrenching pain,
Cannot be unlived, but if faced
With courage, need not be lived again.

Lift up your eyes
Upon this day breaking for you.
Give birth again, To the dream.

When, children, men.
Take it into the palms of your hands,
Mold it into the shape of your most
private need. Sculpt it into
The image of your most public self.
Lift up you hearts
Each new hour holds new chances
For a new beginning.
Do not be wedded forever
To fear, yoked eternally
To brutishness.

The horizon leans forward,
Offering you space
To place new steps of change
Here, on the pulse of this fine day
You may have the courage
To look up and out and upon me,
The Rock, the River, the Tree, your country.
No less to Midas the mendicant.
No less to you now than the mastodon then.

Here on the pulse of this new day
You may have the grace to look up and out
And into you sister's eyes,
And into your brother's face,
Your country,
and say simply
Very simply
With hope—
Good Morning.

Student Worksheet: Spirituals and Angelou

Directions: You will use Handout 2: *Three Spirituals,* and Handout 3: *On the Pulse of Morning,* to respond to the following questions with members of your group. You may need additional space for some of your answers.

1. Read the lyrics of the spirituals on Handout 2. The rock, the river, and the tree are symbols or metaphors for values expressed in the spirituals. What is the meaning of:

   the rock _____

   the river _____

   the tree _____

2. What values are expressed in each of the songs?

3. Read Maya Angelou's inaugural poem *On the Pulse of Morning.* What are the messages of:

   the Rock _____

   the River _____

   the Tree _____

4. Compare your responses to questions 1, 2, and 3. What are the similarities and differences in the messages? What is the consistent theme?

   Similarities:

   Differences:

   Consistent theme:

5. How does this poem reflect the relationship among Americans?

6. How is our relationship with our environment depicted in the poem?

7. Why do you think Angelou used spirituals as the inspiration for this poem?

8. What does this poem say to you?

Global Learning, Inc.

Sense of Place Map

A Sense of Place Map is a symbolic document that depicts your personal connection with the world of your past, your present, and your vision of your future world. It shows the path of your life by creating images of your environment.

Think about places that are important to the story of your life. Create a symbolic document (map, drawing, poem, song, collage, short story) that illustrates places you have been, where you live now, and where you see yourself in the future. Each part of the illustration must be a real place that you have experienced or hope to experience. The focus of this document is to describe what each place means to you and the role it has played in shaping your identity.

Lesson 9

How Does War Impact on the Environment?

Historical Period   Civil War and Reconstruction (1850-1877)
Sherman's March to the Sea

Sustainable Development Topic   Environmental Impact of War

Purpose   This lesson will encourage students to begin to think about the ecological consequences of warfare, thereby extending their perspectives beyond the usual lists of causes and effects of particular wars and events as written from a pre-ecological perspective. The extension activity provides a comparison with an example from the war between the United States and Vietnam.

Objectives   Students will be able to:

1. Identify the environmental results of Sherman's march to the sea from an original source document.
2. Identify ways in which war impacts on the environment.
3. Classify war's impact on the environment according to seven environmental categories.
4. Distinguish among short term, medium term, long term and permanent impacts of warfare on the environment.

Time Required   One class period

Materials Needed   Textbook, Handout 1: *Domestic Life in War-torn Dixie*
Handout 2: *Former Foes* (optional)
Handout 3: *Vietnam and Agent Orange* (optional)
3x5 cards or slips of paper

Teacher Background   "The environment nearly always suffers during war. Animal species become extinct. Forests become deserts or swamps. Jungles dry up. Fertile farmland becomes a mine field. Water becomes contaminated. Native vegetation disappears.

   Global Learning, Inc.

"Despite these results, strangely enough, there is occasionally salvation in the midst of destruction. Some impacts are even positive. During World War II, the German submarine forces effectively shut down the North Atlantic fishing industry. Fish populations rose to an all-time high. 'Off-limits' areas, such as the demilitarized zone between North and South Korea, often become wildlife sanctuaries.

"...Until after the Vietnam War, military planners did not give much thought to the environment. Environmental plans were aimed at lessening the environment's impact on the troops. The military often saw the environment as one more hardship to overcome on the battlefield...." *The Ecology of War,* p.xxvii.

Procedure

1. Prior to the class, assign for homework two readings: an account from their textbook or other materials of Sherman's march to the sea and **Handout 1:** ***Domestic Life in War-torn Dixie***. This is a first hand account by a southern woman who lived near Atlanta in 1864. A current map of the Atlanta area would help students visualize the distances involved.

2. Ask students what images stick out in their minds from Handout 1: *Domestic Life in War-torn Dixie*. Give them some time to discuss their reactions to the reading and to express any feelings it raised in them.

3. Have the class form groups of three for a brainstorming activity. Have each group select a recorder, who will write down whatever is brainstormed on 3x5 cards or on slips of paper—one item per card. Recorders should also share their own ideas during the brainstorm. Remind them of the general rules of brainstorming:

    a. The purpose of brainstorming is to generate as many ideas as possible in a short period of time; we are not worried about quality in brainstorming, but quantity.

    b. We want each person to say what comes to her or his mind.

    c. When we brainstorm, we do not allow any comments, positive or negative, because that will inhibit people from saying what comes to mind.

    d. All ideas are accepted and written down.

4. For 5-7 minutes, have the groups brainstorm answers to the following:

    General Sherman's "march to the sea" has been called "total war," a strategy to defeat the will of the civilians as well as to inflict damage on the military of the Confederacy. As such, this campaign had widespread environmental consequences. Brainstorm as many different ways as you can think of that Sherman's march to the sea impacted on the environment.

5. After the initial brainstorming period, tell students to add to their lists any other ways that they can think of that war impacts on the environment. The purpose of these instructions is to extend student thinking up to the present.

6. After students have finished their brainstorming, put the following categories on the board or on newsprint. Keep students working in their small groups and have them cluster their individual answers on the 3x5 cards according to these categories: **1) earth, 2) air, 3) water, 4) living things, 5) the built environment, 6) natural resources, and 7) manufactured resources.** (Another way to do this if students have brainstormed their lists on a single piece of paper is to have them label each item on their list with the first letter of each category, e.g., E, A, W etc.)

   Note to Teacher: Impacts on the *earth* would include the soil, landforms, types of vegetation, and agriculture. The *air* would include climate, different levels of the atmosphere, and atmospheric gases. The *water* would include freshwater, rivers, lakes, oceans, and the hydrological cycle. *Living things* would include human beings—combatants and noncombatants, other animals, insects, and plants. *Manufactured resources* would include from simple handcrafts to complex industrial goods and services. Both the *natural* and *manufactured resources* would involve their use as well as availability.

7. Go around the class quickly, taking one answer (that has not already been given) per group per category. Are there any categories that do not have any answers? If so, give one or two examples and have the whole class brainstorm some answers.

8. After hearing the newly brainstormed items, write four categories on the top of the chalkboard: *short term, medium term, long term,* and *forever.* Ask each student to write down on a sheet of paper two examples (for each category) of war's environmental impacts that are *short term,* i.e., for the duration of that particular conflict or war; *medium term,* up to 20 years; and *long term,* over 20 years. Are there any impacts that would be *forever*—at least as far as we can tell at this time? After the students have written down their individual examples, write several of these examples on the chalkboard under each of the four categories.

9. Ask the class: *How have the environmental impacts of war changed in the last 50 years or so?* Many of the consequences of war may be the same. However, answers should take note that the human species has developed the technological capacity to inflict more widespread, more long term, and perhaps permanent, injuries upon the environment than during the middle of the 19th century through such

Global Learning, Inc.

inventions as chemical, biological and nuclear weapons. (Of course, other technologies have given us new capabilities for solving some environmental problems.)

10. Conclude the lesson by telling the students that military planners have always had to think about the environment in terms of its impact on their troops and as another obstacle for them to overcome on the battlefield—how to cross this river or "take" that hill. It would take another hundred years after the Civil War and the impact of the modern environmental movement for American military planners to begin to think of their responsibility for protecting and preserving the environment.

"...in August 1970, the deputy secretary of defense gave the various services requirements outlining military compliance with the National Environmental Policy Act of 1969...In 1984, the Department of Defense began the Defense Environmental Restoration Program.... Some critics would argue that the money spent on the program has been little more than an attempt at mollification."

The Ecology of War, pp.xxvii - xxviii.

Student Assessment

Students can be assessed on the basis of their class participation. They can also be asked to write an essay, a short piece of fiction or poetry, or to create a work of art regarding the environmental impacts of war. **Handout 3:** *Vietnam and Agent Orange* could be used as a basis for such an assignment. Students could also compare and contrast the environmental impacts of war in the Civil War and the War in Vietnam as represented by the impact of Agent Orange.

Lesson Extension

1. If more than one class period is available for this lesson, the teacher could give more time to the brainstorming activity, as well as to having students in their small groups create and then present to the class a piece of art, a poem, or a cartoon that reflects their personalized conceptions of the destructiveness of war.

2. The teacher can make an explicit connection to a more contemporary period of time by assigning **Handout 2:** *Former Foes* and **Handout 3:** *Vietnam and Agent Orange* for homework and discussing it in class the following day. Assign a brief reaction paper or an editorial or a letter to the editor regarding the environmental impacts of war.

3. Students may want to compare the environmental impacts they've brainstormed regarding the Civil War with other wars. See the lesson *How Do the Preparations for War Impact on the Environment? The Case of Picatinny Arsenal* for World War II and following, and the lesson *Nuclear Threat at Home:*

The Cold War's Lethal Leftovers regarding the problem of nuclear contamination of military-industrial sites within the United States. See *National Geographic* August 1991 and February 1992 for treatments of the 1991 Gulf War. For a broad overview of the subject, see *The Ecology of War.*

Sources   Bruce Catton. *The American Heritage Picture History of the Civil War.* New York: American Heritage Publishing Co., 1960.

Esper, George. "Fomer Foes." *Star Ledger*, Newark, NJ, 9/12/94.

Lanier-Graham, Susan D. *The Ecology of War: Environmental Impacts of Weaponry and Warfare.* New York: Walker and Co., 1993.

Starr, Jerold M., ed. *The Lessons of the Vietnam War.* Center for Social Studies Education, 3857 Willow Avenue, Pittsburgh, PA 15234, 1991.

Straubing, Harold Elk, ed. *Civil War: Eyewitness Reports.* Hamden, CT: Archon Books, 1985.

Global Learning, Inc.

Domestic Life in War-torn Dixie

General Sherman's scorched earth policy as he marched to the sea included tearing up farm fields and railroads. He destroyed homes, furniture, and personal possessions as his troops descended like locusts. He burned woodlands and silos: butchered livestock. All this activity sorely tested the endurance of the women and children, the elderly, and the crippled, who had remained at home. American money had been turned in for Confederate dollars and Confederate bonds that were almost worthless. There were some rebels who had horded silver and gold, but they were little better off. There was just nothing to buy at any price. Food and clothes were in very short supply. Pride was the powerful ally of the women of the Confederacy. They managed to exhibit super strength, fight the pangs of hunger, and make do because in their own minds, they, too, were soldiers fighting for their new country. A young woman tells the story of her deprivation and hunger, and how she managed to survive. This chapter is taken from *Life in Dixie During the War 1861-1865* by Mary A. H. Gay (The Foote & Davis Co., 1894).

"What is it, Ma? Has anything happened?"

"No, only Maggie Benedict has been here crying as if her heart would break, and saying that her children are begging for bread, and she has none to give them. Give me a little of the meal or hominy that you have, that we may not starve until we can get something else to eat, and then take the remainder to her that she may cook it as quickly as possible for her suffering children."

We had spent the preceding day in picking out grains of corn from cracks and crevices in bureau drawers, and other improvised troughs for Federal horses, as well as gathering up what was scattered upon the ground. In this way by diligent and persevering work, about a half bushel was obtained from the now deserted camping ground of Garrard's cavalry, and this corn was thoroughly washed and dried, and carried by me and Telitha to a poor little mill (which had escaped conflagration, because too humble to attract attention), and ground into coarse meal. Returning from this mill and carrying, myself, a portion of the meal, I saw in the distance my mother coming to meet me. Apprehensive of evil, I ran to meet her and asked:

"What is it, Ma? Has anything happened?"

With flushed face and tear-toned voice she replied as already stated....

I took the bread, and Telitha the bucket, and walked rapidly to Doctor Holmes' residence, where Maggie Benedict, whose husband was away in the Confederate army, had rooms for herself and her children. The Rev. Doctor and his wife had refugeed, leaving this young mother and her children alone and unprotected....

"God helps those who help themselves," is a good old reliable proverb that cannot be too deeply impressed upon the mind of every child. To leave this young mother in a state of absolute helplessness, and her innocent little ones dependent upon the precarious support which might be gleaned from a devastated country would be cruel indeed: but how to end this state of affairs was a serious question.

The railroad having been torn up in every direction communicating with Decatur, there seemed to be but one alternative—to walk—and that was not practicable with several small children.

"Maggie, this state of affairs cannot be kept up: have you no friend to whom you can go?"

"Yes," she replied. "Mr. Benedict has a sister near Madison, who has wanted me and the children to go and stay with her ever since he has been in the army, but I was too independent to do it."

"Absurd! Well, the time has come that you must go. Get the children ready, and I will call for you soon," and without any positive or defined plan of procedure, I took leave of Maggie and her children. I was working by faith, and the Lord directed my footsteps. On my way home, I hunted up "Uncle Mack," and got from him a promise that he would construct a wagon out of the odds and ends left upon the streets of Decatur. The next thing to be done was to provide a horse....

Next morning, before the sun rose, accompanied by the Morton girls, I was on my way to "the cane brakes." I had seen many horses, whose places had been taken by others captured from farmers, abandoned and sent out to the cane-brakes to recuperate or to die, the latter being the more probable....

By twelve o'clock, noon, Uncle Mack appeared upon the scene, pulling something that he had improvised which baffled description, and which, for the sake of the faithful service I obtained from it, I will not attempt to describe, though it might provoke the laughter of the readers. Suffice it to say that as it carried living freight in safety over many a bridge, in honor of this I will call it a wagon. Uncle Mack soon had the horse secured to this vehicle by ropes and pieces of crocus sack, for harness was as scarce a commodity as wagons and horses....

Thus equipped, and with a benediction from my mother, expressed more by looks and acts than by words, I gathered the ropes and started...an errand of mercy which would lead me, as I lead the horse, over a portion of country that in dreariness and utter desolation baffles description—enough to know that Sherman's foraging trains had been over it. Leading the horse which was already christened "Yankee" to Dr. Holmes' door, I called Maggie to come on with her children....

Poor Yankee seemed to feel the importance of his mission, and jogged along at a pretty fair speed, and I, who walked by his side and held the ropes, found myself more than once obliged to strike a trot in order to maintain control of him....

While Maggie hummed a sweet little lullaby to her children, I contemplated the devastation and ruin on every side. Not a vestige of anything remained to mark the sites of the pretty homes which had dotted this fair country before the destroyer came, except, perhaps, a standing chimney now and then. And all this struck me as the willing sacrifice of a peerless people for a great principle, and looking through the dark vista I saw light ahead—I saw white robed peace proclaiming that the end of carnage had come. Even then, as I jogged along, at a snail's pace (for be it known Yankee was not uniform in his gait, and as his mistress had relaxed the tension of the ropes, he had relaxed the speed of his steps), up—a pretty little hill from whose summit I had often gazed with rapturous admiration upon the beautiful mountain of granite near by [i.e., Stone Mountain]. I had so completely materialized the Queen of Peace that I saw her on the mountain's crest, scattering with lavish hand, blessings and treasures as a recompense for the destruction so wantonly inflicted. Thus my hopeful temperament furnished consolation to me, even under darkest circumstances.

Maggie and the children became restless in their pen-up limits, and the latter clamored for something to eat, but there was nothing to give them. Night was upon us, and we had come only about eight miles, and not an animate thing had we seen since we left Decatur, not

Global Learning, Inc.

even a bird, and the silence was unbroken save by the sound of the horse's feet as he trod upon the rocks, and the soft, sweet humming of the young mother to her dear little ones....

Nothing of special interest transpired this second day of our journey. The same fiend of destruction had laid his ruthless hand upon everything within his reach. The woods had been robbed of their beauty and the fields of their products: not even a bird was left to sing a requiem over the scene of desolation, or an animal to suggest where once had been a habitation. Once, crouching near a standing chimney, there was a solitary dog who kept at bay every attempt to approach—no kind word would conciliate or put him off his guard. Poor, lonely sentinel! Did he remember that around the once cheerful hearthstone he had been admitted to a place with the family group? Was he awaiting his master's return? Ah, who can know the emotions, or the dim reasonings of that faithful brute?....

An early start the next day enabled Yankee to carry Maggie and her children and the trunks to Social Circle in time to take the noon train for Madison. So far as Maggie and her children were concerned, I now felt that I had done all that I could, and that I must hasten back to my lonely mother at Decatur....

While waiting for the horse I purchased such articles of food as I could find. For instance, a sack of flour, for which I paid a hundred dollars: a bushel of potatoes, several gallons of sorghum: a few pounds of butter, and a few pounds of meat. Even this was a heavy load for the poor jaded horse. Starting so late I could only get to the hospitable home of Mr. Crew, distant only about three miles from "The Circle"....

A summary of the trip developed these facts: To the faithfulness of Uncle Mack was due the holding together of the most grotesque vehicle ever dignified by the name of wagon: over all that rough road it remained intact, and returned as good as when it started....As for myself, I labored under the hallucination that I was a Confederate soldier, and deemed no task too great for me to try, if it served either directly or indirectly those who were fighting my battles.

[Some weeks later] after mingling renewed vows of allegiance to our cause, and expressions of a willing submission to the consequences of defeat—privations and evil dire, if need be— with my morning prayer, I could not be oblivious to the fact that I was hungry, very hungry. And there was another, [i.e., Ma] whose footsteps were becoming more and more feeble day by day, and whose voice when heard at all, was full of the pathos of despair, who needed nourishment that could not be obtained, and consolation, which it seemed a mockery to offer.

In vain did I look round for relief. There was nothing left in the country to eat. Yea, a crow flying over it would have failed to discover a morsel with which to appease its hunger, for a Sheridan by another name had been there with his minions of destruction, and had ruthlessly destroyed every vestige of food and every means of support. Every larder was empty, and those with thousands and tens of thousands of dollars, were as poor at the poorest, and as hungry, too....

What was I to do? Sit down and wait for the inevitable starvation? No: I was not made of such stuff. I had heard that there had been a provision store opened in Atlanta for the purpose of bartering provisions for munitions of war—anything that could be utilized in warfare. Minnie balls were particularly desirable....

With a basket in either hand, and accompanied by Telitha, who carried one that would hold about a peck, and two old dull case knives, I started to the battlefields around Atlanta to pick up the former missiles of death to exchange for food to keep us from starving....

Former Foes
Aging commanders meet long after guns fall silent.

By George Esper, Associated Press

HANOI—Two old battlefield foes who lost loved ones to war's cruelties came face-to-face in peace for the first time yesterday, two decades after the guns fell silent in Vietnam.

They shook hands and warmly embraced each other.

"I'm very anxious to meet you today and welcome your visit," said legendary Vietnamese Gen. Vo Nguyen Giap. "I know what happened to your family."

Adm. Elmo Zumwalt Jr. turned to Giap. "I look forward to meeting with you, General," he said. "You are a legend in your own time and I know that you share my views that the time has come to bind up our wounds."

Zumwalt, now 73, lives in Arlington, VA. He returned to Vietnam on Friday for the first time in 25 years for a week-long visit in memory of his eldest son, Elmo Zumwalt 3d, and to enlist Hanoi's help in Agent Orange research.

Both he and his son served in Vietnam between 1968 and 1970. The admiral, who was commander of U.S. naval forces in Vietnam then, ordered the spraying of Agent Orange to strip away jungle cover for Giap's Communist troops.

Zumwalt's son was exposed to Agent Orange while commanding a patrol boat in the Mekong Delta, and died in August 1988 at the age of 42 from cancer his father says was caused by Agent Orange. The defoliant also is believed to have caused severe learning disabilities in Zumwalt's grandson, Russell, now 16.

Giap, now 83, defeated the French at Dien Bien Phu in 1954. His wife, Minh Khai, a Communist militant, was arrested for anti-French activities and died in prison. A decade later, Giap held off half-a-million American troops.

With the war stalemated and American casualties rising, the United States withdrew in 1973. Two years later, the North took control of the South....

After their meeting, Giap autographed a copy of his book, "People's War, People's Army," for Zumwalt.

Zumwalt presented him with a signed copy of his own book, "On Watch"...He wrote: "To Gen. Vo Nguyen Giap. With respect to a former adversary and new friend."

Source: *The Star Ledger*, 9/12/94

Vietnam and Agent Orange

Between 1962 and 1971 the U.S. conducted a defoliation program in Vietnam called Operation Ranch Hand. Twin-engine planes, trucks, river boats, even backpacks sprayed almost 18 million gallons of defoliants over about 4.5 million acres of South Vietnam. This area is the size of the State of Massachusetts. The objective of the program was to destroy the plant life that provided ambush cover and food supplies for the enemy. Herbicides also were used to clear the areas around the perimeters of American base camps, landing zones, waterways, and communication lines.

The effects were devastating. Today in Vietnam one sees waste-high scrub brush for hundreds of miles where once there were lush triple-canopy jungles. In some regions it may be several decades before natural vegetation reappears. Returning to their homeland after an earlier evacuation, the people of Bin Hoa were "terrified" to see that "not a blade of grass survived...the trunks of toppled coconut trees protruded along the edges of ditches, leafless bamboo stems stood pointing up at the sky....There were no barking dogs, no bird songs, not even the familiar chirping of insects. The soil was dead."

The most widely used herbicide in Vietnam was called Agent Orange after the color-coded stripe that wound around its 55-gallon steel drum container. Between 1965 and 1970, the U.S. military sprayed nearly twelve million gallons of Agent Orange in Vietnam. Dioxin, a contaminant produced as a by-product of making Agent Orange, is one of the most toxic substances know. U.S. troops in Vietnam operating in sprayed areas may have breathed it, inhaled it from burning brush, drunk or bathed in contaminated water or eaten contaminated food.

Most soldiers who served in Vietnam knew little or nothing about Agent Orange. One of them, Paul Ruetershan, found he had cancer in 1976. Friends called the clean-living Ruetershan a health nut. As he pondered the source of his fatal illness, he began to suspect it might be linked to the herbicides to which he had been exposed in Vietnam.

Ruetershan researched Agent Orange and became convinced that it was the cause of his disease. Before the end of 1977, he and his sister, Jane Dziedzic, formed Agent Orange Victims International. Ruetershan launched the campaign by filing a personal damage claim against the government.

Soon after, Ruetershan met Maude DeVictor, a Veterans Administration (V.A.) counselor in Chicago. DeVictor's own study of Agent Orange documented at least one hundred cases of possible dioxin poisoning. She shared her evidence with Ron DeYoung, a veteran's counselor at a Chicago college. They took the story to a Chicago CBS outlet, where news anchor Bill Kurtis made an hour-long documentary called "Agent Orange, the Deadly Fog." Broadcast on March 23, 1978, it brought forth a flood of claims from veterans all over the country.

On December 14, 1978, at the age of twenty-eight, Paul Ruetershan died. On March 19, 1979, Vietnam veteran Michael Ryan and his wife Maureen, parents of a severely deformed child, joined nineteen other couples in an unprecedented class-action suit against the Dow

Chemical Company and six other manufacturers of herbicides used in Vietnam. They asked that all Vietnam veterans and their families be certified as plaintiffs.

They wanted Agent Orange off the market, information provided about its dangers, a declaration from the companies that they had a responsibility to protect public health and safety, and a fund set up by the companies to award damages to victims.

Faced with the possibility of enormous damages, Dow filed suit against the U.S. government. The company claimed it informed the government about the dangers of dioxin in 1962 and tried to convince the government to use a safer herbicide. That suit was disallowed. However, the government did respond. In December 1979, the U.S. Congress directed the V.A. to study veterans exposed to Agent Orange. Submitted in 1981, the study was rejected as invalid by scientists in Congress' Office of Technology Assessment. Nevertheless, in November, Congress authorized the V.A. to provide medical care to any veteran they find may have been exposed to a toxic substance present in a herbicide.

Late in 1982, the original study proposal was turned over to the Centers for Disease Control in Atlanta. In August 1984, the study, based on families in the area, was released. It found no evidence that Vietnam veterans had a greater risk than other men of fathering babies with major birth defects.

Congress directed the V.A. to conduct further studies as well as to establish a policy regarding claims. In August 1985, the V.A. issued a regulation recognizing only chloracne, a skin disease, as being connected to dioxin exposure. To qualify for help, a veteran had to prove the disease was evident within three months of his or her departure from Vietnam.

In November 1985, the Air Force released the third of three controversial studies of Ranch Hand personnel involved in the spraying missions in Vietnam. The report did not find any statistically significant differences in mortality between Ranch Hand crew members and non-exposed groups.

Despite the lack of conclusive evidence, the suit against the chemical companies was successful. The companies refused to concede any connection between the dioxin in their products and any illnesses or birth defects suffered by veterans and their children. Nevertheless, on May 7, 1984, they agreed to a pretrial settlement of $180 million to be set up in a fund to be administered later by the V.A. Monsanto Chemical explained that, regardless of the scientific evidence, the case had become a "rallying point" for everyone sympathetic to the "cause" of justice for Vietnam veterans. They chose to settle rather than contest an expensive suit in the full glare of "negative media attention" at the risk of "damage to Monsanto's reputation as a concerned, sensitive, socially responsible company."

Many veterans and their supporters reacted angrily to the settlement. For veterans who testified in New Jersey, "money was not the real issue. The issue was and remains concern for their children and families and status of their health." The settlement was appealed.

By 1989, accumulation of interest had swelled the fund to $240 million and all appeals had been exhausted. Attorney's fees and payments to Australian and New Zealand veterans reduced the fund to $222 million. Some $52 million was put into the Agent Orange Class Assistance Program for agencies that serve Vietnam veterans and their families. The balance of $170 million was shared by about 30,000 veterans and 18,000 survivor families considered eligible for the benefits; an average of less than $6,000 per veteran. Veterans' claims against the U.S. government are still being pursued....

...numerous studies have documented significantly higher rates of certain pathologies among Vietnam veterans than among comparison groups of Vietnam era veterans and non-veterans. A May 1990 review of the evidence persuaded V.A. Secretary Edward Derwinski to approve compensation for Vietnam veterans who suffer from non-Hodgkins lymphoma and soft- tissue-sarcomas. The latter disease affects about 1,100 veterans who will be eligible for compensation at a total cost of $8 million per year.

More recently, Rep. Lane Evans (Democrat-IL), co-chair of Vietnam-era Veterans in Congress, introduced legislation, co-sponsored by 160 House members, to compensate veterans or their survivors for the above diseases plus melanoma and basal cell carcinoma. Evans stated: "The fight over methodology has gone on long enough. Veterans who suffer from problems because of exposure need help now. We must take action now to fulfill the promise our country has made."

With so much money at stake, however, it is safe to assume that challenges to scientific evidence in support of legal claims will continue. However, scientists working for the New Jersey Agent Orange Commission recently have developed a method that could fill an important gap in the evidence. The method involves testing blood samples to determine levels of dioxin in Vietnam veterans and a control group of men who did not serve in Vietnam.

Preliminary research indicates excessive levels of dioxin in blood samples from veterans who served in heavily sprayed regions of Vietnam. The Commission will be studying several specific groups, including infantry troops, river boat crews and women veterans. With this measure they might be able to better estimate the link between dioxin in the body and various forms of disease in humans. However, for most veterans there would still be the question of where their exposure to dioxin occurred.

It should go without saying that diseases possibly related to dioxin exposure are a major problem for the Vietnamese people also. Veterans recently returned from tours of Vietnam have described their visit to Ho Chi Minh City's Tu Dzu Hospital where jars of horribly deformed fetuses are stored. In Hanoi, senior officials in the Ministry of Health show slides of children with twisted faces and limbs.

This problem has been studied scientifically with very interesting results. Dr. Ton That Tung of Hanoi University and his colleagues have compared 836 Vietnamese soldiers, who fought in southern Vietnam where the spraying was done, to 236 soldiers who never served in the south. They found that the exposed group had a miscarriage/premature birth rate of 15.3 percent compared to 10.4 percent among those not exposed. Moreover, 3.6 percent of all children fathered by the exposed group suffered congenital birth defects, compared with none in the non-exposed group.

Scientists returning from Vietnam report a serious "persistence of dioxin in the environment and the people." Of great scientific significance is the finding that levels of dioxin in fatty tissue and breast milk were "elevated" among people "potentially exposed in the south" where the spraying was done and even "lower" than in industrial countries among people in the north, never exposed to herbicide spraying. Dr. Arnold Schecter and others feel that this makes Vietnam the obvious site for the most rigorously controlled study of dioxin's relationship to disease in humans. The findings would not only serve the cause of Vietnam veterans, but the health education needs of all people.

Source: Jerold M. Starr, ed., *The Lessons of Vietnam,* 1991.

Lesson 10

The Mining Frontier
Boom and Bust (1849-1890)

Historical Periods Expansion and Reform (1801-1861)
The Development of Industrial United States (1870-1900)

Sustainable Development Topics Intergenerational responsibility, government policy choices, land and water use, and equity issues

Purpose To show students that the General Mining Act of 1872, passed to serve western expansion, also led to environmental and social problems which persist today, and to have the students in a mock Congressional committee hearing analyze some proposed legislative reforms of the 1872 Law in terms of a sustainable future.

Objectives Students will be able to:

1. Analyze primary source accounts of life in the western mining era in the 1849-1890 period in terms of the effects of western mining on the people and on the environment.
2. Analyze three reforms of the General Mining Act of 1872 proposed in 1993 in terms of concern for future generations (intergenerational sustainability).

Time Required Homework and 2 class periods. (If students have not had previous lessons on the concept of sustainable development, they will need more than a quick review. In that case, the lesson will require an extra class period.)

Materials Needed Handout 1: *Three Historical Perspectives on the Gold Rush Era*
Handout 2: *1872 Mining Law: Meet 1993 Reform*
Handout 3: *Three Legislative Proposals*
Handout 4: *Legislative Analysis Sheet*

Teacher Background The mining frontier offers a unique opportunity for using the concept of sustainable development as a framework to analyze the effects of a historical government policy in terms of equity, the environment, economic development and political power.

Global Learning, Inc.

One of the concepts implicit in sustainable development is intergenerational responsibility. Sustainability implies a balance between the basic needs of the inhabitants of the earth and the environment, the resource base which supplies those needs. Intergenerational responsibility implies a concern that the present use of resources will ensure that future generations will be able to meet their needs also.

This is not a new concept. For example, Native American tradition included intergenerational concern in the Great Law of the Haudenosaunee, People of the Longhouse—The Six Nations Iroquois Confederacy (Oneida, Cayuga, Tuscarora, Mohawk, Onondaga and Seneca). "In our every deliberation, we must consider the impact of our decisions on the next seven generations."

One caveat: In analyzing historical decision making, it is easy to slip into judging previous generations outside the context of the knowledge base and experiential concerns of the time. The discussion questions for analyzing the historical documents take this tendency into consideration.

The mining boom, in what was to become the Western U.S.A., began in 1849 with the California gold rush. By 1890 it had ended having provided over $2 billion in wealth, much of which financed the Civil War. At the end of the mining boom, most of the mines had left the hands of the small miner and were now owned by large businesses.

The mining industry left behind some major scars. Many mines were constructed poorly, causing the deaths of workers. Mining left (and still leaves) gullies and polluted rivers and streams as well as soil erosion. Native Americans were driven from their lands by avid gold miners. Between 1852 and 1867, three to four thousand Native American children were taken by slave traders for work as servants and workhands. These and other violations led to renewed fighting and killing between Native Americans and Western settlers.

The General Mining Act of 1872, which essentially allows those who find rock minerals in public territory to buy the land for $5.00 an acre, was passed by Congress for several reasons. The government wanted to encourage western mining as a way to settle the West. At the same time there was a need to bring some "law and order" to the region. The larger mining companies favored passage of the Act as a way to stop claim-jumping and to set standards for filing and holding claims. The law is still in effect and applies to 270 million acres of federal lands—almost one-fourth of all the land in the United States.

Procedure To set the context:

Assign for homework the textbook section on the western mining era and **Handout 1: *Three Historical Perspectives on the Gold Rush Era*.** Tell students to write down three questions they have about the readings for class discussion.

Procedure Day 1 Analyzing the Historical Documents

1. Begin by conducting a discussion about the issues raised in the handout. Start with the questions the students bring. Questions can be grouped and categorized (there might be duplication or similarities). The student questions may be answered in the course of the discussion or be future research questions if answers are not immediately available. Some sample questions to structure the discussion:

    a. What were some of the environmental concerns in the readings? List on board.
    b. What were some of the *equity issues?* List.
    c. Which effects do you think would not have been seen as problematic in the 1870s? (Indicate on the list.) Why?
    d. In your judgment, which of these effects were problematic? (Indicate on the list.) Why? Do you think they are still problematic today?

2. Review the concept of *sustainable development* by asking students for the definition: *development that meets the needs of the present without compromising the ability of future generations to meet their needs.* Discuss briefly. (If students have not had previous exposure to sustainable development concepts, they will need more background work. See the lesson *What Is Sustainable Development? The Chair.*)

    a. Which of these concerns and issues compromised the ability of future generations to meet their needs? How? (E.g., Native Americans who could no longer fish)

3. Tell the class that tomorrow they will serve as a Congressional Advisory Committee. Distribute **Handout 2: *1872 Mining Law: Meet 1993 Reform*** and **Handout 3: *Three Legislative Proposals*,** and assign for homework. Tell students they will need to be familiar with the information in the readings to be able to advise Congress wisely.

Procedure Day 2 Mock Congressional Advisory Committee Hearing

1. List any questions students have. Discuss briefly. If answers are not readily available, save for future research.
2. Divide the class into groups of four. Tell students that they are being asked to serve on a congressional committee to advise the legislature on reforms to the General Mining Act of 1872. Each group will need to pick a **recorder** to keep the group's notes.

Global Learning, Inc.

3. Distribute **Handout 4:** *Legislative Analysis Sheet*, to the group recorders. (The correct answers for question 3 are 1. 0, 2. $240 million, 3. $150 million, 4. $60 million.)

4. Ask all to read again the three legislative reform proposals which they received for homework and, as a group, to analyze the reform proposals in terms of working toward a sustainable future using the legislative analysis sheet. (Allow 15-20 minutes.)

5. Each group decides which legislative proposal they want to support and writes a one- paragraph statement of support for their choice. Each group picks a **reporter** who presents the group's statement.

6. The teacher records the groups' choices.

7. Discussion:
   a. What are the areas of agreement among the student groups?
   b. Where are the areas of disagreement?
   c. Can students make the case that their choices take future generations into account?

8. Conclude by having everyone in the class vote individually, by paper ballot, on which reform proposal they would advise Congress to adopt.

Student Assessment   Students can be asssessed on the basis of their class participation. They can also write a paragraph supporting their final vote on a preferred reform proposal.

Lesson Extensions   Students may be encouraged to send their analysis and statement of support for a particular legislative reform proposal to their local Congressperson or to the congressional committees that have a bearing on the legislation, i.e., Agriculture, Commerce, and Resources with its Subcommittees on Energy and Mineral Resources and on Fishing, Wildlife and Oceans. The telephone number for general information in Congress is (202) 225-3121.

Set a report-back time to see how the congressional process is working on reform of the General Mining Act of 1872. You may want to bring this up in the Progressive Era or our contemporary time frame. Contact your local Congressperson's office or the Mineral Policy Center, Room 550, 1325 Massachusetts Avenue, NW, Washington, D.C. 20005, (202) 887-1872, for an update on the General Mining Act of 1872.

Sources   Letto, Jay. "1872 Mining Law: Meet 1993 Reform," *E Magazine*. September-October 1993.

Todd, John. *The Sunset Land*. Boston: Lee and Shepard, 1870.

Three Historical Perspectives on the Gold Rush Era

I. A Federal Agent Assesses Mining's Impact on Native Americans, 1853

Diamond Springs
El Dorado County
December 31, 1853

The Indians in this portion of the State are wretchedly poor, having no horses, cattle, or other property. They formerly subsisted on game, fish, acorns, etc., but it is now impossible for them to make a living by hunting or fishing, for nearly all the game has been driven from the mining region or has been killed by the thousands of our people who now occupy the once quiet home of these children of the forest. The rivers or tributaries of the Sacramento formerly were clear as crystal and abounded with the finest salmon and other fish. I saw them at Salmon Falls on the American river in the year 1851, and also the Indians taking barrels of these beautiful fish and drying them for winter. But the miners have turned the streams from their beds and conveyed the water to the dry diggings and after being used until it is so thick with mud that it will scarcely run it returns to its natural channel and with it the soil from a thousand hills, which has driven almost every kind of fish to seek new places of resort where they can enjoy a purer and more natural element. And to prove the old adage that misfortunes never come singly the oaks have for the last three years refused to furnish the acorn, which formed one of the chief articles of Indian food. They have often told me that the white man had killed all their game, had driven the fish from the rivers, had cut down and destroyed the trees and that what were now standing were worthless for they bore no acorns. In their superstitious imaginations they believe that the White man's presence among them has caused the trees (that formerly bore plentifully) to now be worthless and barren. In concluding this brief report, I deem it my duty to recommend to your favorable consideration the early establishment of a suitable reservation and the removal of these Indians thereto, where they can receive medical aid and assistance which at the present time they so much require.

All of which is very respectfully submitted.

Hon. Thos. J. Henley
Supt. of Indian Affairs
San Francisco, Cal.

E.A. Stevenson
Spec. Indian Agent

Global Learning, Inc.

II. Excerpts from "Sunset Land," a promotional settlement account by John Todd, a New England minister. (1870)

...The discovery of gold, and the amount obtained, have given a stimulus to commerce, to agriculture, to every department of life. They have created impulses that have advanced civilization, and shaken up nations, and poured one country into another, till we hardly know what will be next. The arts have advanced, architecture has made new discoveries in applying its skill, manufacturers have been called upon to supply more people, and with better garments; and if a few have played the fool by sudden riches, the great mass of the people have been greatly benefited....

Since this outpouring of the silver and the gold from the mines, we are every way improved; we have better clothing, better houses, better carriages, better school- houses and churches, and schools and colleges, better books and libraries, better ships and steamboats, better goods manufactured, and everything better. Not only so, but where one used to have these good things, ten have them now. The whole plane of human comforts and enjoyments has been raised up many degrees....

...As to the amount of precious metals that have been dug out of the soil of California during the twenty years, it is difficult to form an estimate on which you can rely. As near as I can judge, I should put the gold at one thousand hundred tons. The silver mining is now in its infancy, but the yield is enormous. You go into the express office on the arrival of the daily steamer, and you are amazed at the enormous amount of huge silver bars that have just come in--sometimes three tons of these in a single day! These are almost all sent off in the bars to China, and other parts of the world....

III. Excerpts from "Sunset Land," a promotional settlement account by John Todd, a New England minister. (1870)

...Nothing can be more dreary than a territory where the soil has been washed out as low as the water will run off. Ten thousand rocks of all shapes, and forms, and sizes are left; acres and acres, and even miles, of the skeletons of beauty, with a flesh all gone, and nothing but hideousness remaining. I have heard it asserted, that the placer mines are about exhausted, and that, hereafter, nothing but the rich companies, who have great mills to crush the quartz rock, can gain a living. I do not believe this is true. While capital and skill can gain much faster in quartz-mining, I have no doubt that it will take generations, if not a thousand years, before the gold is so washed out of the soil of California, that mining will not be a paying business. In the quartz mines, a very huge water-wheel, made to turn by the smallest amount of water possible, pumps the water from the mine as fast as it accumulates; the ore is then dug or blasted out, broken into pieces about as large as the fist, then put into an iron mortar, and stamped with iron pestles, till it is so reduced to powder, that water will wash it out in the trough, where the quicksilver lies in wait to catch the gold. This amalgam, quicksilver and gold, is next put into a covered retort of iron, with a pipe allowing the fumes of the quicksilver to escape, which pipe is cooled by passing through cold water, till the quicksilver fumes are condensed, and it drops down, the pure metal it was, leaving the gold in the retort. In this process, about twenty-five per cent of the quicksilver is lost. There are about four hundred and fifty quartz mills already in operation in the State, and the number is constantly increasing. In the placer mines the poorest man may go to work, only paying for the use of water. In the quartz-mining, vast capital can and must be employed. When the little claims on mining land have been staked out, the spirit of speculation comes in to buy and sell these claims. I have seen many houses bought for the sake of the soil that might be dug out under them. The useless house is left standing on sticks.

1872 Mining Law: Meet 1993 Reform
The Last Great Land Giveaway May Soon Be Over

"Mining operations on federal lands produce $3 to $4 billion worth of minerals a year-- and the public doesn't get a cent."

One hundred and twenty-two years ago, Ulysses S. Grant was President, Charles Darwin continued work on his evolution theory, George Pullman introduced the "sleeper car," and the General Mining Law of 1872 was enacted. Since then, we've had 24 new presidents, evolution has become a science, and the sleeper car has lost out to air travel. But the mining law remains. Passed by Congress primarily to bring law and order to a 19th century "Wild West" shooting itself apart over mining claims, the 1872 Law also sought to lure immigrants and Easterners to settle the vast stretches of public land in the West. In 1993, however, the miners are usually wealthy and the mining companies often foreign-owned, and just about everybody—except mining companies and their powerful lobby—thinks the law has long overstayed its welcome.

As incredible as it may sound, under the archaic law, miners can stake a "claim" and mine any federal land, except within National Parks and Wilderness Areas, simply by declaring that they think the land holds valuable minerals. They pay the government no rent on the land and no royalties on the minerals extracted, but they may lease the land to others and charge them rent and royalties. And if "valuable minerals" are found, the claimholder may "patent" or purchase title to the land for $5 or less an acre. Referred to as "the last of the great land giveaways," the law has sold off 3.2 million acres of public land—an area the size of Connecticut.

But the worst aspect of the law may be that it allows the managing agencies—the Bureau of Land Management (BLM) and the Forest Service—no recourse for environmental protection. Mining can take place in sensitive areas, and there is no provision for reclamation of damaged land. The result: 52 mines on the Environmental Protection Agency's (EPA) Superfund National Priorities List of the worst toxic waste sites in the country; 424,000 acres of unreclaimed federal land left by hardrock mining; and 10,000 miles of rivers polluted from mining operations, as estimated by the U.S. Bureau of Mines. Says Jim Lyon of the Mineral Policy Center in Washington, DC, "no one really knows" the whole scope of the damage. "Probably the worst problem from hardrock mining is degraded water quality from heavy metals and mine drainage. Once it starts, it's almost impossible to stop, it can severely impact on a large area, and it will take generations to clean up."

Of the thousands of abandoned sites, only a handful are being restored. It's much more common for a company to abandon the mine site, file for bankruptcy to avoid future liability costs, and leave the public with the cleanup bill. The Atlas Asbestos Mine Superfund site in Fresno County, California, for example, was listed on the EPA's National Priorities List in 1984. Located on 435 acres of BLM land, it has three open pit mines and numerous piles of asbestos waste. After abandoning the site in 1979, Wheeler Properties filed for bankruptcy, leaving the public with the cleanup bill. Soil erosion on the steep slopes has prevented revegetation, and wind erosion and water runoff have caused the levels of asbestos in nearby surface water to exceed EPA standards for human health. It now threatens the drinking water in the California Aqueduct and nearby communities. In 1991, the EPA approved a $4.29 million effort to contain asbestos at the site to prevent further contamination, but the agency is still seeking responsible parties to help pay the costs.

Apart from all the destruction, lost government revenues from the law has opened some eyes. According to the Mineral Policy Center, mining operations on federal lands produce $3 to $4 billion worth of minerals each year—and the public doesn't get a cent. Royalties, which nearly every other developed country charges, would add hundreds of millions of dollars to the federal treasury.

The 5,000-acre Stillwater Mine outside Yellowstone National park holds platinum and palladium deposits worth $30 billion. The Johns Manville and Chevron companies have jointly applied to buy the land for $20,000—less than $5 an acre. "Clearly, the American people, who own the $30 billion worth of minerals, ought to get a fair return on that," Lyon says. "And the land should not be sold," he added. "That's in violation of the Federal Land Management Act, which says that the land policy should encourage the retention of public land, not create inholdings."

The Clinton Administration, under the aegis of deficit reduction, last spring asked for a 12.5 percent royalty on minerals extracted from federal lands, but Western Democrat Senators convinced the President to back down.

Industry has countless arguments against real reform. They claim that royalties and expensive environmental measures will close down mining operations everywhere. They present scenarios of thriving communities turned into ghost towns, skyrocketing consumer prices and general economic disaster. But Lyon replies: "Mining has never been a sustainable industry. It's always been boom or bust. We think that the idea of reform putting the industry out of business is a red herring." The 1872 Mining Law only covers one-third of hardrock mining in the U.S. The rest is on private, state, or tribal lands, where the industry has no trouble paying royalties, and companies often lease lands to each other, charging royalties ranging from five to 20 percent. Even the family of Senator Max Baucus (D-MT) gets royalties for mining on its land. Yet Baucus has told Clinton that collecting royalties from federal lands will break the industry. "If royalties are good enough for the Baucus family ranch," Lyon asked, "why aren't they good enough for the American people?"

Source: Jay Letto. E Magazine. September-October 1993.

For more information, contact: Mineral Policy Center, 1325 Massachusetts Avenue NW, Washington, DC 20005, (202) 887-1872.

Three Legislative Proposals

I. House of Representative Bill: *The Mineral Exploration and Development Act of 1993* **(H.R. 918), introduced by Representative Nick Rahall (D-West Virginia)**

1. Calls for an 8% royalty on gross production.
2. Abolishes patenting (this means that all land would be retained by the federal government).
3. Charges a per claim fee of $100 a year for companies to hold the mineral rights.
4. Environmental Standards

    a. A company has to demonstrate, up front, that its mining practices will not harm the environment.
    b. Gives regulators authority to stop damaging operations of mining companies.
    c. Establishes strong inspection and enforcement provisions allowing citizen lawsuits to give the public the opportunity to compel enforcement and to stop bad operations.
    d. Establishes an abandoned-mine cleanup program to be funded by the royalties, permit fees and penalties.

II. Senate: *Mining Law Reform Act of 1993* **(S.257), introduced by Senator Dale Bumpers (D-Arkansas)**

1. Royalties of 5% of the gross value of minerals found (1/3 to be set aside in trust to clean up abandoned mines).
2. Requires reclamation plans along with the bonds or other forms of security to make sure that reclamation is performed once mining is completed.
3. Gives federal agencies new authority to protect the environment in mining areas.
4. Eliminates patents (federal government retains the land).

III. Senate: Hardrock Mining Reform Act of 1993 (S.775), introduced by Senator Larry Craig (R-Indiana)

1. 2% royalties to the government on the gross value of minerals found.[*]

2. No change in the "right to mine" provision of the 1872 Mining Law. This clause grants superior status to mining over all other values on public lands.

3. Requires a "plan of operations" for all mining activities which would expose such activities to improved scrutiny under the National Environmental Protection Act. Critics say, however, that groundwater protection (one of the worst environmental effects of mining operations) is not prevented by Federal law.

4. No goals and standards for reclamation of worked-out mine sites is included.

5. Would allow a continuing of the purchase of public lands for mining up to six months after the Bill would be passed. Thus public lands would continue to be converted to private holdings. Critics estimate that $86 billion dollars worth of public ores are now being "patented" or purchased. They claim that mining companies are rushing to purchase public lands before any reforms can be made by the legislature.

6. Mining industry could continue to take a "percentage depletion allowance" on its Federal income tax equal to 15% (for gold) of the gross value of mine operation.

---

[*] Based on 1992 figures for gold, 2% royalty would work out to about $0.21 per ounce of gold. By comparison, Senator Bumper's Bill, S.257, would collect $27.60 per ounce.

One large mining company has costs of $210.00 per ounce for gold mining. The company is currently selling gold for $397.00 per ounce. The net profit for this company in 1993 was $175 million dollars.

Under current law, companies are not liable for conducting environmental cleanup after mining operations.

Global Learning, Inc.

Legislative Analysis Sheet

1. List the issues you think will be adequately addressed by each legislative proposal. Give reasons for your choices.

   Rahall   Bumpers   Craig

2. List the issues that you think will not be adequately addressed in each proposal. Give reasons.

   Rahall   Bumpers   Craig

3. Calculate the revenues to the government (and indirectly to the taxpayer) for mineral mining on federal lands. Base your calculations on $3 billion worth of minerals' being mined in one year.

    a. Under the General Mining Act of 1872
       (which is still in effect)   _____

    b. Under the Rahall House Bill   _____

    c. Under the Bumpers Senate Bill   _____

    d. Under the Craig Senate Bill   _____

4. What do you think are the major road blocks to reform? List and give reasons.

Global Learning, Inc.

Lesson 11

Environmental Impacts of the Transcontinental Railroad

Historical Period	The Development of Industrial United States (1860-1900)
Sustainable Development Topics	Environmental and social impacts of economic development
Purpose	This lesson helps students analyze the environmental impact of the building of the transcontinental railroad by first introducing students to a contemporary Environmental Impact Statement for a recently completed section of interstate highway. Students will see that such impacts include economic and social dimensions, as well as the natural order.
Objectives	Students will be able to:

1. Analyze the elements of an environmental impact statement for a highway.
2. Apply this analysis to a previous historical period, namely, to the building of the transcontinental railroads.
3. Make a public policy recommendation and support it with reasons.
4. Distinguish among facts, opinions, and value judgments.

Time Required	Homework and 2 class periods, or 3 with the video excerpt
Materials Needed	Handout 1: *OPEN ROAD* Handout 2: *Interstate I-287: Summary of Environmental Impacts* Handout 3: *The Golden Spike: The Story of the Transcontinental Railroad*

The HBO video *Earth and the American Dream* (optional—available from Direct Cinema, P.O. Box 10003, Santa Monica, CA 90410; 800-525-0000; $85 rental, $95 purchase)
Newsprint, markers, masking tape
Topographical map of the United States
Highway map of New Jersey or the metropolitan New York area

Teacher Background

Railroads were introduced into the United States in the late 1820s, and within 25 years, voices were beginning to call for a link between the Pacific coast and the sometimes incompatible systems of the region east of the Mississippi River. The slavery issue postponed a commitment to this transcontinental link, and the Civil War slowed it down, but in 1862 President Lincoln signed the Pacific Railway Act and provided generous land grants to the two railroads—the Central Pacific and the Union Pacific, in order to finance the undertaking with private funds. The call of "Manifest Destiny" deafened most ears to any potential cries of injustice and fueled a remarkable engineering feat. At the same time, this human activity had massive impacts on the North American continent, impacts many of us are still learning about.

Procedure

Assign **Handout 1: *OPEN ROAD*** for homework. Using a highway atlas or map of New Jersey, have students draw a map of the complete Route 287 from Staten Island to Port Chester on an 8½ x 11" sheet of paper, indicating the most recently completed section. Also include routes I-80, I-78, US-46, NJ-23, I-87, the New Jersey Turnpike, and the Garden State Parkway.

Procedure

Day 1

1. Ask the class: *What were the reasons for building Interstate Route 287 in New Jersey?* (to save time and money by avoiding the congested routes closer to New York City)

2. *What happened in 1971 that contributed to the delays in completing this highway?* (National Environmental Policy Act required extensive environmental reviews of all federal projects.)

3. Write on the board: **Environmental Impact Statement**. Ask students to brainstorm what they think would go into an EIS. Remind students of the rules of brainstorming:

   a. The purpose of brainstorming is to generate as many ideas as possible in a short period of time; we are not worried about quality in brainstorming, but quantity.

   b. We want each person to say what comes to her or his mind.

   c. When we brainstorm, we do not allow any comments, positive or negative, because that may inhibit people from saying what comes to mind.

Global Learning, Inc.

    d. All ideas are accepted and written down.

4. Ask students to group the results of their brainstorming and give each category a name.

5. Distribute **Handout 2: *Interstate I-287: Summary of Environmental Impacts***. This is the actual summary of the 1982 environmental impact statement mentioned in Handout 1. Ask students to compare their brainstormed list and categories with those on this summary.

6. Tell the students that they are going to take a "quantum leap" back into history to the 1860s. Using this highway environmental impact summary, they are going to prepare an Environmental Impact Statement for the building of the transcontinental railroad. Either show the ten minute section, "Prairies will be coverd with your speckled cattle and festive cowboys—1850-1900," from the video *Earth and the American Dream,* or have all students read their textbook section on the transcontinental railroad. If you show the video, be prepared for a lively discussion before focusing again on the building of the railroad. This discussion will probably take the rest of the class period and steps 7-12 will need to be completed on an additional day. Drawing the routes of the railroads can then be assigned as homework.

7. On a topographical map of the United States, trace the route of the Union Pacific and the Central Pacific railroads from Omaha across southern Nebraska and Wyoming, northern Utah and Nevada, and central California to Sacramento—or vice versa! Point out where Promontory, Utah is (just east of the northern tip of the Great Salt Lake). Ask what geographical challenges would face the builders of these railroads. Have students identify which of the present-day states were still territories in 1862 and which had become states by the completion of the railroads (Nevada [1864], Nebraska [1867], Wyoming [1890], and Utah [1896]). (If time permits, you can assign these tasks for students to do individually or in pairs on an outline map of the United States. A map can be found in Handout 2 of the lesson, *Nuclear Threat at Home.*)

8. Form small groups of 2 or 3 students. From Handout 2 eliminate the categories of *traffic operations, historic properties,* and *recreational facilities.* Assign each group 3-4 of the remaining categories so that each category has at least two small groups working on it. On a large sheet of newsprint, have each group list questions for each assigned category that they would ask to ascertain the environmental impact of the building of the Central Pacific and the Union Pacific railroads.

9. Have all groups post their lists of questions. Have the whole class agree on a few questions for each category that might apply to the transcontinental railroad.

10. Assign each group a set of categories to research and to draft a summary environmental impact statement, e.g.:

   a. Natural ecosystems, communities and neighborhoods (including Native Americans), and short-term employment;

   b. Wetlands, air quality, long-term employment, and construction operations;

   c. Land use, property acquisition and relocation, noise quality.

11. Information can be obtained from **Handout 3: *The Golden Spike: The Story of the Transcontinental Railroad*,** topographical maps of the region, in encyclopedias under the headings of railroads/history or of the Union Pacific and Central Pacific railroads, and from books on the history of railroads in the United States. Sample titles are listed below under sources.

12. You may want to give students more than one evening to conduct this research.

Procedure Day 2

1. Have the groups that researched the same set of categories meet together to combine and refine their summary statements. Have them post their results on newsprint so the whole class can read them.

2. Conduct a general discussion of the combined results.

3. Conclude the lesson by assigning the following essay: *If you were a member of a congressional advisory committee in 1862, but knew the results of the class' Environmental Impact Statement, would you support or oppose the building of the transcontinental railroads? Give your reasons and indicate which are factual, which are opinions, and which are value judgments. Discuss the relationship between economic development concerns, environmental impacts, and equity issues. What recommendations would you make to lessen or eliminate the negative impacts of the railroad, keeping in mind the technology of the 1860s?*

Lesson Extension This lesson provides an opportunity for students to explore the issue of equity, or fairness, regarding past events over which they had no control, but from which they have benefitted by virtue of such factors as our current national unity and standards of living. The loss of Native Americans' lands and traditional lifestyles and the treatment of Chinese laborers after the completion of the railroads are two major examples of equity

Global Learning, Inc.

issues. *What rights and responsibility, if any, do we share today as a result of inequities in our country's past?* Using the following perspectives as a starting point and modifying them according to their own views, students could discuss this question in small groups, or write an essay elaborating on the following perspectives, or create a visual or poetic response.

Perspective 1: What happened in the past may or may not have been fair, but I was not alive then and it has nothing to do with me.

Perspective 2: What happened in the past was unfair. We can understand it within its historical context and try to support the descendants of those affected groups as they struggle to reclaim their cultural heritage. The United States Government today is morally and legally responsible to honor its historic treaties with Native American nations, even if it costs our government significant amounts of money.

Perspective 3: I am a member of one of the groups (racial, ethnic, gender, religious...) who have been historically discriminated against. Even today we must fight against negative stereotypes and discriminatory practices that make it more difficult for us to achieve success and acceptance as equals in this society. I just want the huge uphill playing field to be leveled out so I can compete on par with everyone else for a decent lifestyle. To me, that's what equal opportunity is supposed to be.

Perspective 4: Life's not fair. Our present-day country is what it is, partly as a result of past injustices. But those who have wealth and power deserve to keep them, as long as they don't abuse other people's rights. Indeed, the wealthy invest in businesses and help create jobs and opportunities for upward social and economic mobility for both the poor and the middle class. Their contributions to economic growth are necessary if present-day injustices are ever going to be overcome.

Student Assessment   Students can be assessed based on their written work, their group work, and their class participation.

Sources   Douglas, George H. *All Aboard! The Railroad in American Life.* New York: Paragon House, 1992.

Encyclopedia Americana, Vols. 15 and 23. Danbury, CT: Grolier Inc., 1994.

Frank, Al. "OPEN ROAD: Long-awaited Rt. 287 link cleared for speedy travel." Newark, NJ: *The Star Ledger.* Nov. 20, 1993.

Holbrook, Stewart H. *The Story of American Railroads*. New York: Crown Publishers, 1947.

Interstate Route 287 from U.S. Route 202, Montville, NJ to the New York Thruway, Suffern, NY, FINAL Environmental Impact Statement and Section 4(f) Evaluation, U.S. Department of Transportation Federal Highway Administration and New Jersey Department of Transportation. September 1982.

Withuhn, William L., ed. *Rails Across America: A History of Railroads in North America*. New York: SMITHMARK Publishers, Inc. 1993.

Global Learning, Inc.

OPEN ROAD

Long-awaited Rt. 287 link cleared for speedy travel

The Star Ledger
Saturday, Nov. 20, 1993
By Al Frank

Motorists finally got a high-speed corridor to the New York Line through New Jersey's midsection as the last 20.5 mile stretch of Route 287 opened yesterday.

The passage through Morris, Passaic and Bergen Counties, four decades in the making, was fully opened to traffic after 2 p.m., approximately 40 minutes after Gov. Jim Florio and other dignitaries snipped a red, white and blue ribbon and the Lancers Marching Band of Lakeland Regional High School in Wanaque played the National Anthem.

"I understand about Rome not being built in a day, but 40 years is a little much," Florio quipped in a reference to the time it took to complete the interstate.

The opening did not come cheap. The state Department of Transportation (DOT) said contractors were paid $5 million in overtime to complete the project before winter.

But Florio said the investment was well worth the jobs and saved travel time [that] the completed highway is expected to generate.

Although the dedication program put the cost of the new section at $900 million, the price tag was $720 million, according to the Federal Highway Administration, which paid the tab.

The amount was $30 million less than estimated a year ago, albeit higher than the $145 million cited 30 years ago and the $490 million projected in a 1982 environmental impact statement.

But getting to use the highway, rather than its cost, was on the minds of motorists who lined up yesterday to give the "missing link" from Montville to Suffern, N.Y., a test spin.

"I've waited 15 years for this and have been excited for the last five, because you could see it coming," said Eric H. of Parsippany-Troy Hills. He said the new section will cut 20 minutes a day from his commute to [the] felt manufacturer [in] Bloomingdale, where [he] is a vice president.

"It will also cut 25 minutes one-way to our manufacturing facility" in Newburgh, N.Y., H. said, explaining trucks previously had to use back roads around the Wanaque Reservoir....

While serving as a major corridor through the state's suburban central and northern counties—and the catalyst for extraordinary growth during the 1960s and 1970s—the purpose of Route 287 was to provide an alternate to frequently congested arteries near Manhattan.

Virtually every other city in the nation can be avoided by circumferential interstates, like Routes 495 around Washington and 285 circling Atlanta. Bypassing New York by taking

Route 287, the 89 miles between the New Jersey Turnpike and New York Thruway, will save 50 minutes in driving time, according to the 1982 environmental impact statement....

The [crescent-shaped bridge over the Wanaque River] was the setting for yesterday's ceremony, held under leaden skies and intermittent drizzle. The location was 15 miles north of the original section of Route 287, a two-mile link between Routes 10 and 80 in Parsippany that was completed in 1957.

Construction on other segments between Montville and the New Jersey Turnpike in Edison was finished during the next 14 years. But the northernmost segment to the New York border was stalled when the 1971 National Environmental Policy Act required extensive environmental reviews of all federal projects.

As a result, wetlands destroyed during the Route 287 construction had to be replaced.

That process was to have been finished before the highway was opened, but that would have meant a two-year delay if the Army Corps of Engineers had not agreed to postpone the completion date. It did so Monday night, after [Transportation Commissioner Thomas] Downs agreed to a new timetable.

Even so, environmentalists are not unhappy, said Ella Filippone, executive administrator of the Passaic River Coalition, who opposed the project.

"We recognized that we had to let the highway open," Filippone said. "It would have been ridiculous to let it lay unused while we finished the wetlands."

In exchange for not objecting to the new wetlands deadline, Filippone said the coalition got the DOT to agree to quarterly tests of highway runoff at 22 points for the next three years.

She said the tests will look for some 13 substances like petroleum hydrocarbons, oil and grease, lead and road salts and whether they are filtering into waterways like the Towaco wellfield and the Pequannock and Ramapo rivers.

Filippone said the concession was important and also showed that environmental groups are not obstructionists.

"Now, our problems with the highway are being solved and I'm a real happy person," she said....

While most are expecting the highway's opening to ease congestion along local roads, Kinnelon Police Chief Daniel Colucci and other officials offered a conservative prediction.

"I'm not sure we're going to get a decrease," Colucci said, adding that motorists used to taking back roads may continue to avoid congestion from construction south of Montville and near the Route 80 interchange.

But Shelton, who began his DOT career in 1961 with the highway and will retire next year, said he foresaw few problems.

"I don't see major tie-ups; at least 23 hours a day there will be no backup," he said....

DIRECTIONS: *Using a highway atlas or map of New Jersey, draw a map of the complete Route 287 from Staten Island to Port Chester on an 8½ x 11" sheet of paper. Indicate the most recently completed section described in the newspaper article above. Also include routes I-80, I-78, US-46, NJ-23, I-87, the New Jersey Turnpike, and the Garden State Parkway.*

Interstate I-287:
Summary of Environmental Impacts

The following summary presents the various environmental impacts, both beneficial and adverse, associated with the construction of the Preferred Alignment for I-287.

a. Long-Term Impacts

Traffic Operations

The proposed project will complete the Interstate system in the area and will cause traffic to be diverted not only from local streets, especially U.S. Route 202, but also from routes beyond the immediate area, including Route 17 and the Garden State Parkway. It will provide for significant reduction in regional travel times, significant improvement in intra-urban service and complete an Interstate link that the Federal government considers essential for proper National Defense preparedness. Under the No-Build Alternative, congestion on the local road network will become severe, especially on north-south through routes.

Natural Ecosystems

Impacts on aquatic biota in the project area will occur because of erosion and sedimentation, pollutants in runoff, channelization, and removal of bank vegetation. The most significant impact to the terrestrial ecosystem will be the removal of vegetation and wildlife habitat resulting from construction and subsequent use of the roadway. Approximately 745 acres of woodland, 50 acres of abandoned fields, and 8 acres of agricultural fields will be taken, 30% of which would be paved. No plants or animals on the Federal List of rare and endangered species are known to be affected by the project.

Wetlands

Construction of the Preferred Alternative will result in the loss of approximately 36 acres of wetland habitat. In compliance with Executive Order 11990, Preservation of Wetlands, given that there exist no practicable alternatives to avoid construction in wetlands, all practicable measures will be incorporated to minimize harm to wetlands. During design, an interagency task force including the U.S. Environmental Protection Agency, the U.S. Department of Interior (Fish and Wildlife Service), U.S. Army Corps of Engineers, and N.J. Department of Environmental Protection will be formed to develop a wetlands mitigation plan.

Noise Quality

The noise quality analysis indicates that the primary impact of the proposed project will occur immediately adjacent to the proposed alignment. Noise level increases and/or decreases on local roads with access to I-287 will be insignificant and not apparent to the human ear. Adjacent to I-287, 429 buildings will be impacted by noise levels in excess of the

Design Standards of 70 dBA (decibels—70 dBA are equivalent to a vacuum cleaner)....If noise barriers are constructed, the number of buildings impacted is reduced to 231.

Air Quality

The air quality study has shown that the completion of the proposed project will produce no violation of the National Ambient Air Quality Standards. Carbon monoxide emissions are expected to be lower in the "Build" Alternative than in the "No-Build" Alternative. Hydrocarbon emissions are higher in the "Build" Alternative in 1984 but lower in 1994. This project is consistent with the State Implementation Plan.

Employment

Total employment in the five-county Region attributable to I-287 should increase by approximately 7,000 by the year 1995 if the project is built. The largest single sector employment increase would occur in wholesaling and retailing (approximately 28% of the total). Another 19% would occur in the chemical industry.

Land Use

I-287 will cause additional economic growth to the Region, thereby increasing pressure for land development in the Preferred Alternative corridor, especially in the vicinity of proposed interchanges.

The Preferred Alternative is compatible with the land use plan of Passaic County. It is, however, less compatible with the land use plans of Morris and Bergen Counties. The Tri-State Regional Planning Commission has found the Preferred Alternative consistent with Tri-State plans and programs.

Historic Properties

Based upon the survey undertaken for this project, it has been determined that 4 historic structures potentially eligible for the National Register and 5 historic archaeology sites which are potentially eligible would be impacted, in many instances very minimally, by the proposed project. One historic structure will be physically taken by the project and 3 archaeology sites will experience some physical taking.

Recreational Facilities

Four public parks within the study area will be physically affected by the proposed project. These are the Morris County Sunset Valley Golf Course (Pequannock, Kinnelon), Mountainside Park (Pequannock), Campgaw Mountain County Reservation (Mahwah), and Darlington County Park (Mahwah).

Communities and Neighborhoods

Community service provision would generally be improved by the project because of increased inter- and intra-area accessibility. The proposed project would not impede access between any parts of communities. However, it might change what are perceived as neighborhood boundaries and thus affect social interaction patterns.

Global Learning, Inc.

b. Short-Term Impacts

Property Acquisition and Relocation

A total of 198 families and 73 businesses would be displaced as a result of acquisition for the right- of-way. Sufficient relocation housing and other property is expected to be available for those who must relocate. Approximately 120 jobs could be permanently lost due to quarry takings. The negative impact of right-of-way takings on the local tax base will not be severe except in Riverdale, which will lose approximately 23.5% of its tax base....

Construction Operations

The most significant impacts during construction would be soil erosion and noise. While heavy construction could involve severe soil erosion, construction contract specifications will require specific erosion control measures that will substantially reduce this impact. Minor relocations of local streets are expected during construction.

Employment

The construction and engineering of I-287 would generate, directly and indirectly, almost 5,500 man- years of employment. More than half of this increase would occur in the construction sector.

Source: *Interstate Route 287 from U.S. Route 202, Montville, NJ to the New York Thruway, Suffern, NY, FINAL Environmental Impact Statement and Section 4(f) Evaluation*, U.S. Department of Transportation Federal Highway Administration and New Jersey Department of Transportation. September 1982.

The Golden Spike:
The Story of the Transcontinental Railroad

The railroad president swung the sledge hammer and missed, hitting his foot instead of the Golden Spike. A worker took over, hit the Golden Spike square on its head, and in so doing, at Promontory, Utah, linked the Atlantic coast of the United States to the Pacific coast on a bed of iron rails.

What happened to the Golden Spike? It was removed to a museum, but the railroad remained to change the course of history in North America. Its construction would be one of the greatest projects undertaken by human beings since Chinese workers built the Great Wall. Later, in the 20th century, the Panama Canal and the Interstate Highway System would rival these great feats of engineering and construction.

The railroad changed almost everything in its path. It helped to reduce the buffalo herds of the Great Plains from 60 million in 1850 to about 500 in 1900. Buffaloes provided food for workers and, later, targets for "sportsmen" riding the trains. Prairie fires, started accidentally by the mainly Chinese and Irish workers and by sparks from the railroad's locomotives, roared over the Plains. As a result, the Native Americans lost most of their food, their clothing, and their shelter.

For the new Americans who came to settle in what would become states in the United States, the railroad provided the transportation to get to their new homes and then to ship their grain and cattle to markets in Chicago and in the eastern cities. The economy of the United States rapidly expanded, helping to make the nation's people prosperous.

The railroad was built without the use of mechanized equipment. The entire project uniting the Union Pacific Railroad being built westward from the Nebraska Territory and the Central Pacific Railroad eastward from California, took only seven years to complete. Only the Rocky Mountains and the Sierra Nevada slowed its progress. There were no power drills to bore holes in the granite mountains for blasting and no steam shovels to cut passes. The Chinese workers working eastward felled trees, cleared the earth, moved mountains of dirt by wheelbarrow or one-horse dump cart, drilled and blasted 13 tunnels, cut ties, shoveled snow, and built trestles—all by hand. The railroad companies, competing for compensation based on the amount of track laid and unrestricted by government regulations, offered prizes to the workers who could lay the most miles of track.

Both railroads crossed lands that had been occupied for thousands of years by Native Americans. In California, a century of Spanish, Mexican and American occupation had decimated their numbers and relegated the few survivors to the status of ranch hands and fugitives. The Washoes and Piutes of Nevada had been considerably reduced in number by intermittent warfare with settlers earlier in the 1860s. Minor conflicts accompanied the passage of the Central Pacific through their lands—mostly grading crews shooting at the Native Americans—and the company was careful to distribute food, liquor, free passes, small amounts of money and a few jobs among tribal leaders to ensure their cooperation.

Global Learning, Inc.

The Union Pacific faced a different situation. The tribes of the Great Plains, the Northern Cheyenne and the Sioux, were well organized, mobile, and able to resist the encroachment of the railroad onto their land. These groups had been engaged in almost constant conflict with overland emigrants and settlers since the start of the California Gold Rush, and the Army frequently found itself in the position of trying to stop the newer Americans from exterminating the original inhabitants of the land. Native American anger was strong, and the coming of the railroad made matters much worse, but actual attacks against railroad construction workers were not common. The few real instances were greatly magnified in the eastern press and persist as legends even today.

Discounted in the rush to link the east and west coasts were the Native Americans, whose lands the railroad crossed. Also discounted were the buffalo and many other forms of wildlife whose habitat changed so swiftly and dramatically. But private enterprise flourished, and the economy of the United States became the world's largest.

At the time, few citizens of the United States questioned the long-range consequences of the transcontinental railroad. A hundred years later, environmentalists would argue that the impact of railroads was more positive than the impact of their younger cousin, the Interstate Highway System, and students would have a hard time imagining what it would be like to have neither.

Lesson 12

Energy Transitions and U.S. History

Historical Period	The Development of Industrial U.S. (1870-1900)
Sustainable Development Topic	Social and Economic Development
Purpose	To show students how historical changes in energy systems, including the transition from wood to coal during this period of United States history, have affected society and to help students relate those observations to the current debate over future energy sources.
Objectives	Students will be able to:

1. Define "energy transition" and identify past energy transitions.
2. Identify similarities and differences between the current energy transition and past transitions such as that from wood to coal and from coal to oil.
3. Identify changes in social and economic characteristics which have resulted from or could result from past and future changes in the dominant source of energy.

Time Required	1-2 class periods
Materials Needed	Handout 1: *Energy Transitions and Social Change* Handout 2: *Prove It!* Eight large pieces of chart paper or newsprint and markers
About the Lesson	The initial student activity in this lesson requires students to read a selection on energy transitions and social change with the purpose of discovering "evidence" to support a number of statements provided on Handout 2, *Prove It!* This helps focus the student on what is important in the passage as well as fosters an inner dialogue within the reader which improves comprehension.

Following whole class discussion of individuals' evidence, there is the opportunity for students to work in groups to identify specific

changes energy transitions have produced, or could potentially produce, across a range of social and economic characteristics.

Optional lesson extensions provide for further research into energy sources which may prove dominant in the future, and the creative depiction of student-identified social changes caused by energy transitions.

Teacher Background   It is possible to periodize history in many ways. One important periodization would be in terms of the sources of energy which humans have used to accomplish their purposes. "Energy ages" can be identified in terms of the principal source of energy: human power, animal power, wood, coal, and oil. And while certain parts of the world have been at different stages, and while some parts of the world have essentially skipped some ages (e.g., the age of coal), this broad classification provides insights into the history of civilization as well as the history of energy use specifically.

Actually the broad "energy ages" suggested above can be somewhat deceiving. They after all represent the principal source of energy which humans have used at different points in time. In reality much of history has involved the diversification of energy sources. Thus in the age dominated by wood, wind and water also came to be tapped as sources of energy. Likewise, even when wood provided a society's dominant source of energy, those energy sources which pre-dated the dominance of wood (e.g., human and animal power) obviously continued to be important.

- **Energy Transitions**—Thinking about history in terms of dominant energy sources, however, does help to place recent energy history into perspective. While the phrase "energy crisis" is rarely used to describe the situation in which the world currently finds itself, it is undoubtedly true that the world has entered a period of energy transition. That is, we have entered a period in which the global society's principal energy source is shifting away from oil. That we are less clear about the source of energy toward which we are moving is an indication of the political importance of the energy issue.

  As the list of "energy ages" suggests, this is not the first energy transition which humans, or even Americans, have faced. Significant energy transitions occurred as humans moved from human to animal power. The shift to an energy system based on wood was probably less noticeable. Wood had been an energy source long before the domestication of animals. Its uses simply grew as new applications were discovered (e.g., metal smelting). For the most part, these new applications could not use animal or human power and be effective.

The transitions from wood to coal and from coal to oil were more noticeable. These are also transitions which have been a part of the American experience. In the United States the shift from wood to coal occurred in conjunction with industrialization. Coal did not emerge as the dominant energy source within the United States, however, until after 1890. Oil did not emerge as the dominant energy source until after 1950. While the transition to oil has been a recent phenomenon all over the world, European countries for the most part experienced the transition from wood to coal before the United States.

- **Energy Transitions and Cultural Change**—Changes in energy sources have always been accompanied by social as well as economic changes. The introduction of new energy sources makes new technologies available. In many cases these new technologies have a significant impact on the very way in which a society is ordered.

  The domestication of animals and the shift from an energy system based on human labor to one based on animal power had such an effect. Animals were first used in transportation. As such they increased greatly people's ability to move goods over large distances. This increased mobility encouraged the first true trading systems. Similarly the use of draft animals in farming greatly expanded the acreage which a single farmer could cultivate. This expanded productivity made it possible for a larger proportion of the population to engage in occupations outside of farming.

  Equally fundamental changes have occurred with the transition from wood to coal and from coal to oil in recent times. The growth of the coal industry was necessary for industrialization based on steel production. Industrialization has been associated in turn with significant social changes including urbanization, the growth of unions, the consumer society, and the global trading system, among others. The shift from coal to oil made possible the emergence of automobile based transportation systems. It has also made possible air transportation, which has played a key role in the expansion of global systems.

- **Differences in Energy Transitions**—Past energy transitions provide some perspective on the kinds of social changes which can accompany shifts from one dominant energy source to another. At the same time, there are important differences between the current energy transition and past ones.

  Perhaps the most important single difference lies in the fact that the current energy transition is occurring in response to the declining availability of oil as opposed to the increasing

124   Global Learning, Inc.

attractiveness or utility of some alternative energy source. Most shifts in energy use in the past have involved the latter, "pull" phenomenon. Animals replaced human power because animals were an attractive alternative. As metal smelting increased and with the invention of the steam engine, wood provided an obvious and available energy source. Thus, its dominance grew. Even oil use increased because oil was an attractive alternative to coal.

In contrast, the current energy transition is propelled by a "push" phenomenon. The transition will occur because of shortages in the dominant fuel: oil. There is relatively little agreement about the energy source which should or can replace it.

Shortage-based transitions are not unknown. The British, for example, shifted from wood to coal as a result of shortages. In the 1500's the British Admiralty began to experience a shortage of native hardwood timber needed for shipbuilding. The Admiralty pushed for conservation laws which restricted the wood available for heating and industrial use. As a result coal became increasingly important as an energy source.

However, in the British case, coal had been known and in use as an energy source for four hundred years. The shift, in other words, was necessitated by shortages of wood. But the abundance and utility of coals was never in question. Today there are serious questions as to the desirability of an energy system based primarily on nuclear power. There are considerable questions as to the viability of an energy system based on the utilization of solar energy.

Procedure

1. Ask the students to volunteer which single *technological development* they feel has had the most impact on their day-to-day lives. When soliciting responses, restrict the students to volunteering the development only, not the change itself.

2. Provide students with three minutes to write down *the nature of the change* which their identified development has caused and to project how their lives would be different in the absence of the development. Allow students to change their choices if they realize during the discussion that their initial choice was not appropriate.

3. Discuss with the class the changes they wrote.

4. Suggest that basic to such technologically inspired change is the availability of an appropriate energy source to initiate and sustain such developments. The discovery and development of that energy source contributes significantly to the societal changes through resultant technology. For example, the shift from coal to oil made possible the internal

combustion engine. This energy-based technological development resulted in the emergence of an automobile based transportation system which has increased our society's sense of individuals' independence, fueled the decentralization of cities and the growth of suburbs, and created the oil-based political realities of today.

5. Distribute **Handouts 1** and **2**. Tell the students to discover and write down as much evidence for the statements on Handout 2 they can find in the information provided in Handout 1. They are to be as specific as possible, quoting if possible, and providing multiple examples of evidence if they are present.

6. As the students are working on the assignment, circulate as necessary to help individuals with vocabulary or conceptual difficulties.

7. Conduct a whole class discussion of the evidence students have generated. Encourage students to add to their evidence sheets as new information is provided or to delete evidence shown to be inadequate.

8. Place eight chart papers around the room with one of these social/economic topics listed at the top of each:
transportation, size of population,
cities, farming and food production,
trade, manufacturing,
housing, interdependence (economic, social, political).

9. Divide the students into eight groups and have them group around one of the chart papers. Read one of the energy transitions from below. Have each group record on the chart paper for that topic as many changes to that topic as they can brainstorm that were caused, or that would be caused, by that energy transition.
Energy transitions:
human to animal/wood,
wood to coal,
coal to oil,
oil to nuclear,
oil to solar.

10. After a few minutes of brainstorming, have the students move to another chart paper and topic and repeat the process with the second energy transition. Repeat the process of moving and brainstorming until all the energy transitions have been covered. Encourage students to be as specific as possible. List these transitions on the chalkboard for continual review during this phase of the activity.

11. Conclude the lesson with a whole class discussion of the results of the above activity. Ask for clarification of those items which are confusing. Encourage students to challenge

those entries which seem inappropriate. Seek reasons for the item's inclusion from the group which wrote it.

Lesson Extensions

1. Conduct research on energy resources which may be important or even dominant in the future. Write an essay identifying problems involved in developing or using that energy source. Essays should identify social, political, or economic changes which might be necessary to develop that energy source.

2. Creatively illustrate (picture, poem, song, etc.) one of the changes identified on the chart paper in the above activity. Encourage an impressionistic response rather than a realistic portrayal of the societal change.

Student Assessment   The following questions may be used in addition to observation of student performance (all questions refer to Handout 1):

1. The chart portrays history in terms of "ages." What "ages" are identified? Why is there no line between Animal and Wood ages?

2. How might you explain this particular progression or sequence of dominant energy sources? Why did human power precede wood or animal power? Why did these two precede coal and coal precede oil?

3. What differences and similarities between the current energy transition and past ones does the article suggest? Have other energy transitions been due to forces "pushing" society away from the dominant energy source? Or to the lure of a new energy source? Has the new energy source been relatively more or less centralized than past energy sources?

4. A major theme of the reading is that changes in energy have an effect on society. What are some examples of social changes associated with:
   a. the domestication of fire?
   b. the domestication of animals?
   c. the change to coal?
   d. the change to oil?

Lesson adapted from Robert B. Woyach et al., *Bringing a Global Perspective to American History.* Mershon Center, The Ohio State University, 1983.

Energy Transitions and Social Change

Broad agreement can be found for the notion that the world is in the midst of an energy system transition. The current domination by conventional oil and natural gas is giving way to domination by one or more other primary energy sources.

History provides examples of other transitions. In 1850, the United States derived nearly 90% of its energy from **wood.** Throughout the Civil War and well into the robber baron era of the late 19th century, wood remained the dominant fuel. In 1890, **coal** finally provided 50% of our energy (with wood still providing almost all the rest). Coal's dominance peaked in 1910 when it provided 70% of all energy produced and consumed in the U.S. Increasing scarcity of wood played some role in the transition. Almost certainly more important, however, were the dramatic benefits the emerging industrial system reaped from coal use, specifically in steel-making and transportation (railroads and steamboats).

A whole new era in economics and politics arose with coal. The country began its movement to the city. The era spawned entrepreneurial giants, not in coal itself, but in industries it supported, such as steel and railroads. These industries in turn gave rise to a period of labor organization. A young and weak United Mine Workers (UMW) called its first strike in 1900. The energy system based on coal set in motion powerful social forces.

Already in 1910, **oil and gas** provided about 20% of U.S. energy needs. Sixty years later, in 1970, they reached the 70% level that coal had attained in 1910. In 1990, the level had dropped to 65%. Oil, too, left a trail of major economic, social, and political change. Whereas coal companies always remained relatively small, oil's history began with a single major company, Standard Oil.

The Current Transition

Another transition is, however, beginning. This does not mean that oil production will fall. In fact, U.S. coal consumption is now greater than in 1910. It is coal's *relative* position which has declined. Global oil production and consumption will continue to rise for some years. But its *relative* position is beginning to decline.

There are both similarities and differences between the coming transition and past ones. For example, the coming transition is the result of forces pushing the world away from dependence on oil.

This push began sooner than was geologically necessary. Geologists estimate that less than 25% of the ultimately recoverable oil in the world has been used. But the concentration of oil supplies in the Persian Gulf has allowed oil producing countries to restrict production and obtain higher prices. Thus in the mid-1970's oil production did not keep pace with rising demand. As long as oil producers can restrict production in this way and as long as oil supplies around the world are vulnerable to disruption by military action, the world will be pushed away from its dependence on oil.

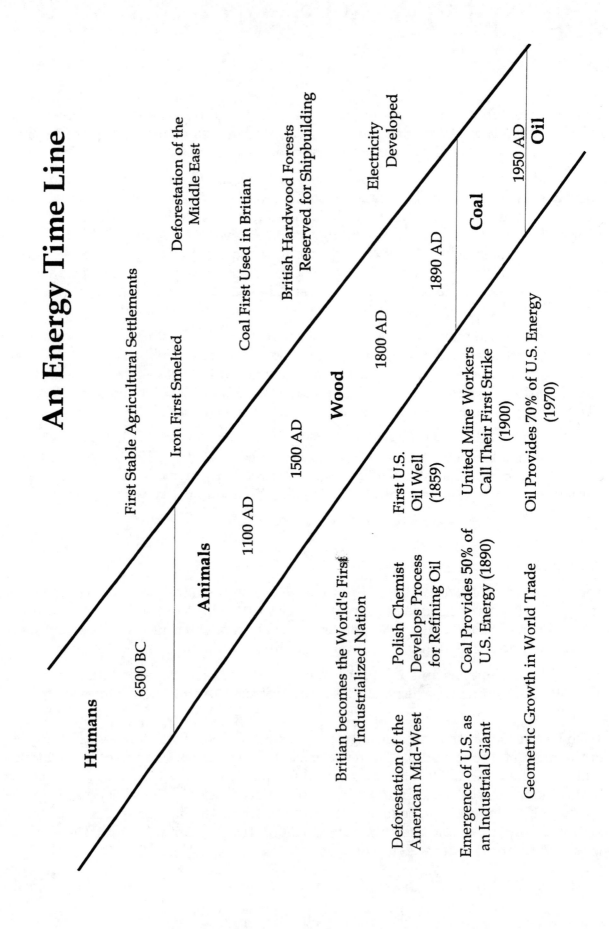

An Energy Time Line

Humans
6500 BC
First Stable Agricultural Settlements

Animals
1100 AD
Iron First Smelted
Deforestation of the Middle East

Wood
1500 AD
1800 AD
Coal First Used in Britian
British Hardwood Forests Reserved for Shipbuilding
Electricity Developed

Coal
1890 AD
1950 AD

Oil

Britian becomes the World's First Industrialized Nation

Deforestation of the American Mid-West

Polish Chemist Develops Process for Refining Oil

First U.S. Oil Well (1859)

United Mine Workers Call Their First Strike (1900)

Emergence of U.S. as an Industrial Giant

Coal Provides 50% of U.S. Energy (1890)

Oil Provides 70% of U.S. Energy (1970)

Geometric Growth in World Trade

The greater use of wood, animal power and even oil in past transitions were largely due to the great attractiveness of these energy sources rather than to a shortage of previously dominant energy sources. Oil replaced coal, but coal reserves far exceed oil reserves. And humanpower was still available long after animals were domesticated as beasts of burden.

On the other hand, the coming transition is similar to past transitions from wood to coal. In Britain and again in the United States shortages of wood helped to spur greater use of coal. In the case of coal, however, new technologies, especially for making steel and using electricity also "pulled" society toward greater use of coal.

The current transition is also unlike past transitions in that while the transition from oil is apparent, there is little agreement about the dominant energy source of the future. **Nuclear power** is one alternative. **Solar power,** harnessed in a variety of ways, is another.

A trend toward nuclear power would be consistent with historical trends. Most other energy transitions have led to the use of **more centralized energy sources.** Animals and wood were more centralized than human power, although they were both still quite decentralized. That is, they were generally available to everyone but still less available than human muscle power. Coal was even more centralized. Coal seams are not evenly distributed around the country or around the world. Thus it is possible for some people to control the use of coal. Oil is even more centralized than coal. Uranium deposits are more centralized than oil.

A trend toward solar power on the other hand, could reverse this historic trend. Solar power is **highly decentralized.** And while some methods of harnessing solar power are more centralized than others, the energy source itself is highly decentralized.

Energy Transitions and Social Changes

Most of the debate surrounding new energy sources is couched in terms of economic and environmental issues. Nuclear energy, for instance, is attacked primarily on environmental grounds. Its costs have soared, partly because of environmental regulations.

Underlying the energy debate, however, is another set of issues not well understood. These issues affect choices between solar and nuclear power, between nationalizing or leaving the oil industry private, between public transit and private autos. **The root of the issues lies in values concerning how society is best organized.** We must remind ourselves again of the fundamental impact which energy has on society.

The importance of **humans' domestication of fire**—that is, the beginnings of an energy system based on combustion of wood—is symbolized in the Greek myth of Prometheus. Prometheus stole fire from the gods and gave it to humans. He also taught humans various arts and sciences. The abilities to cook, to maintain shelters secure against wild animals, to develop some metallurgy followed from the new energy system. The growth of early civilizations is hardly conceivable without fire.

The transition to coal cannot be compared to the domestication of fire. But the impact was profound. Alexandre Eifel would not have been able to construct his tower in Paris in 1889 had it not been for the technological advances in the iron and steel industry. These stemmed in large part from the relatively concentrated and even heat of coal. That construction project symbolized the advances that made possible **our present cities and the**

railroad system. We have commented earlier on the relationship between the coal industry and the rise of the labor movement.

The transition to oil and natural gas can take at least partial credit for a number of phenomena: the existence of some of the world's largest corporations (in oil and automobiles), the undertaking of history's largest construction project (the U.S. interstate highway system), the suburbanization of the U.S. and the growth of major cities everywhere.

Our oil based energy system has also increased global interdependence. It has led to the world's first global energy supply system, the development of aviation and other transportation technologies. It has even led to the great expansion of the U.S. global role, including recent strengthening of commitments and military intervention in the Persian Gulf.

The Debate Over Energy Systems

We are now in the early and probably critical stages of another energy transition. **No collective social choice was exercised in earlier transitions.** There were no public institutions which both recognized the occurrence of the transition and had the tools to shape it. This time, there are. And the debate is underway. Claims and counterclaims of technological feasibility, cost, and environmental impact fly through the media. These factors are important. But they also often conceal the policies upon which various groups' positions are built.

Consider some of the social implications of a nuclear power-based society. One of the most obvious is a significant governmental role in the system. Government would need to deal directly with safety issues, including providing and transporting fuel and disposing of wastes. Custody over weapons-grade nuclear material or centuries-long waste disposal control will not be left to private industry. Nuclear power requires a centralized power plant. And nuclear "parks" with massive generating capabilities (subject to government regulation) have been proposed. Nuclear power also requires highly capital intensive distribution by power lines, which is a natural monopoly. Private utilities in that position are subject to constant governmental scrutiny, including price control. It is no accident that those countries which have made the largest commitment to nuclear power have strong centralized political systems. They share a faith in government planning for the economy. These include not only the United States, but the former U.S.S.R., which once had the world's most ambitious nuclear program, and France, with its active government planning history.

Consider, in contrast, an energy system based upon small-scale solar collection systems. The nuclear system would favor urbanization to increase efficiency in distribution systems and even the use of waste heat from the plants. The solar system favors rural living for collection purposes. It favors continued development of the "sunbelt" over the "snowbelt" in the U.S. Installation and maintenance would require a large labor force. But the need to custom-build solar systems would support a crafts (skilled) rather than assembly line (unskilled) labor force. Since solar systems cannot generate as much energy per plant as nuclear systems, they favor smaller-scale industrial processing. Thus government's role in the energy can be much reduced. And large-scale industrial entities also have less reason to exist. It is no accident that such an energy system received support from those opposed to big government and large corporations. Solar energy is also suggested by those who favor more decentralized and, in many respects, more traditional life styles.

Consider a coal-based energy system. Almost certainly such a system would combine reliance on coal-generated electricity with a synthetic fuel industry producing gaseous and liquid fuels. In many respects, the society based on such a system appears more similar to our current one than do those based on nuclear power or decentralized solar plants. Specifically, the industry would be capital and technology intensive. It would provide benefits to highly concentrated capital. Government would need to subsidize the development of new energy capital in some cases. It would certainly need to subsidize private risk associated with major investments in relatively new energy processes, such as coal liquefaction. The system would require the fewest changes in our current energy consumption patterns, including the use of private automobiles and gas-heated private houses. It should not surprise us that many major U.S. corporations see this system as our best answer.

Adapted from: Barry B. Hughes, "Energy as a Global Issues," in *Global Issues: Energy,* James Harf et al., eds., (Columbus, OH: Consortium for International Studies Education, 1980)

Prove It!

Use Handout 1: *Energy Transitions and Social Change,* to find evidence to support each of the following statements. Be as specific as possible. Cite as much pertinent evidence as you can find—the more the better.

1. We have entered a period in which the global society's principal energy source is shifting away from oil.

2. History shows significant energy transitions have occurred in the past.

3. The current energy system transition is occurring in response to the declining availability of oil as opposed to the increasing attractiveness of some other fuel source.

4. A move towards nuclear power is consistent with the centralized/decentralized nature of earlier transitions.

5. Past energy transitions provide some perspective on the kinds of social changes which can accompany shifts from one dominant energy source to another.

6. A move towards either nuclear, solar, or coal power within the U.S.A. would have uniquely different social ramifications.

Lesson 13

Save the Earth! But How?

Historical Period The Progressive Era (1900-1930)
T. Roosevelt Administration

Sustainable Development Topics Human/environment interaction, use of resources, views of the environment

Purpose To identify and evaluate various perspectives about the human/environment relationship and how those perspectives affect government policy.

Objectives Students will be able to:

1. Identify four 19th and 20th century American ideas about the environment and its use.
2. Compare these views for differences and similarities.
3. Trace the effect of these views on national policy.
4. Consider the effect of fragmentation of public opinion on effective policy making.

Time Required Two to three days

Materials Needed Handout 1: *George Perkins Marsh: Man and Nature*
Handout 2: *Theodore Roosevelt: Opening Address by the President*
Handout 3: *George L. Knapp: The Other Side of Conservation*
Handout 4: *John Muir on Wilderness*
Handout 5: *Summary of Positions*
Handout 6: *An Act to Establish a National Park Service*
Handout 7: *Questions for Critical Thinking*
Newsprint and colored markers
Student text regarding the Roosevelt administration and the federal conservation program

Teacher Background You will find an article at the end of the lesson by Carl Moneyhon, an historian at the University of Arkansas on the environmental movement of the period for your personal background. You might like to outline some important facts for your students at the *conclusion* of the student activity as most student texts deal very briefly with Roosevelt's conservation program and present it as a conflict free idea whose time had come. Prior to this lesson, students should have a basic knowledge of the time period and the effects of western expansion and industrial development. Begin the lesson with a brief review of this background.

Procedure   Day 1

1. Divide students into four groups and distribute enough copies of *one* of the **handouts** for each student in the group. At this time you will also distribute a piece of newsprint and markers to each group. You should have a "Marsh" group, a "Knapp" group, a "Roosevelt" group, and a "Muir" group.

2. Instruct students that they should read their handout and identify how the author describes the relationship between humans and the environment. Once they have read the handout, they will work together to create a visual representation, e.g., a drawing or a political cartoon, of the relationship between humans and their environment. Assure them that they will not be graded for artistic ability. The goal is to accurately depict the human/environment relationship described in their reading. You might want to assign specific jobs in the group, i.e., artists, reporter, scribe. It is very important that all students work together in formulating their ideas for the drawing.

3. Once it becomes apparent that all cartoons are ready for presentation, ask the reporters from each group to present their group's drawing and to provide an explanation of the view expressed in the reading.

4. Next you will distribute **Handout 5: *Summary of Positions*** to all students. Ask students to read the summaries of the differing ideas about the environment and resource use. They should write the name of one of the four authors whose view of the environment most closely resembles the identification in the space provided at the end of each identification. Students may make this an individual or group effort. Ask students to volunteer their answers.
   The correct answers are:
   Conservation=Roosevelt; Preservation=Muir;
   Ecology=Marsh; Laissez Faire=Knapp.

5. Distribute **Handout 6: *The National Parks Act***. Ask students to read the act for homework and to write an editorial commenting on the act from the perspective of one of the authors they reviewed in class. These editorials will be presented in class.

Global Learning, Inc.

Procedure   Day 2

1. Randomly divide the class into groups of four or five. They should bring their editorials to the group meeting and swap theirs for another's. Distribute copies of **Handout 7: *Questions for Critical Thinking*** and instruct students that they should complete #1-3 individually and #4-7 as a group.

2. When the groups finish rewriting The National Parks Act, you may want to outline briefly the characters and the conflict about the conservation of resources during the Roosevelt administration as explained in the Moneyhon background article. Ask students to present their revised version of the act and discuss how conflicting opinions affect the direction of national policy.

Extension Activity   The issue of the use, conservation or preservation of the natural environment contributed to the split between Theodore Roosevelt and William Howard Taft in what was known as the Ballinger-Pinchot Affair. Differences between Roosevelt's view of a strong and expansive presidency versus Taft's more delimited, conservative view also surfaced in this controversy. (See chapter 4, "Crisis Over Conservation" in *The Presidency of William Howard Taft* by Paolo E. Coletta, Lawrence, KS: University Press of Kansas, 1987, encyclopedias, or other books on Taft.) Students could compare and contrast the Ballinger-Pinchot dispute with more contemporary controversies regarding the role of government in permitting or limiting the use of public lands, for example in the spotted owl versus timber interests in the Pacific Northwest in the 1990s.

A second extension activity would be to use the lesson, *Save the Earth II!* This lesson asks students to evaluate a contemporary environmental controversy from the standpoints of several different environmental organizations.

Sources   Knapp, George L. *North American Review,* 191 (1910).

Marsh, George Perkins. *Man and Nature.* New York: Charles Scribners Sons, 1864.

Moneyhon, Carl H. "The Environmental Crisis and American Politics, 1860-1920," in Lester J. Bilsky, ed. *Historical Ecology: Essays on Environmental and Social Change,* Port Washington, NY: Kennikat Press, 1980.

Muir, John. *The Yosemite.* New York: Century, 1912.

The National Parks Act [H.R. 15522], 1916.

Roosevelt, Theodore. *Proceedings of a Conference of Governors in the White House.* Washington, D.C. Government Printing Office, 1909.

George Perkins Marsh: Man and Nature (1864)

In reclaiming and reoccupying lands laid to waste by human improvidence or malice, and abandoned by man, or occupied only by a nomad of thinly scattered population, the task of the pioneer settler is of a very different character. He is to become a co-worker with nature in the reconstruction of the damaged fabric which the negligence of the wantonness of former lodgers has rendered untenantable. He must aid her in reclothing the mountain slopes with forests and vegetable mould, thereby restoring the fountains which she provided to water them...

Man has too long forgotten that the earth was given to him for usufruct* alone, not for consumption, still less for profligate waste. Nature has provided against the absolute destruction of any elementary matter, the raw material of her works; the thunderbolt and the tornado, the most convulsive throes of even the volcano and the earthquake, being only phenomena of decomposition and recomposition. But she has left it within the power of man irreparably to derange the combinations of inorganic and organic life...

The fact that, of all organic beings, man alone is to be regarded as essentially a destructive power, and that he wields energies to resist which, nature—that nature whom all material life and all inorganic substance obey—is wholly impotent...

Purely untutored humanity, it is true, interferes comparatively little with the arrangements of nature, and the destructive agency of man becomes more and more unsparing as he advances in civilization, until the impoverishment, with which his exhaustion of the natural resources of the soil is threatening him, at last awakens him to the necessity of preserving what is left, if not of restoring what has been wantonly wasted.

---

* usufruct, (n) the legal right to use another's property and enjoy the advantages of it without injuring or destroying it.

 Global Learning, Inc.

Theodore Roosevelt: Opening Address by the President (1909)

Nature has supplied to us in the United States, and still supplies to us, more kinds of resources in a more lavish degree than has ever been the case at any other time or with any other people. Our position in the world has been attained by the extent and the thoroughness of the control we have achieved over nature; but we are more, and not less, dependent upon what she furnishes than at any previous time of history since the days of primitive man...

The wise use of all of our natural resources, which are our national resources as well, is the great material question of today. I have asked you to come together now because the enormous consumption of these resources, and the threat of imminent exhaustion of some of them, due to reckless and wasteful use...calls for common effort, common action.

We want to take action that will prevent the advent of a woodless age, and defer as long as possible the advent of an ironless age...

Natural resources...can be divided into two sharply distinguished classes accordingly as they are or are not capable of renewal. Mines if used must necessarily be exhausted. The minerals do not and can not renew themselves. Therefore in dealing with coal, the oil, the gas, the iron, the metals generally, all that we can do is to try to see that they are wisely used. The exhaustion is certain to come in time. We can trust that it will be deferred long enough to enable extraordinary inventive genius of our people to devise means and methods for more or less adequately replacing what is lost; but the exhaustion is sure to come.

The second class of resources consists of those which can not only be used in such a manner as to leave them undiminished for our children, but can actually be improved by wise use. The soil, the forests, the waterways come in this category. Everyone knows that a really good farmer leaves his farm more valuable at the end of life than it was when he first took hold of it. So with the waterways. So with the forests. In dealing with mineral resources, man is able to improve on nature only by putting resources to beneficial use which in the end exhausts them; but in dealing with the soil and its products man can improve on nature by compelling the resources to renew and even reconstruct themselves in such manner as to serve increasingly beneficial uses--while the living waters can be so controlled as to multiply their benefits...

In the past we have admitted the right of the individual to injure the future of the Republic for his own present profit. In fact there has been a good deal of demand for unrestricted individualism, for the right of the individual to injure the future of all of us for his own temporary and immediate profit. The time has come for a change. As a people we have a right and the duty, second to none other but the right and duty of obeying the moral law, of requiring and doing justice, to protect ourselves and our children against the wasteful development of our natural resources, whether that waste is caused by actual destruction of such resources or by making them impossible of development hereafter.

George L. Knapp:
The Other Side of Conservation (1910)

For some years past, the reading public has been treated to fervid and extended eulogies of a policy which the eulogists call the "conservation of our natural resources." In behalf of this so-called "conservation," the finest press bureau in the world has labored with zeal quite unhampered by any considerations of fact or logic; and has shown its understanding of practical psychology by appealing, not to popular reason, but to popular fears. We are told by this press bureau that our natural resources are being wasted in the most wanton and criminal style; wasted, apparently, for the sheer joy of wasting. We are told that our forests are being cut at a rate which will soon leave us a land without trees; and Nineveh, and Tyre, and any other place far enough away are cited to prove that a land without trees is foredoomed to be a land without civilization. We are told that our coal-mines would be exhausted within a century; that our iron ores are going to the blast-furnace at a rate which will send us back to the stone age within the lifetime of the men who read the fearsome prophecy. In short, we are assured that every resource capable of exhaustion is being exhausted; and that the resource which can not be exhausted is being monopolized...

I propose to speak for those exiles in sin who hold that a large part of the present "conservation" movement is unadulterated humbug. That the modern Jeremiahs are as sincere as was the older one, I do not question. But I count their prophecies to be baseless vaporings, and their vaunted remedy worse than the fancied disease. I am one who can see no warrant of law, of justice, nor of necessity for that wholesale reversal of our traditional policy which the advocates of "conservation" demand. I am one who does not shiver for the future at the sight of a load of coal, nor view the steel mill as the arch-robber of posterity. I am one who does not believe in a power trust, past, present, or to come; and who, if he were a capitalist seeking to form a trust, would ask nothing better than just the present conservation scheme to help him. I believe that a government bureau is the worst imaginable landlord; and that its essential nature is not changed by giving it a high-sounding name, and decking it with homage halos.

...There is just one heritage which I am anxious to transmit to my children and to their children's children--the heritage of personal liberty, of free individual action, of "leave it to live by no man's leave underneath the law." And I know of no way to secure that heritage save to sharply challenge and relentlessly fight every bureaucratic invasion of local and individual rights, no matter how friendly the mottoes on the invading banners.

Global Learning, Inc.

John Muir on Wilderness (1912)

Hetch Hetchy Valley, far from being a plain, common, rock bound meadow, as many who have not seen it seem to suppose, is a grand landscape garden, one of nature's most precious mountain temples. As in Yosemite, the sublime rocks of its walls seem to glow with life, whether leaning back in repose or standing back in thoughtful attitudes, giving welcome to storms and calm alike, their brows in the sky, their feet set in the groves and gay flowery meadows, while birds, bees, and butterflies help the river and waterfalls to stir all the air into music—things frail and fleeting and types of permanence meeting here and blending, just as they do in Yosemite, to draw her lover into close and confiding communion with her.

Sad to say, this most precious and sublime feature of the Yosemite National park, one of the greatest of all our natural resources for the uplifting joy and peace and health of the people, is in danger of being dammed and made into a reservoir to help supply San Francisco with water and light, thus flooding it from wall to wall and burying its gardens and groves one or two hundred feet deep. This grossly destructive commercial scheme has long been planned and urged (though water as pure and abundant can be got from sources outside of the people's park, in a dozen different places), because of the comparative cheapness of the dam and of the territory which it is sought to divert from the great uses to which it was dedicated in the Act of 1890 establishing Yosemite National Park...

"Damming and submerging it 175 feet deep would enhance its beauty by forming a crystal-clear lake." Landscape gardens, places of recreation and worship, are never made beautiful by destroying and burying them. The beautiful sham lake, forsooth, would be only an eyesore, a dismal blot on the landscape, like many others to be seen in the Sierra. For, instead of keeping it at the same level all year, allowing Nature centuries to make new shores, it would, of course, be full only a month or two in the spring, when the snow is melting fast; then it would be gradually drained, exposing the slimy sides of the basin and shallower parts of the bottom, with the gathered drift and waste, death and decay of the upper basins, caught here instead of being swept to a decent natural burial along the banks of the river or in the sea. Thus the Hetch Hetchy dam-lake would be only a rough imitation of a natural lake for a few of the spring months, an open sepulcher for the others....

These temple destroyers, devotees of ravaging commercialism, seem to have a perfect contempt for Nature, and, instead of lifting their eyes to the God of the mountains, lift them to the Almighty Dollar.

Dam Hetch Hetchy! As well dam for water-tanks the people's cathedrals and churches, for no holier temple has ever been consecrated by the heart of man.

Summary of Positions

Conservation

- Emphasis on the role of science and technology in achieving a solution to environmental destruction.
- Promotes efficient use of resources and exploration of alternative resources.
- Humans can better control and improve the environment through innovation.
- Popular view among scientists, industrialists, and politicians.

Preservation

- Believes that economic development does not always lead to progress.
- What is best in life is found in nature.
- A romantic, spiritual view of nature wherein nature and its preservation are essential to human existence.
- Identifies science and technology as impediments to the natural relationship between humans and their environment.

Ecology

- Identifies the relationship between humans and the environment as symbiotic.
- People must consider nature as an equal partner in determining the costs and benefits of development options.
- The environment is in balance naturally; people only serve to upset that healthy balance.
- Humans should work to identify, understand, and improve their relationship within the natural world, not to exploit and destroy it through science and technology.

Laissez Faire

- Professes a "wait and see" attitude toward human use of the environment; address the consequences of human development when they occur.
- Resources were created for human use and development as humans are God's highest creation.
- To enhance the ability of individuals to meet their needs and improve their lives is the purpose of the American government.
- Nature will take care of itself.

Global Learning, Inc.

An Act to Establish a National Park Service (1916)

Be it enacted by the Senate and House of Representatives of the United States of America in Congress assembled, That there is hereby created in the Department of the Interior a service to be called the National Park Service, which shall be under the charge of a director, who shall be appointed by the Secretary...The service thus established shall promote and regulate the use of the Federal areas know as national parks, monuments, and reservations hereinafter specified by such means and measures as conform to the fundamental purpose of said parks, monuments, and reservations, which purpose is to conserve the scenery and the natural and historic objects and the wild life therein and to provide for the enjoyment of the same in such manner and by such means as will leave them unimpaired for the enjoyment of future generations...

SEC.3. That the Secretary of the Interior shall make and publish such rules and regulations as he may deem necessary or proper for the use and management of the parks, monuments and reservations under the jurisdiction of the national Park Service...He may also, upon terms and conditions to be fixed by him, sell or dispose of timber in those cases where in his judgment the cutting of such timber is required in order to control the attacks of insects or diseases or otherwise conserve scenery or the natural or historic objects in any such park, monument, or reservation. He may also provide in his discretion for the destruction of such animals and of such plant life as may be detrimental to the use of any said parks, monuments, or reservations. He may also grant privileges, leases, and permits for the use of land for the accommodation of visitors in the various parks, monuments, or other reservations herein provided for, but for periods not exceeding twenty years; and no curiosities, wonders, or objects of interest shall be leased, rented, or granted to anyone on such terms as to interfere with free access to them by the public: *Provided, however,* That the Secretary of the Interior may, under such rules and regulations and on such terms as he may prescribe, grant the privilege to graze livestock within any national park, monument, or reservation herein referred to when in his judgment such use is not detrimental to the primary purpose for which such park, monument, or reservation was created, except that this provision shall not apply to the Yellowstone National Park.

Questions for Critical Thinking

Answer questions 1-3 individually.

1. State the problem being discussed.

2. Review each group member's editorial and read for the following:
   - statements which are opinion
   - statements or data that are irrelevant
   - statements or data that are untrue or unsupported
   Underline opinion statements. Place (parentheses) around irrelevant or false statements.

3. Restate the problem using only those sections of the editorials that are not underlined or in parentheses. Your goal is to arrive at an unbiased, factual statement.

Answer questions 4-7 in your group.

4. Compare the problem statements of the various editorials. Identify the various views of the group members.

5. Point out errors, inconsistencies, and voids that appear in the editorials.

6. What are the effects of opinions, values, and misinformation on understanding problems and their solutions?

7. Rewrite the National Parks Act making changes to it that consider the different views of the problem.

Global Learning, Inc.

Conservation as Politics
Carl Moneyhon

The late nineteenth century saw four major ideas concerning society and environment develop, each with a wide following. These major modes of thought may be characterized as *conservation, preservation, ecology,* and *laissez faire.* While adherents to each concept recognized the general problem, their goals varied, indeed were often contradictory, and, therefore, a general reform movement to solve environmental problems was virtually impossible. Even within these groups general agreement concerning goals and means to ends proved difficult. For Americans, therefore, there was a general perception of a crisis, but little agreement on its definition or on measures to alleviate it.

Of the four major ideologies, *conservationism* received the greatest publicity during this period. Its spokespersons were the most vocal and political. The concept promised to meet the crisis with minimal modification of existing American society. Conservationists emphasized the role of scientific and rational institutions in achieving a solution. Proper application of these techniques, they believed, would abate the problem by providing new resources to avoid shortages and making more efficient use of the natural wealth that was already available. This particular approach found its strongest adherents among scientists, professionals such as physicians and scholars, and some industrialists—men who possessed the technical knowledge that they believed would save the nation. Elements of conservationist thought were found in a host of programs developed during the late nineteenth century. Typical was the effort of Bernhard E. Fernow and Gifford Pinchot to bring scientific methods of tree farming into currency in the timber industry. Through careful cultivation, development of new kinds of timber, and proper harvesting, they believed the nation's timber resources could be preserved practically intact for future generations as well as the current. Perhaps no better statement exists of the kind of thought that embraced the conservationists than that of the economist Simon Patten. In *The New Basis of Civilization* he indicated his belief that science and technology would provide the ultimate means for humans to overcome the limits of environment. He wrote:

> Artificial culture and experimental science have already fundamentally altered the elemental relations existing two hundred years ago between population and environment. Yet to say that the methods which have made man physically independent of the local food supply are artificial is to underrate the powers of the new forces by implying that they are constantly opposed by fundamental natural forces which in the end must again triumph. The final victory of man's machinery over nature's materials is the next logical process in evolution, as nature's control of human society was the transition from anarchic and puny individualism to the group acting as a powerful, intelligent organism. Machinery, science, and intelligence moving on the face of the other may well affect it as the elements do, upbuilding, obliterating, and creating; but they are man's forces and will be used to hasten his dominion over nature.

The conservationists believed that promised shortages could be avoided, that the social status quo could consequently be maintained, with the innovation made possible by science and technology.

As a practical program, a variety of governmental agencies designed to apply the conservationist solution to problems appeared after the 1870s. The first of these was the United States Fish Commission created in 1871. Congress created it specifically to discover what was happening to the coastal fisheries and what might be done to prevent their destruction. Its first commissioner, Spencer Fullerton Baird, was a scientist who pushed the commission into a general study of marine biology and fish culture. As a result of these studies, Congress funded programs to replenish fish stocks and also moved to restrict fishing. Conservationism was also apparent in the work of the Division of Forestry created in 1881 within the Department of Agriculture. Under Franklin B. Hough, Bernhard E. Fernow, and Gifford Pinchot the division collected information on scientific tree culture and disseminated that information throughout the United States. At the request of the nation's chief foresters, Congress passed laws to preserve timber resources. Typical of these was the 1891 legislation allowing the president to set aside parts of the public domain for forest reserves. The most encompassing legislation passed through Congress in 1897, and authorized a system of management for these national forests under the direction of the Department of the Interior.

By 1900, however, conservationists confronted a dilemma. Their piecemeal approach to conservation provided only limited results. While they could respond to problems as they arose, the number of crisis situations continued to mount. Further, they became aware of the interrelationship of environmental problems. Realizing that the situation required a broad approach, conservationists, encouraged by the leadership of President Theodore Roosevelt, attempted to expand their ideal into a general reform. Roosevelt became the center of this movement when he brought to his administration prominent advocates of conservation, such as Gifford Pinchot, W.J. McGee, and Charles Van Hise. In 1908 the president called together a conference of governors to secure broad support for various conservation measures that he hoped to push through Congress. The general thrust of these measures would be to create a general conservation policy, the first step which would be the organization of a National Conservation Commission to inventory resources that would allow better planning. Roosevelt further envisioned annual conservation conferences in Washington to help develop a broad national policy. Emphasizing his concern, Roosevelt told the assembled governors that the conservation of natural resources was "the weightiest problem now before the Nation." He warned them that without quick measures, the nation's natural wealth was "in danger of exhaustion."...

The move to a general policy split the conservationists for development of a program raised major questions as to means and ends. All could agree that the environment must be managed, but they could not agree as to who should do the managing and whose purpose should be served by it. In short, there was no agreement as to who constituted society or what defined social interest. As a result two major groups emerged among the conservationists. The first, consisting of Roosevelt, Pinchot, Van Hise and others, came to believe that planning and definition must be in the hands of society through government. The second pushed the view that the response must be by society through individuals and private interests of the community. As a result, the conservationists, even though they agreed on the nature of the environmental problem and the solution to the problem, split over the question of social welfare....

Divisions within the conservationist camp created problems, and these were further complicated by the opposition of people who saw the crisis but had an alternative solution—the *preservationists*. This group represented a large number of Americans who

Global Learning, Inc.

viewed the environment somewhat romantically. Some were outright reactionaries. They believed that physical development did not always lead to progress. They argued that the best in life might be found in nature rather than in the words of man. Preservationism was not a new idea in the United States; in fact, it had a long tradition that could be traced in the ideas of Thoreau, George Catlin, and others. By the late nineteenth century men like Frederick Law Olmsted, Charles W. Eliot, and John Muir had become its carriers. They believed that nature possessed a spiritual quality necessary for the survival of humankind and argued for wilderness, for the preservation of the undeveloped. Muir wrote, "Everybody needs beauty as well as bread, places to play in and pray in, where nature may heal and cheer and give strength to body and soul alike." Eliot, president of Harvard and chairman of the National Conservation Congress in 1909, cooperated with the conservationists but believed nature was more than a resource for human utilization; it was worth preserving for itself. To him the city and the factory system created evils too great for the human body to endure and which only a resort to nature could cure. Frederick Law Olmsted, whose career included laying out natural sanctuaries in the heart of cities, suggested that the contemplation of nature was necessary for the health and vigor of humankind. Without it humans had, "softening of the brain, paralysis, palsy, monomania, insanity, mental and nervous excitability, moroseness, melancholy or irascibility, and incapacitation of the individual for proper exercise of intellectual and moral forces."

The preservationists' position was not an easy one for an individual at the turn of the century. To adopt it usually involved serious problems, for many could appreciate the advantages made possible by urban and industrial civilization. Yet at the same time they feared it and looked to the past, to a natural order for solace in the face of the upheaval of the industrial age. The paradoxes involved in the preservationist view appear prominently in the thought of John Burroughs. In *The Summit of the Year* he criticized the conservationist approach, the scientific way of looking at the world. It provided a mixed blessing:

> Well, we can gain a lot of facts, such as they are, but we may lose our own souls. This spirit has invaded school and college. Our young people go to the woods with pencil and note-book in hand; they drive sharp bargains with every flower and bird and tree they meet; they want tangible assets that can be put down in black and white. Nature as a living joy, something to love, to live with, to brood over, is now, I fear, seldom thought of. It is only a mine to be worked and to be through with, a stream to be fished, a tree to be shaken, a field to be gleaned. With what desperate thoroughness the new men study the birds; and about all their studies yield is a mass of dry, unrelated facts.

However, Burroughs could not see a way out of the dilemma. He did not like what was happening, but he did not believe the world could forget what it had now learned. He concluded that people ultimately "must face and accept the new situation....We shall write less poetry, but we ought to live saner lives; we shall tremble and worship less, but we shall be more at home in the universe." All preservationists were not as willing as Burroughs to accept compromise with "progress." In political battles of the Roosevelt and Taft years they would frequently stand against the convervationists and their opposition, as the internal split within conservationism, would work to preclude the development of a broad approach to ecological crisis.

A third approach to the apparent crisis of the late nineteenth century embraced elements and values of both conservationism and preservationism but had its unique elements. Its uniqueness would make its adherents uncooperative with those of the other two ideas. This approach may be called *ecological*. The concept of ecology involved the idea that humans were integrally involved with nature in an interdependent relationship. Ecologists, therefore, argued that the demands of nature must play as great a role in determining a proper course for society to follow as the needs of humans. The earliest spokesperson for this view in the United States was George P. Marsh, a diplomat who had served in Europe and witnessed first-hand the devastation that resulted from ignoring the demands of nature. In 1864 he published *Man and Nature* in which he warned Americans that they were creating problems for themselves by destroying their environment and cautioned them not to interfere with the "spontaneous arrangements of the organic and inorganic world." Marsh believed that nature possessed a natural balance and that humans, if they dealt unknowingly with it, could destroy that balance and make the world unfit for life. Looking at what Italians had done to their mountains, the destruction of timber and the resulting erosion and flooding, Marsh saw ample proof of his view's validity. He told Americans that they must stop. "We are even now breaking up the floor and wainscoting and doors and window frames of our dwelling, for fuel to warm our bodies and to seethe our pottage, and the world cannot afford to wait till the slow and sure progress of exact science has taught it better economy."

Marsh presented a strong challenge to the entire American concept of life and nature. He suggested that humans might not have the right to do with nature what they wanted but rather that they needed to understand what nature wanted. Perhaps it was too radical a departure for the time; consequently its adherents remained a small group, generally confined to the academy. Still, it was a point of view important among a potentially influential group of people. Unfortunately, it provided another approach to the American environmental problem and thus fragmented social response. The ecologists, because of their definition of the problem, had to move slowly. They had to discover what the correct relationship with the world should be. Nathaniel Shaler argued for education, for only through the study of nature would an answer to environmental problems be discovered. Shaler, however, found this goal hindered by the very institutions designed for study. He wrote of scientific education in the United States:

> We now present the realm to beginners as a group of fragments labeled astronomy, geology, chemistry, physics, and biology, each, as set forth, appearing to him as a little world in itself, with its own separate life, having little to do with its neighbors. It is rare, indeed, in a very considerable experience with youths to find one who has gained any inkling as to the complex unity of nature. Seldom it is, even with those who attain mastery in some one of these learnings, that we find a true sense as to the absolute oneness of the realm, or the place of man as the highest product of its work.

The ecologists perceived themselves in an adversary relationship with the rest of the community, including conservationists and preservationists, and believed that they had the only answer to the situation.

Conservationism, preservationism, and ecology represented activist approaches to environmental pressures. A fourth approach was the adoption of a wait-and-see attitude, a belief in *laissez faire*—let the situation develop and find out what happens. Accompanying this point of view was a basic optimism, a trust that nature or God would work things out. Its exponents adopted basic hostility toward those groups seeking to intervene in the process. George L. Knapp condemned the conservationists as "unadulterated humbugs" who sought to undermine the best in American life. In an article for the *North American Review* he wrote:

That the modern Jeremiahs are as sincere as was the older one I do not question. But I count their prophesies to be baseless vaporings, and their vaunted remedy worse than the fancied disease. I am one who can see no warrant of law, or justice, nor of necessity for that wholesale reversal of our traditional policy which the advocates of "conservation" demand. I am one who does not shiver for the future at the sight of a load of coal, nor view a steel-mill as the arch-robber of posterity.

While there might be immediate shortages, existing institutions would meet the crisis. The optimism of the advocates of laissez faire was strikingly expounded by Congressman Martin Dies of Texas before Congress on August 30, 1913. Dies strongly opposed efforts to prevent the construction of a dam across the Hetch Hetchy Valley in California, and speaking to the point he said:

I sympathize with my friends in California who want to take a part of the public domain now....I am willing to let them have it.

That is what the great resources of this country are for. They are for the American people. I want them to open the coal mines in Alaska. I want them to open the reservations of this country. I am not for preservations or parks. I would have the great timber and mineral and coal resources of this country opened to the people....Let California have it, and let Alaska open her coal mines. God Almighty has located the resources of this country in such form as that His children will not use them in disproportion, and your Pinchots will not be able to controvert and circumvent the laws of God Almighty.

The ideology of the advocates of laissez faire appears clearly in the statements of both Knapp and Dies. It represented, at least in part, a reassertion of two traditional American ideas. The environment existed for humans to subdue and develop, and to be subdued and developed by private initiative, by individuals whose pursuit of their own interests worked in the interest of the American people. In addition, God had a special concern with the people of the United States, and God would not allow anything bad to happen. While a crisis might exist, there was no need to change American ways.

Resources were diminishing. Wild life was disappearing. Everybody could see that something was happening. Something had gone wrong. But no consensus emerged as to what should be done. If planning was to be done, who would be responsible? If technological innovation was necessary, who would sponsor it? What approach should be taken? The problem raised by the crisis was no longer one of science. What had emerged was a political dilemma in which a variety of views contested for acceptance and no one could claim majority support. Everyone claimed to speak for public interest, for the national good and welfare, but the various groups proposing solutions offered different definitions of both the public interest and how to secure it. Consequently, reform efforts ran into trouble in the national political arena. In one episode after another environmental reformers found themselves unable to cooperate with one another. As a result, perhaps, the forces for laissez faire won the day....No broad reform plan emerged, no directed solution to the problem. Instead the nation met crises as it had in the past, piecemeal and responsively. This placed adjustments in each case in the hands of those directly tied to specific shortages. Thus, power companies developed waterways, steel companies sought new sources of iron ore, and so on. In the short run this probably averted the crisis. Private industry and enterprise was interested in efficient utilization of resources. It also managed to develop alternative sources for the energy and raw materials whose destruction had been feared.

But in the long run what took place? The discovery of new sources of diminishing materials spurred American growth, and the American population quickly expanded to consume whatever could be produced. Thus, society was still tied to the same pattern of utilization of resources that had created the initial crisis. That portion of the problem had only been delayed. However, in addition the crisis had prompted less visible change in the American community. The status quo had not been maintained; change had not been stopped.

In fact, Americans confronted the very crisis feared by Frederick Jackson Turner. By the success they achieved in solving the immediate problems, private entrepreneurs secured greater control over the resources that they needed and, consequently, greater economic and political power. Within this situation the chance of the individual either to gain economic power or exercise power outside of these corporations was diminished. The crisis forced change, whether Americans planned for it or not.

Lesson 14

The Grapes of Wrath

A Study in Contrasts

Historical Period   The Great Depression and World War II (1930-1945)

Sustainable Development Topics   Conflicting attitudes toward one's environment

Economic disparity in agriculture between family farms and agribusiness

Cost-benefit analysis of agribusiness

Objectives   Students will be able to:

1. Analyze how tenant farmers use the land and contrast with how agribusinesses/banks use the land.
2. Analyze costs and benefits of agribusiness in terms of the consumer, family farms, and tenant farmers.
3. Identify changes that can be made to help solve problems facing the United States' agricultural system of both family and corporate farms.

Time Requirement   One pre-lesson homework assignment and one to two classes

Materials Needed   Handout 1: *Grapes of Wrath* Reading
Handout 2: *Grapes of Wrath* Worksheet
Handout 3: *Agribusiness*
The Problem Solving Model at the beginning of this book

Lesson Background   This lesson was developed to illustrate the role of land management and agribusiness in the 1930s. From this reading the class will eventually be able to understand the many different problems that faced the agriculture industry during the 1930s and thus, can gain an appreciation of the many problems that face agriculture today. The reading selection from *The Grapes of Wrath* was picked for its stark contrast in how the land was viewed by small tenant farmers and the large land owners. With the contrasting view of the land as a backdrop, the piece describes the use of destructive farming methods used for the sake of profit. Finally, the piece identifies some of the options that the tenant farmers had after being kicked off the land.

The reading introduces the issue of sustainable development in many different ways. It introduces to the student the idea of land use and development. It also looks at the growing role of agribusiness in the farming industry at the expense of more traditional farming methods. It is as important today as it was during the 1930s to understand the precarious position of the farm industry and that what is good for the consumer is not necessarily good for the tenant farmer.

To understand the unique and consistent problems with agriculture during the 1930s please see the following sources:

1. *The New Deal 1932-1940,* William Luchtenberg
2. *The Coming of the New Deal,* Arthur Schlesinger
3. *The Grapes of Wrath,* John Steinbeck

Procedure

1. **Pre-class assignment**—Have students read the passage from **Handout 1: *The Grapes of Wrath*.** After doing the reading the students should also answer the questions on **Handout 2** to gauge comprehension and to facilitate discussion for the next day.

2. **In class**—Divide the class into groups of four people (more or less as you see fit). In these groups have the students review the homework reading for comprehension and beginning the lesson. After reviewing the handout, have the groups verbally create an overall reaction to the reading. Ask: *How might you have felt as one of the tenant farmers? As one of the bankers? If you had to choose between these two, which would you have chosen to be?*

3. Pass out **Handout 3: *Agribusiness*** or project it on an overhead projector. The definition of agribusiness for this lesson: *Farming and related processing and marketing concerns, operating as a large scale business.* In their groups, have the students explain what the arrows from part to part mean in the diagram. *What would happen to other parts of this system if a change is introduced, e.g., if petroleum prices increase, or if people stop buying a particular commodity?*

4. *What are the* **costs** *and* **benefits** *of agribusiness on individual segments of the society such as consumers, family farmers, and tenant farmers? On the Land?* The teacher can illustrate the group responses on a matrix/student organizer on the board.

Global Learning, Inc.

	Costs	Benefits
Consumers		
Family Farmers		
Tenant Farmers		
the Land...		

5. After going through the cost-benefit analysis, have the groups identify problems with the agricultural industry in the 1930s. These problems can encompass such aspects as: soil conservation, crop pricing, work conditions, consumer protection, or tenant farmers protection. Use step one, defining the problem, from the **Problem Solving Model: Contemporary Period** at the beginning of this book so that the students write out complete problem statements.

6. After identifying several problems with the agricultural system, each group will take on a single issue to develop a comprehensive plan that they think would solve their problem. See steps two through six in the **Problem Solving Model** for assistance. Make sure at least three perspectives are represented among the groups. For example, one group will represent the needs of *the banks and large landowners.* Another group will develop a plan for the needs of *family and tenant farmers* who are not covered by the Agricultural Adjustment Act. Another group will represent the needs of *the consumer.* Each group will develop a plan for their own part of the whole system. (For number 6 it is suggested that you see *The Coming of the New Deal,* by Arthur Schlesinger, who uses a fine illustration of the causes and developments of the Dust Bowl.)

7. After each group comes up with a plan, it is the job of a group spokesperson to present an outline of the particular group's proposal to the rest of the class. After the proposals have been presented and outlines left on the board, students can negotiate, as representatives of their groups, to create a comprehensive agricultural plan with which all groups are satisfied.

8. At the debriefing period after the negotiations, two points need to be addressed. The first point is to ask the individual groups: *to what extent were you successful in the negotiations?* Have the groups elaborate on their experiences. If a group falls short of their expectations, have the group explain what the particular impediments were. Through critical thinking questions explore with the students why their group's interests were so antagonistic to other groups' interests. As the teacher, you should always bring the students back to the historical realities of the 1930s. The second point to be

addressed by the class in the debriefing period is whether the students see any problems with the comprehensive plan and how those problems might be fixed to the satisfaction of the different parties.

Student Assessment   Students can be assessed on the basis of their completed worksheet (Handout 2), their original written plan, their class participation, and their effectiveness in getting the whole class to incorporate their group's elements within the comprehensive agricultural plan.

Global Learning, Inc.

Grapes of Wrath Reading

The owners of the land came onto the land, or more often a spokesman for the owners came. They came in closed cars, and they felt the dry earth with their fingers, and sometimes they drove big earth augers into the ground for soil tests. The tenants, from their sun-beaten dooryards, watched uneasily when the closed cars drove along the fields. And at last the owner men drove into the dooryards and sat in their cars to talk out their windows. The tenant men stood beside the cars for a while, and then squatted on their hams and found sticks with which to mark the dust.

In the open doors the women stood looking out, and behind them the children—corn-headed children, with wide eyes, one bare foot on top of the other bare foot, and the toes working. The women and the children watched their men talking to the owner men. They were silent.

Some of the owner men were kind because they hated what they had to do, and some of them were angry because they hated to be cruel, and some of them were cold because long ago they found out that one could not be an owner unless one were cold. And all of them were caught in something larger than themselves. Some of them hated the mathematics that drove them, and some were afraid, and some of them worshiped the mathematics because it provided a refuge from thought and feeling. If a bank or finance company owned the land, The Bank—The Company-needs-wants-insists-must have—as though the Bank or the Company were a monster, with thought and feeling, which had ensnared them. These last would take no responsibility for the banks or the companies because they were men and slaves, while the banks were machines and masters all at the same time. Some of the owner men were proud to be slaves to such cold and powerful masters. The owner men sat in their cars and explained. You know the land is poor. You scrambled at it long enough, God knows.

The squatting tenant men nodded and wondered and drew figures in the dust, and yes, they knew, God knows. If the dust only wouldn't fly. If the top would only stay down on the soil, it might not be so bad.

The owner men went on leading to their point: You know the land's getting poorer. You know what cotton does to the land; robs it, sucks all the blood out of it. The squatters nodded—they knew, God knew. If they could only rotate crops they might pump blood back into the land.

Well, it's too late. And the owner men explained the workings and thinkings of the monster that was stronger than they were. A man can hold if he can just eat and pay taxes; he can do that.

Yes, he can do that until his crops fail one day and he has to borrow money from the bank.

But-you see, the bank or a company can't do that, because those creatures don't breath air, don't eat side-meat. They breath profits; they eat the interest on money. If they don't get it they die the way that you die without air, without side-meat. It is a sad thing, but it is so. It just is so.

The squatting men raised their eyes to understand. Can't we just hang on? Maybe the next year will be a good year? God knows how much cotton next year. And with all the wars— God knows what price cotton will bring. Don't they make explosives out of cotton? And uniforms? Get enough wars and cotton'll hit the ceiling. Next year, maybe. They looked up questioningly.

We can't depend on it. The bank-the monster has to have profits all the time. It can't wait. It'll die. No, taxes go on. When the monster stops growing, it dies. It can't stay one size.

Soft fingers began to tap the sill of the car window, and hard fingers tightened on the restless drawing sticks. In the doorways of the sun-beaten tenant houses, women sighed and then shift feet so that the one that had been down was now on top, and the toes working. Dogs came sniffing near the owner's cars and wetted on all four tires one after another. And chickens lay in the sunny dust and fluffed their feathers to get the cleansing dust down to the skin. In the little sties the pigs grunted inquiringly over the muddy remnants of the slops.

The squatting men looked down again. What do you want us to do? We can't take less share of the crop—we're half starved now. The kids are hungry all the time. We got no clothes, torn an' ragged. If all the neighbors weren't all the same, we'd be ashamed to go to meeting.

And at last the owners came to the point. The tenant system won't work anymore. One man on a tractor can take the place of twelve or fourteen families. Pay him a wage and take all the crop. We have to do it. We don't like to do it. But the monster's sick. Something has happened to the monster.

But you'll kill the land with cotton.

We know. We got to take the cotton before the land dies. Then we'll sell the land. Lots of families in the East would like to own a piece of land.

The tenant men looked up alarmed. But what'll happen to us? How'll we eat?

You'll have to get off the land. The plows will go through the doorway.

And now the squatting men stood up angrily. Grampa took up the land, and he had to kill the Indians and drive them away. And Pa was born here, and he had to kill weeds and snakes. And then a bad year came and he had to borrow a little money. An' we was born here. There in the door—our children born here. And pa had to borrow money. The bank owned the land then, but we stayed and we got a little of what we raised.

We know that-all that. It's not us, it's the bank. A bank isn't like a man. Or an owner with fifty-thousand acres, he isn't like a man either. That's the monster.

Sure, cried the tenant men, but it is our land. We measured it and broke it up. We were born on it, and we killed on it, died on it. Even if it's no good, it's still ours. That's what makes it ours—being born on it, working it, dying on it. That makes ownership, not a paper with numbers on it.

We're sorry. It's not us. It's the monster. The bank isn't like a man.

Yes, but the bank is only made of men.

No, you're wrong there-quite wrong there. The bank is something else than men. It happens that every man in a bank hates what a bank does, and yet the bank does it. The bank is something more than men, I tell you. It's a monster. Men made it but they can't control it.

                                                                 Global Learning, Inc.

The tenants cried, grampa killed Indians, pa killed snakes for the land. Maybe we can kill banks—they're worse than Indians and snakes. Maybe we got to fight to keep our land, like pa and grampa did.

And now the owner men grew angry. You'll have to go....We'll get our guns like grampa when the Indians came. What then? Well-first the sheriff, and then the troops. You'll be stealing if you try to stay. You'll be murderers if you kill to stay. The monster isn't men, but it can make men do what it wants.

But if we go, where will we go? How'll we go? We got no money.

We're sorry, said the owner men. The bank, the fifty-thousand acre owner can't be responsible. You're on land that isn't yours. Once over the line maybe you can pick cotton in the fall. Maybe you can go on relief. Why don't you go on west to California? There is work there, and it never gets cold. Why, you can reach out anywhere and pick an orange. Why, there's always some kind of crop to work in. Why don't you go there? And the owner men started their cars and rolled away.

The tenant men squatted on their hams again to make the dust with a stick, to figure, to wonder. Their sunburned faces were dark, and their sunwhipped eyes were light. The women moved cautiously out of the doorways toward the men, and the children crept behind the women, cautiously, ready to run. The bigger boys squatted beside their father, because that made them men. After a time the women asked, what did he want?

And the men looked up for a second, and the smolder of pain was in their eyes. We got to get off. A tractor and a superintendent. Like factories.

Where will we go? the women asked.

We don't know. We don't know.

And the women went quickly, quietly back into the houses and herded the children ahead of them. They knew that a man so hurt and so perplexed may turn in anger, even on people he loves. They left the men alone to figure and wonder in the dust.

After a time perhaps the tenant man looked about-at the pump put in ten years ago, with a goose-neck handle and iron flowers on the spout, at the chopping block where a thousand chickens had been killed, at the hand plow lying in the shed, at the patent crib hanging in the rafters over it.

The children crowded about the women in the houses. What we going to do, Ma? Where we going to go?

The women, said we don't know, yet. Go out and play. But don't go near your father. He might whale you if you go near him. And the women went on with the work, but all the time they watched the men squatting in the dust-perplexed and figuring.

Grapes of Wrath Worksheet

Your Name _____

Answer the following questions in complete sentences.

1. What was the tenant farming system?

2. Why are the tenant farmers being removed from the land?

3. Why do the tenant farmers refer to the land that they farm as their own?

4. What is the attitude of the tenants toward the banks and agribusiness?

5. What is the significance of referring to the banks and agribusiness as "the monster?"

6. How would this story be different if it were told from the perspective of the owner men in the cars?

Agribusiness

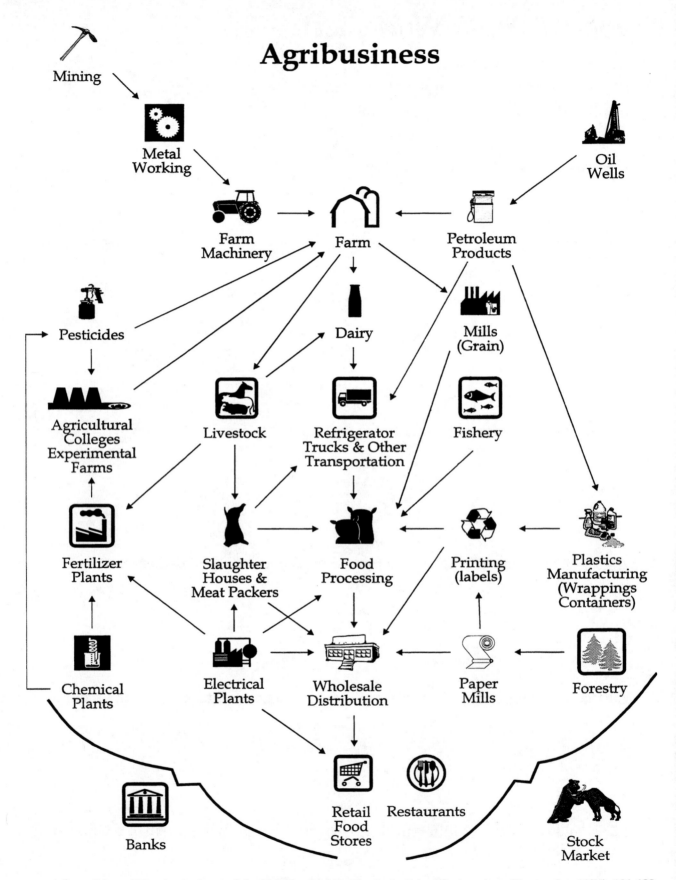

Adapted from "The Agriculture of the U.S." by Earl O. Heady in *Scientific American* (September 1976): 121-122.

Lesson 15

How Do the Preparations for War Impact on the Environment?

The Case of Picatinny Arsenal

Historical Period   The Great Depression and World War II (1930-1945)
Recent United States (1975-present)

Sustainable Development Topic   Environmental Impact of War

Purpose   War and the preparation for war have had profound impacts on the natural environment. Students will use *primary source documents* to investigate two cases involving the problem of water pollution in two different historical periods, as well as efforts to resolve this problem at Picatinny Arsenal in northern New Jersey. Students will also explore how human efforts to correct environmental contamination have evolved from the middle of World War II to the present.

Objectives   Students will be able to:

1. Distinguish among *egocentric, piecemeal, environmental* and *ecosystem approaches* to problem solving.
2. Analyze primary source documents from the archives of Picatinny Arsenal and from the U.S. Environmental Protection Agency in terms of environmental consequences of past decision making and in terms of systematic problem solving.
3. Make judgments about the difference between the environmental and the ecosystem approaches to problem solving and support their judgments with data.

Time Required   2 to 3 class periods

Materials Needed	Handout 1: *Sustainable Development: The Ecosystem Approach* Handout 2: *Picatinny Arsenal—A Brief Overview* Handout 3: *History of Water Pollution Problems—Arsenal Streams* Handout 4: *Picatinny Arsenal's Superfund Sites,* or Handout 5: *Bad Water Stirs Fears in Rockaway Twp.*
Teacher Background	Handout 5 is provided in case the teacher feels that Handout 4 is either too difficult or too time consuming to read. In such a case, the teacher can use Handout 4 as background to lead a discussion on Handout 5.
Procedure	Assign **Handouts 1** and **2** for homework, including the student organizer for Handout 1 and the location map at the end of Handout 2.

Procedure Day 1

1. Begin the class by putting the four categories on the board: **egocentric, piecemeal, environmental,** and **ecosystem** approaches. Ask students to list characteristics or qualities of each approach under each heading. Work with the students to get a general description of each approach. Have the students record these descriptions on their student organizer for Handout 1 for use with the next readings.

2. Distribute **Handout 3** to half the class and **Handout 4** to the other half. [NOTE: You have an option of using the newspaper article in **Handout 5** if you think Handout 4 is either too difficult or too long for your students.] Tell the students that they are reading original source materials and note that the language is somewhat formal and technical. Let students reading the same Handout work in pairs to answer the worksheets for that reading. If time permits, have students begin to work in class and finish the worksheets as homework. Tell the class that each student will be responsible tomorrow for teaching the contents of their worksheets to another student who has not read their reading.

Procedure Day 2

1. Create new pairs of students, one who worked with Handout 3 and one who worked with Handout 4 or 5. Have each student explain their reading and completed worksheet to the other student. Tell the students that they must know the content of *both* handouts when they are done.

2. Conduct a discussion with the class. From those who read Handout 3, ask for examples of the **egocentric** and **piecemeal** approaches to the environment, and discuss the results with the whole class.

3. From those who read Handout 4, ask who answered question 5 as if the efforts to clean up Picatinny Arsenal are an example of the **environmental** approach and who think these efforts are an example of the **ecosystem** approach. Have the students support their positions with information from the reading and from the class' original description of these two positions. Involve the whole class in the discussion.

4. Ask the class to compare and contrast the problem of water pollution as described in these two readings. Draw out the increased level of complexity and technological sophistication in recent times. Ask them what changes have occurred since 1944 that account for the differences. Bring out such points as the fact that more chemical compounds have been created, we are more aware of how all things within an ecosystem are interconnected, the ability to measure items by ppm (parts per million), ppb, or even ppt results from recent technological inventions—such as HDLC (the high density liquid chromatograph) and mass spectrophotometer in the 1960s.

5. Conclude by asking for examples of ways in which war and the preparation for war affect the environment that they had not thought about before this lesson.

Student Assessment   Students can be assessed on the basis of their completed worksheets, class participation, or an essay question asking them to compare and contrast the problem of water pollution as described in these two readings. To achieve accountability in both halves of the pairs, remind students that they are required to know the content of both Handouts 3 and 4 (or 5).

Extension   Students who want to explore further the impact of the military and military bases on the environment can contact the following sources:

Department of Defense, Directorate for Defense Information, 3400 Defense Pentagon, Washington, DC 20301-3400, Room 2E777; Telephone 703-697-6462.

Regional Office of the EPA: Boston, 617-565-9447;
New York, 212-264-2980;
Philadelphia, 215-597-9817;
Atlanta, 404-347-3004;
Chicago, 312-353-3209;
Dallas, 214-655-2204;
Kansas City, 913-551-7003;
Denver, 303-391-6999;
San Francisco, 415-744-1581;
Seattle, 206-553-1207.

Center for Defense Information, 1500 Massachusetts Ave. NW, Washington, DC 20005 (202) 862-0700

Sources   *The History of Picatinny Arsenal.* Picatinny Arsenal, March 31, 1931.

"History of Water Pollution Problems—Arsenal Streams." Picatinny Arsenal, 1944.

Kaye, Seymour M. *Encyclopedia of Explosives and Related Items.* Patr 2700, Volume 8, US Army Armament Research and Development Command, Dover, NJ, 1978.

Osby, Liu. "Bad Water Stirs Fears in Rockaway Township," *Daily Record.* 2/13/91.

US Environmental Protection Agency. "Fact Sheet, Picatinny Arsenal," September 1993.

US Environmental Protection Agency. "Picatinny Arsenal, New Jersey, EPA ID# NJ3210020704," February 1994.

Vallentyne, J.R. & A.M. Beeton. *The Ecosystem Approach to Managing Human Uses and Abuses of Natural Resources in the Great Lake Basin.* Great Lakes Laboratory for Fisheries and Aquatic Sciences, Department of Fisheries and Oceans, 1986. Taken from E.D.I.T. File 10, *Environment First: The Idea of Sustainable Development.* Common Heritage Programme, 200 Isabella Street, Suite 300, Ottawa, Ontario, Canada K1S 1V7.

Approaches to the Environment Student Organizer

List several characteristics or examples of each approach:

Egocentric	
Piecemeal	
Environmental	
Ecosystem	

Global Learning, Inc.

Sustainable Development
The Ecosystem Approach

Ecosystems are natural or artificial subdivisions of the biosphere with boundaries arbitrarily defined to suit particular purposes. It is possible to speak of your personal ecosystem (you and the environment on which you depend for sunshine, air water, food, and friends), the Great Lakes basin as an ecosystem (interacting communities of living and nonliving things in the basin), or our planetary ecosystem, the biosphere....

There is a simple, yet profound difference between "environment" and "ecosystem." The notion of environment is like that of **house**—something external and detached. In contrast, ecosystem implies **home**—something we feel part of and see ourselves in even when we are not there. A home has an added spiritual dimension that makes it qualitatively different from a house. It is a happier place because of the caring and sharing relationships among its inhabitants.

The emergence of an **ecosystem approach** to planning, research, and management is not accidental. It is the most recent phase in a historical succession of management approaches from **egocentric** to **piecemeal** to **environmental** and now to an **ecosystem approach**....The ecosystem approach emerged in the 1970s with the realization, in part from the discovery of toxic chemicals in human food chains, that people and environments can only be managed effectively in relation to ecosystems of which they are parts....

Some examples of the evolution from indifferent to ecosystem management styles may help to clarify what is meant by ecosystem approach and to show the extent to which it is now in development:

> **Organic waste.** First it was dumped wherever convenient—best of all in streams or lakes. Next, because of downstream problems, we developed energy-consumptive sewage treatment systems. Now, an ecosystem approach focuses on recycling energy efficiently, and material recovery from sewage.

> **Eutrophication.** First it was ignored. When the odors became too strong, nutrient-rich effluents were diverted downstream. Then phosphorus was removed from sewage effluents. An ecosystem approach promotes low-phosphate detergents, more efficient use of fertilizers, and nutrient recycling.

> **Toxic chemicals.** At first toxic chemicals were used indiscriminately. Then they were dealt with one by one with regulations after the fact, as in the case of pesticides. An ecosystem approach requires designing with nature, particularly for long-lived compounds.

Source: J.R. Vallentyne & A.M. Beeton.*The Ecosystem Approach to Managing Human Uses and Abuses of Natural Resources in the Great Lake Basin.*

Picatinny Arsenal—A Brief Overview

How might Picatinny Arsenal impact on its environment?

Picatinny Arsenal is a development arsenal concerned with research and engineering of military propellants, explosives and hardware for Army weapons of all kinds and for the adaption of nuclear and non-nuclear warheads to missiles. At the installation, about 5,500 people are employed in research and development of munitions and weapons. The Arsenal encompasses more than 1,500 buildings on 6,491 acres.

The Arsenal is located in Rockaway Township in the central portion of northern New Jersey, five miles north of Dover. This places it at the outer rim of the New York metropolitan area. It occupies a ten mile long valley, lying between mountain ridges which serve as natural barricades. The valley also has a natural water supply. These are the three attributes for which the site was selected: nearness to the world of commerce; means of protection of the surrounding area from the hazards inherent in its work; and the availability of the one extremely vital natural resource—water.

The name Picatinny has been variously ascribed to mean "peak with broken rocks and cliffs" or "water-by-the-hill" as the name given by the Lenape Native Americans to the brook flowing under what is now called Picatinny Peak.

The site of the Arsenal has a long industrial history. Middle Forge, one of the first forges in New Jersey, was established there in 1749. The forge later became part of Mount Hope Iron Works, which provided cannon shot and other iron implements for the Revolutionary War. The need of a depot where powder and explosives might be stored in large quantities, and where powder mills might be erected, was seriously felt by the Army during and after the Civil War. In 1880, the U.S. War Department established the Picatinny Powder Works at the site, and, since 1907, as a result of expanding activities, the facility has been known as Picatinny Arsenal. During World War I, the Arsenal produced many types of ammunition, from .30 caliber rifle ammunition to 16 inch projectiles. During World War II production was expanded to include bombs, high explosives, pyrotechnics (e.g., rockets and flares), and other ordnance items. At the time of Pearl Harbor no other plant in the United States was capable of making anything larger than small arms ammunition. Picatinny provided detonators to the Atomic Energy Commission for inclusion in the Manhattan Project, which developed the Atomic Bomb.

In the 1950's, 60's and 70's, the Arsenal's Nuclear Division produced nuclear projectiles, missiles and subsurface munitions, i.e., mines. Also during this period, a new assortment of antipersonnel weapons were developed and were utilized during the Vietnam War. In recent years, the Arsenal's mission has shifted to research and development of large caliber munitions, such as so-called "smart" munitions and mines, "lethal mechanisms" including chemical energy warheads and kinetic energy penetrators, and new optical, infrared and radar devices.

List three ways that Picatinny Arsenal might impact on its natural environment.

Global Learning, Inc.

Handout 2

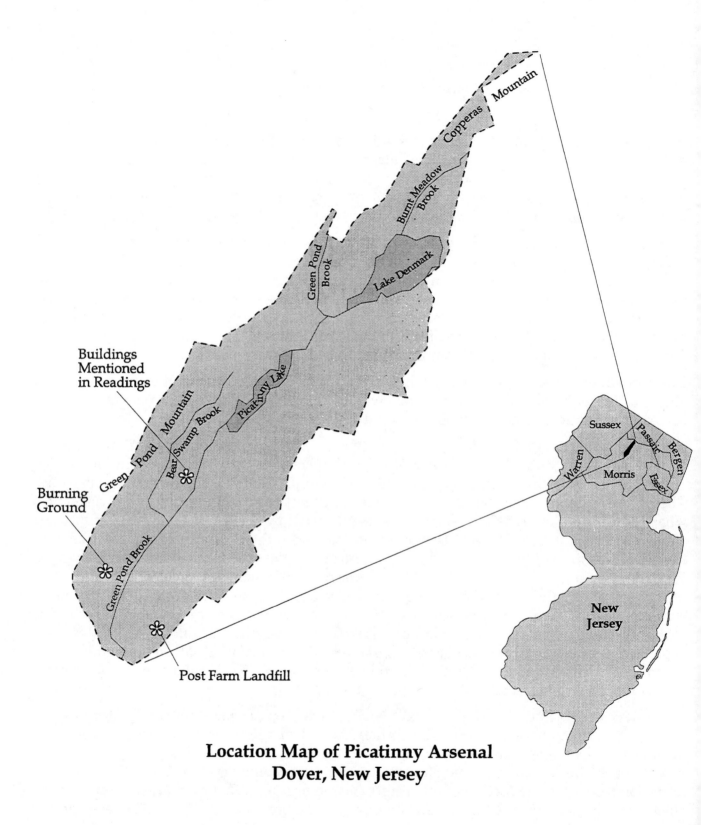

Buildings
Mentioned
in Readings

Burning
Ground

Post Farm Landfill

Copperas Mountain

Burnt Meadow Brook

Green Pond Brook

Lake Denmark

Green Pond Mountain

Bear Swamp Brook

Picatinny Lake

Green Pond

Green Pond Brook

Sussex

Warren

Passaic

Bergen

Morris

Essex

New Jersey

**Location Map of Picatinny Arsenal
Dover, New Jersey**

Picatinny Arsenal
History of Water Pollution Problems—Arsenal Streams

*The following quarterly report was filed by the Arsenal's historian in 1944. It contains illustrations of both the **egocentric** and **piecemeal** approaches to the environment. Before reading this report, review the questions on the third page of this handout.*

Green Pond Brook is a branch of the Rockaway River, which in turn is a source of supply of potable water for Jersey City, NJ. [The Jersey City Water Works' Boonton Reservoir lies less than 15 miles downstream. This reservoir provides drinking water to more than 350,000 people in four communities.] As Green Pond Brook flows through the Arsenal, the Sanitary Engineers have maintained a very close supervision on the quality of water outflow of this brook as it flows from these premises. A field inspector also of the Department of Public Works has made and continues to make inspections along our streams for the detection of possible sources of pollution and for the purpose of making recommendations that will help to hold pollution down to a minimum.

The department's main concern has been for the control of oil, turbidity [cloudiness and muddiness], tetryl [a yellow powder used as an explosive], acidity, color and bacteriological purity. These items are listed from the most difficult to control to the least difficult....

It should be stated before going into detail that while the Arsenal has made every effort within reason to satisfy the state and that they in turn appeared to feel that we were doing all in our power to satisfy them, the problem was never completely controlled.

The source of oil flow into the streams was traced to the Metal Components Shop, the steel chip bins between the third and fourth wings of Bldg. #31, the Garage Bldg., large air compressors in Bldg. #31 and Bldg. #266, and the Arsenal Parking lots. Occasionally larger quantities of oil flow were traced to construction activities along the streams, the innocent emptying of crank case oil in unauthorized places and a general contamination of various areas by intensive trucking activities and the tracking of small quantities of grease and oil by pedestrians through the Metal Components Group Area.

The Area around the chip bins was floored with concrete slabs constructed with retaining ledges and sloped surfaces so as to retain oil drippings and special oil catch basins. The bins proper were also piped to collecting drums as a means of collecting oil dripping immediately after discharge into their storage space. This arrangement saved a considerable amount of useable oil which was reprocessed for further use. The steel and other chips were later loaded into railroad cars for shipment to the outside. [The railroad looped the entire arsenal.] It was noted that even after chips had been held for a considerable length of time in the bins, oil would still collect in cars and drip on the ground wherever the loaded cars were spotted to await transit....

The Garage Bldg. has been operated with unusual care and very closely supervised by the officer in charge in order to prevent undue contamination. All crank case oil was collected in drums, transported to the Power House and burned as fuel. Even with all of these precautions small quantities of oil eventually reached the brook through floor drains, normal spillage and general tracking of oil by pedestrians in the area which surrounds the garage. A distributing tank which was located at the end of Bldg. #24 also caused some contamination, although this tank was equipped with a metal catch pan. Car washing at various locations around Bldg. #33 also contributes to the general oil nuisance. A remedy for this was partly put into use by the erection of a special car washing concrete platform with an oil catch basin adjacent to it. This project was never inclosed however, because of lack of funds and the urgency of other more important projects and its use was gradually abandoned in favor of the more convenient location around Bldg. #33.

Various large compressors and pumps around the Arsenal were checked and safeguarded against oil spatter by the installation of oil collecting pans.

The various Arsenal parking lots were responsible for a large portion of the oil pollution in the streams, particularly after heavy showers. This was caused by the large number of old and defective buses that were parked during the three shift periods of each work day and private cars, all of which deposited oil on the ground. As these lots were graded for proper drainage, the fast run-off carried portions of the surface oil and some portion of the oil which has seeped into the filled ground during every rain storm.

Two methods of control were adopted, first, a close supervision of all the Arsenal activities was maintained to prevent the leakage of oils and to prevent unlawful disposal in Arsenal streams. All waste oils were collected and disposed of by burning in the Power House or filtered for reuse. The burning of waste oils in the burning ground with garbage and other process wastes was abandoned. A special oil-absorbing powder called Redi-Dry was spread over contaminated areas and floors wherever conditions warranted it. Secondly, the oil which eventually escaped through the first precautions was partly collected within special catch basins. In addition, planks were placed across the brooks to hold back oil film which was collected by skimming. The collection catch basins and the collection pools were also skimmed daily or as required. It should be noted that a very small quantity of oil may spread to almost molecular thinness and pollute, in appearance at least, a large stream area.

[The report continues with a discussion of the problems of, and proposed solutions for, turbidity, tetryl, acidity, water color, bacteriological purity.]

Picatinny Arsenal—1944
History of Water Pollution Problems—Arsenal Streams

1. What were the sources of the oil pollution problem at Picatinny Arsenal in 1944?

2. How did oil from these sources wind up in the Arsenal's streams and lakes?

3. What source of drinking water did this oil pollution threaten to pollute?

4. What were the Arsenal's three main approaches to solving this problem?

5. Give one example from the report of an egocentric approach to the environment.

6. How does this report illustrate a piecemeal approach to the environment?

Global Learning, Inc.

Picatinny Arsenal—1944
History of Water Pollution Problems—Arsenal Streams Answer Sheet

1. What were the sources of the oil pollution problem at Picatinny Arsenal in 1944?

   metal components shop
   steel chip bins
   Garage Bldg.
   large air compressors
   parking lot run off
   construction activities along streams
   dumping crank case oil on the ground
   leaks from trucks, buses and cars
   pedestrians tracking grease and oil

2. How did oil from these sources wind up in the Arsenal's streams and lakes?

   Oil floats on water. Rain would lift the dripped or spilled oil from the ground and from paved surfaces, and it would run into the streams.

3. What water supply source did this oil pollution threaten to pollute?

   Jersey City's Boonton Reservoir

4. What were the Arsenal's three main approaches to solving this problem?

   1) Prevention of both leaks and unlawful disposal, through close supervision of all Arsenal activities
   2) Collection of spilled oil in catch basins
   3) Skimming the brooks with planks

5. Give one example from the report of an egocentric approach to the environment.

   "the innocent emptying of crank case oil in unauthorized places"
   car washing at convenient locations without regard to the resulting pollution

6. How does this report illustrate a piecemeal approach to the environment?

   The approach to the problem does not get to the heart of the problem. It seems to assume that the manufacturing and transportation activities must continue basically as is and that the environmental task is to minimize the damages. Of course, this assumption is understandable given not only the era but also the fact that World War II was raging with its demands on the Arsenal and general resource shortages in the country. The solutions, however, are rudimentary and do not completely solve the problem, even though the planners appear to be doing the best they know how.

Picatinny Arsenal's Superfund Sites
U.S. Environmental Protection Agency, Region II

*The following reading is taken directly from two fact sheets compiled by the U.S. Environmental Protection Agency (EPA) in September 1993 and February 1994. Before you read, review the questions on the last page of the handout. As you read, keep in mind the distinction between an **environmental** and an **ecosystem** approach to managing and problem solving.*

Site Contamination

Between 1976 and 1989 Picatinny Arsenal and the U.S. Army Environmental Center have identified 156 areas of concern at Picatinny. [These 156 areas have been placed on the EPA's "Superfund" National Priorities List.] They include areas for testing rocket fuels, munitions, and propellants; areas where chemicals and shells were buried; lagoons; landfills; drum storage areas; and a sludge bed. Ground water contamination has been confirmed near Buildings 24 and 95 where plating operations took place during the 1970's and early 1980's. The major contaminant of concern, trichloroethylene (TCE),[*] is found in a ground water plume emanating from the Building 24 area at concentrations as high as 25 ppm (parts per million). The leading edge of this plume, with concentrations as high as 5 ppb (parts per billion), is discharging into Green Pond Brook which flows off site. [The Brook flows into the Rockaway River, which flows into the Jersey City Reservoir in Boonton, about 15 miles from Picatinny. This reservoir provides drinking water to more than 350,000 people in four communities.] Contamination, in the form of an explosive, RDX, was discovered in off-site residential wells in October of 1990. RDX is a suspected carcinogen. Meetings were held with the affected residents and Picatinny is supplying drinking water to 3 households. The Army has agreed to extend the municipal water line to the 17 affected residences by Spring 1994.

Monitoring wells and soils adjacent to unlined lagoons, which until 1981 held wastewater from metal plating and etching facilities, are contaminated with volatile organic compounds and heavy metals. Polychlorinated biphenyls (PCBs) and an organic pesticide were found in the sediments of the Green Pond Brook. In 1982, the brook was dredged, and the materials were piled nearby. Site studies have found metals, explosives, and trace amounts of dioxin in a defined area; access to that area has been restricted. The contaminated groundwater, soil, and sediments could pose a health hazard if accidentally ingested. Contaminated groundwater has apparently migrated off-site at the southern boundary where low levels of explosive compounds have been found in private wells. In addition, the contaminants from the site could pollute the waters of Green Pond Brook, Lake Denmark, and Picatinny Lake.

---

[*] TCE is a solvent used in dry cleaning. It was used at Picatinny in the machine shop as a popular degreaser. It is a Class B1 carcinogen. The maximum allowable levels in water is 1 ppb. 25 ppm is 25,000 times greater than this standard.

Global Learning, Inc.

Cleanup Approach

The site is being addressed in a phased long-term remediation. The 156 areas of concern have been divided into 3 phases to be studied in succession. Phase I generally encompasses the highest priority sites which are located at the southern portion of the Arsenal....

Response Action Status

Building 24 Area: In 1989, with agreement of the EPA and the State, the Army selected the following remedy for preventing groundwater contaminated with volatile organic compounds (including TCE) from discharging into Green Pond Brook: (1) extraction of contaminated groundwater through wells; (2) installation of a pre-treatment system for the removal of metals and solids from the water; (3) air stripping to remove volatile organic compounds; (4) filtering to remove volatile organic compounds from the air stripper exhaust and additional volatile organic compounds from the air stripper effluent; (5) discharging treated water via a holding tank and piping it to Green Pond Brook; (6) operation and maintenance of the system; and (7) effluent monitoring. A pump and treat system was activated October 1992 and has been operating satisfactorily since that time...

Burning Ground Area: Explosively contaminated sludge and sediment from manufacturing processes are sent to the burning grounds to be incinerated in pans (formerly incinerated on ground surface). The Army is investigating this area of the site to determine the nature and extent of contamination in soil, groundwater, surface water, and sediment. Field sampling has been completed and the Remedial Investigation Report for this area is to be submitted March 1994.

Buildings Contaminated with Explosives: There are approximately 450 abandoned buildings at Picatinny Arsenal which are severely contaminated with explosives. The extent of the contamination can be seen from the fact that a worker was reportedly killed a few years ago when the building he was working in exploded. Picatinny feels that the only way to remove this threat to human health is to burn the buildings which they have started to do. The question remains to what degree these buildings or remains of buildings should be investigated as sources of contamination to the environment. This group of buildings is addressed in the Phase II Remedial Investigation (RI) workplan.

Remaining Areas: A Remedial Investigation Concept Plan was completed for 156 areas in 1991 including the previously mentioned areas. The plan prioritized areas for investigation and potential cleanup. To facilitate this process, these 156 areas have been broken into three phases. The Phase I Remedial Investigation (RI) workplan was approved September 1993 and field sampling is currently underway. The Phase II RI workplan was submitted May 1993 and field sampling is expected to start Fall 1994. The Phase III RI workplan, which will cover the remaining sites at Picatinny Arsenal, will be submitted 10 months after the Phase II RI workplan is approved. Additionally, the off-site well contamination in the vicinity of the southern boundary is being investigated under Phase I.

Site Facts: Picatinny Arsenal is participating in the Installation Restoration Program, a specially funded program established by the Department of Defense in 1978 to identify, investigate, and control the migration of hazardous contaminants at military and other Department of Defense facilities. An Interagency Agreement [on how the restoration work was going to be done, who was responsible for what aspects of it, and possible penalties for noncompliance] was signed by the Army and the EPA in May 1991.

Environmental Progress

Construction of the groundwater cleanup remedy for Building 24 has been completed and activated. Preliminary concerns regarding heavy metal levels in the treatment plant discharge did not prove warranted as they were found to be under permit levels. A removal action has been carried out at the Post Farm Landfill to remove buried drums. Additionally, off-site residents, whose well water was found to be contaminated with explosives, will be provided with an alternative water supply. As previously mentioned, field sampling in support of the Burning Grounds Remedial Investigation has been completed. The Army is planning to discontinue open burning of its explosive wastes at the Burning Grounds by 1995 when an incinerator is scheduled to come on-line. The Phase I and Phase II Remedial Investigation workplans, encompassing over 100 of the 156 areas of concern identified at Picatinny Arsenal, have been submitted to EPA with field sampling underway for Phase I. While further investigations leading to the selection of final remedies for the remaining contaminated areas are being conducted, the EPA has determined that there is no immediate danger to the nearby residents or the environment.

Global Learning, Inc.

Picatinny Arsenal's Superfund Sites

1. Describe the two problems regarding off site drinking water that have been identified at Picatinny Arsenal.

2. What solutions have been proposed or implemented to address these two problem areas?

3. Draw a diagram of the procedure being used to keep the volatile organic compounds like TCE in the Building 24 Area from draining into Green Pond Brook.

4. The Army has developed a plan to clean up the contaminated sites at Picatinny, called a Remedial Investigation Concept Plan. Outline the contents of this plan according to the three different time phases. Give dates when work was scheduled to be started or completed. Include several examples of tasks for each phase.

5. Would you describe the efforts to clean up contaminated sites at Picatinny Arsenal as an example of the environmental approach or the ecosystem approach to managing and problem solving? Support your choice with information from this reading.

Bad Water Stirs Fears in Rockaway Township

By Liv Osby, *Daily Record,* Morris County, N.J. Wednesday, February 13, 1991

Concerns about health, property values and livelihoods were on the minds of Union Turnpike residents yesterday after Picatinny Arsenal revealed it had discovered an explosive compound in some of the region's drinking water.

"They told us that it's possibly contaminated and they don't want us drinking the water until they're sure," said Brad McConley, whose father, William McConley, lives at one of the homes where contamination was found.

"Whenever there's bad water, you worry," he said. "But we have bottled water for drinking anyway."

Picatinny officials announced Monday that an explosive compound known as RDX was confirmed in one well and suspected in two others, including the well at the McConley home and used car business on Route 15 south.

For years the Army has been monitoring 18 private wells on Union Turnpike and Route 15 in the township to determine whether any pollutants from the weapons research and development facility migrated off the base. Monday's announcement provided the first evidence of that off-site migration.

"The Army has been doing this work to pick up any change so action can be taken before there is any potential health impact," township Health Officer Steve Levinson said.

Township and Army officials took additional water samples yesterday, Levinson said. While RDX, or hexahydro-trinitrotriazine, is a suspected carcinogen, neither Levinson nor Picatinny spokesman Pete Rowland had information about any other possible health effects. Army officials say there is no danger of explosion.

"I'm worried about my tenants," said landlord Tom Schoonmaker, who owns two homes on Union Turnpike, noting tenants called him about breaking their leases after learning of the contamination yesterday.

Schoonmaker also owns a landscaping and excavating company on Union Turnpike, Tomco Inc., and said yesterday that the business has used bottled water since it opened three years ago.

"We won't drink or cook with the water. We can't make coffee or tea," Schoonmaker said. "We won't shower in it or even wash dishes in it. It smells terrible."

Indeed, water flowing from Tomco's hot water faucet yesterday had the sulfur-like, smell of rotten eggs. Schoonmaker's secretary, Eleanor Palmieri, added that white clothes turned brown the one time she washed clothes at the business.

While the township recommended that the residents of homes with contamination drink bottled water, Rowland said the Army will not supply bottled water to those whose wells tested negative for contaminants, such as Tomco Inc.

He said water in the region has a high iron content, which could account for the brown water. Levinson said a rotten egg smell often is produced by an electric hot water heater, adding that ground water odors normally are reported by more than one resident.

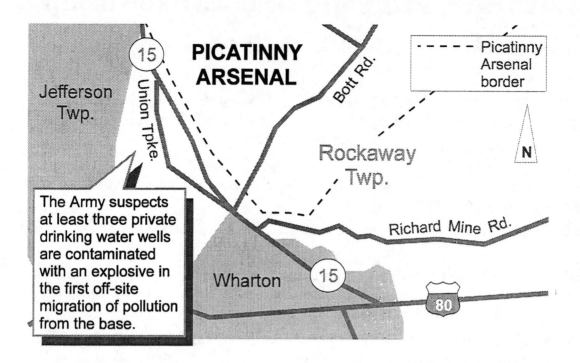

1. What environmental problem from Picatinny Arsennal is affecting people in Rockaway Township?

2. How many homes are affected?

3. Describe the concerns that this problem has raised for the residents.

4. What steps have been taken to solve this problem?

Answer Sheet

1. What environmental problem from Picatinny Arsenal is affecting people in Rockaway Township?

   An explosive, RDX, from the Arsennal has contaminated the wells and drinking water of people living on Union Turnpike, just south of the Arsennal.

2. How many homes are affected?

   18

3. Describe the concerns that this problem has raised for the residents.

   Health: RDX is a suspected carcinogen.

   Inconvenience: The water smells so it can't be used for cooking and cleaning. It also turns washed clothes brown, although there may be other explanations for these problems.

   Property values will be depressed if their wells are contaminated.

   Livelihoods: Tenants have called a landlord about breaking their leases. The landscaping business must use bottled water instead of tap water.

   According to the Army, there is no danger of explosion.

4. What steps have been taken to solve this problem?

   The Army has been monitoring 18 private wells for years.

   The Army is providing bottled drinking water to affected households.

   (Ultimately the Army paid to have these houses tied into the municipal drinking water supply instead of their using their own wells.)

Lesson 16

The Contributions of Major Religions and Philosophies to a Universal Environmental Ethic

Historical Period   Postwar United States (1945-1975)
Recent United States (1975-present)

1972 UN Conference on the Human Environment in Stockholm, or the resulting creations of the United Nations Environment Programme and the United States Environmental Protection Agency, or modern environmental citizens' movement, or the 1992 Earth Summit in Rio de Janeiro.

Sustainable Development Topic   Social Development

Purpose   An ethic may be thought of as an ideal of human behavior and an environmental ethic as an ideal human behavior with respect to the environment, both natural and built. A newly emerging environmental ethic appears to support the growing national and international concern about the environment. The purpose of this lesson is to explore this ethic's roots through a comparative study of the ways in which the world's major religions and philosophies have embraced environmental concerns and to identify the principles they hold in common, i.e. universally. More and more of the world's religions are also finding their expression within the United States, so this lesson will introduce students to the increasing diversity within American society.

Objectives   The students will be able to:

1. Identify the role ethics play in human behavior particularly as they relate to environmentally responsible behavior.

2. Describe the nature of a universally held ethic.
3. Identify various religions' and philosophies' contributions to a universal environmental ethic.
4. Identify some commonalities among religions with regard to basic environmental concerns.
5. Express a personal environmental ethic.

Time Required 2 class periods

Materials Needed Handout 1: *Origins of an Environmental Ethic*
Handout 2: *Building Blocks of a Universal Environmental Ethic*

Teacher Background This lesson makes use of a *concept formation teaching strategy*. It allows students to explore the religious or philosophical origins of a universal environmental ethic by making connections among specific items of information.

First students generate data based on a reading. Next they categorize the data, initially according to predetermined criteria, subsequently by student generated criteria. By uniting descriptive labels for student criteria with multiple specific examples, students form a deep understanding of the concept. This increases motivation and provides students with the opportunity to organize the information into a coherent whole, to move from a mess to a model. This lesson concludes with the opportunity for students to move beyond the data and create a personal environmental ethic.

Procedure

1. Ask students, *Why do some laws have a high compliance rate in spite of limited enforcement efforts* (e.g. the vast majority of Americans comply with the Internal Revenue Code despite the chance of an income tax audit being about 5% on average) *and other laws see poor compliance despite attempts at strict enforcement* (e.g. illegal drug usage or speeding on interstate highways)?
2. The ensuing discussion should elicit the understanding that universal obedience to any law must mean that the principle of that law is supported by individual moral sensibility and conscience.
3. Establish the concept of **ethics** as *the ideal of human behavior based on moral sensibility and conscience*. Ethics operate regardless of the presence of law or law enforcement.
4. Move the discussion to the environment by asking students why they think most people don't litter even when no one is present to enforce littering laws.
5. Identify this as environmentally ideal personal behavior: the individual acts in accordance with an internalized environmental ethic, a matter of sensibility and conscience

Global Learning, Inc.

which is present regardless of external enforcement. The ethic is to a great degree universal since most people do not litter no matter what the circumstances.

6. Solicit from students some additional examples of voluntary universal compliance with an environmental ethic.

7. Ask students to think about where such universal environmental ethics might come from; *what are the building blocks that serve as a foundation for such an ethic?* Suggest that the answer might lie in an analysis of environmental ethics across the borders of religions and philosophies.

8. Go over the list of religions with the class. Ask if members of the class are practitioners of any of them, or if they know people who are, or if they know where in the region there are practitioners.

9. Distribute **Handouts 1** and **2**, but first cut Handout 2 in half so each "building block" is on its own sheet of paper. Direct students to read Handout 1 with a partner. Each team of students is to write as many foundation tenets of an environmental ethic as they can identify. Each tenet is to be written on an individual foundation block from Handout 2. The name, or names of the religion or philosophy from which the tenet derives should also be recorded.

10. As student teams volunteer their individual building blocks in a whole class setting, tape them on the chalkboard grouped by religion or philosophy.

11. When all have been properly categorized by religion, have students work in small groups (3 to 5 students) at reorganizing the foundation tenets into new categories based on student generated criteria. *Which of these statements belong together and why?* Encourage students to notice relationships, search for common attributes, and identify commonalties across religious boundaries. When new groupings have been agreed on, students should provide new descriptive labels for the categories. Encourage students to explore how groups of statements could go together to form larger groups. Provide time to share new groupings with the entire class.

Student Assessment Have students select an individual religion or philosophy, summarize its tenets, and explain why, of the ones presented, it bears the clearest message for today's world in terms of its contribution to a universal environmental ethic.

Lesson Extension The slogan *think globally, act locally* is now used worldwide to ask humans to focus on the impact of their actions. Have each student create a personal environmental ethic by borrowing from the ones presented or by creating totally new tenets.

Source Student readings are adapted from "A Universal Environmental Ethic—The Ultimate Goal of Environmental Education," in *Connect—the UNESCO-UNEP Environmental Education Newsletter*, Vol. XVI, No. 2, June 1991; 7, place de Fontenoy, 75352 Paris 07 SP, France.

Teacher Synopsis of Handout In the context of modern social interaction, strict obedience to the letter of the law must be complemented and supplemented by individual moral sensibility and conscience. While laws may reflect our culture's newly developing sensibility to the environment and may control or inhibit our behavior and actions on many occasions, an environmental ethic which we have personally created and reinforced will discourage us from acting against the environment even in private. The following synopsis of religions' views toward the environment suggests that there are some principles in common across the borders of time and space which may move world cultures toward a universal environmental ethic.

Hinduism The two major elements in Hinduism which contribute to the development of a universal environmental ethic are empathy and compassion regarding all living things and a sense of harmony with the environment resulting in its protection and enhancement.

Jainism This religion has an explicit environmental ethic since *ahimsa* is the doctrine of extreme concern for other living things. This concern contributes to the universal environmental ethic for which the exercise aims.

Buddhism A non-violent and gentle attitude towards nature, animals and fellow people provides the essence of a universal environmental ethic.

Zen Buddhism Zen provides a strong philosophical and experiential basis for an environmental ethic based on the aesthetic qualities of nature.

Taoism Taoism fits well the world view of ecology in which nature is a dynamic whole in which humans have their fitting and appropriate place.

Confucianism The virtues of regard for others, justice, wisdom, and faithfulness to one's posterity all contribute to a universal environmental ethic.

Global Learning, Inc.

Judeo-Christian   There are three possible environmental ethics consistent with the Judeo-Christian world-view, depending on its interpretation: 1) an indirect, anthropocentric, utilitarian ethic associated with mastery; 2) a more direct biocentric ethic associated with stewardship; 3) a direct biocentric ethic associated with citizenship. These last two are both direct and biocentric, but they differ in their practical implications. The former would permit benign management of Nature and wise use while the latter would imply a *laissez faire*, live-and-let-live approach, incompatible with the current more positive attitude toward environmental protection and improvement. The stewardship interpretation is perhaps the most practical one consistent with the Judeo-Christian tradition and the most effective for contributing to a universal environmental ethic.

Greeks   The Greek philosophical tradition can contribute an essential component of an environmental ethic—scientifically sound environmentalism.

Islam   The Islamic tradition supports a direct biocentric ethic of the stewardship type and an indirect anthropocentric environmental ethic.

An ethical attitude toward the environment personally and professionally, individually and collectively, and universally valid is the goal of the new environmental education. Students can learn to find their roots in these world cultures and religions and to anchor their beliefs solidly in them.

Origins of an Environmental Ethic
A Chronological View of Major World Religions and Philosophies

Hinduism Hinduism is one of the world's oldest religions. In it, gods are identified with and seen through the forces and processes of nature—sky, earth, thunder, rock, wood, and so on. There is a belief in an inner, unseen, abstract reality which lies beyond the world which is disclosed to our senses. For humans and other living things, *Atman* is the spirit or inner self which is in contrast to the body. All other things we can identify in the world are manifestations of the inner being *Brahman*. Atman and Brahman have come to be conceptually united so that the inner being of all things is soul or spiritual being. These objective and subjective knowledges are consolidated so that to know oneself fully means to know or see into the nature of all things.

The empirical world is unimportant since it is only the outward form of the spirits. This world is also to be despised and avoided since it lures the human soul into the illusion of believing the visible world to be real, and thus distracts the soul from merging itself with the one great transcendental soul, i.e. from achieving *nirvana*. Yet the essential soul of each person is the same in the sense that each is part of the great transcendental soul of Atman/Brahman and there is no distinction between self and other. Since other people are also victims of the deceit, frustration and suffering that occurs in the empirical world, a Hindu feels empathy and compassion for others and also feels connected to them as well as to other natural environmental beings since ultimately there are no others in the one great indivisible Being.

An ecological world view which represents the world holistically—as a unity of oneself and one's surroundings—thus corresponds with the Hindu world view of empathy and compassion for all living things. And the Hindu sense of oneness and harmony with the environment leads to its protection and enhancement.

Global Learning, Inc.

Jainism In contrast to Hinduism, Jainism is dualistic rather than monistic; there is a clear dichotomy between soul and body, mind and matter. Each soul, moreover, maintains its own integrity and is not part of a universal soul. Every living thing is endowed with such a soul which is crusted over with flesh or other covering until its consciousness is dimmed and becomes confused with sensory perceptions of various sorts. Underneath, however, all souls are equally pure and perfect in and of themselves.

At the core of Jainism is the doctrine of *ahimsa,* the determination not to kill or harm any living thing which contains a soul as perfect or complete as one's own and which is as liable to suffering as oneself. The Jains are famous for the extremes to which they go to honor this doctrine. Meat eating is especially prohibited since animal consciousness is thought to be higher than plant consciousness. Food must be inspected before eating to assure that insect eggs or mites are not consumed inadvertently. Similarly, water must be strained, not to protect one's health, but to avoid consuming any organisms in the water. Mahavira, the founder of Jainism, only ate leftover food which had been prepared for someone else since he did not personally want to cause any injury to plants or to their seeds. One ought even to sweep one's path before walking so that the feet do not injure or kill any living things.

Buddhism The core moral values in Buddhism include abstention from killing living creatures, abstention from stealing, abstention from lying, and abstention from taking intoxicants. These precepts—respect for life and property, truthfulness, and a sober lifestyle—embody the basic requirements for living a proper life and establishing a good community. The teachings of Siddharta Gautama, known as the Buddha, condemned the infliction of suffering and pain on living creatures. Hunting was criticized, and kings were expected to provide protected territory not only for human beings, but also for the beasts of the forests and the birds of the air. Although the Buddha did not carry the principle of *ahimsa* as far as the Jains did, his preaching against taking life shows sympathy for all creatures.

We can infer from the Buddha's teachings a pro-conservationist conception of nature which is critical of those who exploit the environment for short-term gain and of those who live a life of unlimited consumerism. The non-violent character of the religion and the gentle attitude toward nature, animals, and fellow people all point to a strong environmental ethic.

Zen Buddhism   In Zen, the world is seen as the delightful expression, both the work and play, of a benign and loving common essence or spirit which exists in all things. In Zen poetry and art, especially, there is a very strong tradition of a nature aesthetic; the poet or artist contemplates the fleeting yet eternal moment of *satori*, the beauty of a moment in time which is also the eternal beauty. The aesthetic value of nature has long been a powerful human motive for its conservation.

Taoism   The word *tao* literally means a way or a road. It is the way of the universe, the orderly and harmonious unfolding of phenomena, the orderly development of things. If this road is allowed to run its course, it results in natural fulfillment and perfection. Taoism stresses the perfection of harmony between humanity and nature. It also provides the basis for looking at technological development. Taoists think that the traditional Western forms of high technology should be abandoned for forms of low technology or what is often called appropriate technology, one that attempts to cooperate and adapt to nature instead of commanding and controlling it. Taoists bend the natural processes to human advantage and adapt human ways of life to the environment.

Like the Zen Buddhism to which it is related, Taoism sees the environment as having a unity among natural things and these things having unity with humanity. Nature is a separate and dynamic whole in which humanity has its fitting and appropriate place.

Confucianism   Confucius accepted the Tao but he focused on promoting order in human society. Just as nature is orderly and harmonious, so ought human society to be equally so. Confucianism supports an anthropocentric view of the environment: since destroying, degrading, or defiling the environment would in most cases impose hardships on other people, it must be avoided. If not, it would violate the first two Confucian virtues—regard for others and justice. The third virtue is wisdom, and environmental destruction would be seen as unwise and imprudent. The fourth virtue, faithfulness to one's children or one's children's children or to one's even more remote posterity, would also prohibit defacing the environment.

Judeo-Christian Tradition There has recently been intense controversy about the environmental attitudes of the Judeo-Christian tradition, most of it centering on the relationship between God, humans, and nature in the opening two chapters of Genesis in the *Bible*. One reading of Genesis called the *mastery interpretation* says that humans are created in the image of God, given control over nature and commanded to subdue it. This implies a God-given right to exploit the Earth without moral restraint (except in the case where exploitation would adversely affect humans themselves). Humans are unique among God's creatures and are given unique rights and privileges. They are to the rest of the world's creatures as God is to them. Thus if God is the lord and master of humanity, so humans are the lords and masters of nature.

The second reading, called the *stewardship interpretation* of Genesis, opposes the mastery view and says that since humans are created in God's image, they not only have special rights and privileges, but also special duties and responsibilities. Foremost among these is their responsibility to rule the Earth wisely and kindly. To abuse, degrade, or destroy the Earth is to violate the trust that God placed in humanity.

The most recent teaching of the Roman Catholic Church is contained in Pope John Paul II's Encyclical on the Environment (1990). It stresses humanity's stewardship of nature. People are guardians and protectors of the environment, not its owners. A way of loving one's fellow humans is to protect the natural resources on which they depend.

**Greek Mythology
and Philosophy**

As Greek mythology and philosophy was spread throughout the Mediterranean basin by the Macedonian and Roman empires, it became the primary source of Western culture and civilization. Its rather rational view of the world led eventually to the development of Western science.

Plato's philosophy presented a divine soul in an alien, mortal body, a kind of earthly prison or tomb. This dualistic concept of Plato became very influential in Western civilization and religion. Pythagoras believed in the transmigration of souls from humans to animals and vice versa, thus extending the sphere of human relationships to non-human natural beings. His thoughts may be more relevant to the modern animal rights movement than to environmental ethics discussions. Other Greek philosophers, meanwhile, studied the physical world, the characteristics of nature. Democritus developed the atomic theory of matter which stated that atoms were indivisible, solid particles composing all material objects.

The result of most Greek thinking was a concept of nature as materialistic and mechanical, and of humans, because of their souls, as essentially divine, both separate from and superior to nature. In Western thought, this duality has reinforced the notion of human incompatibility with the environment rather than harmony. The combination of Platonic-Pythagorean dualism and Democritean atomism lies at the root of some present environmental problems. In another way, however, the Greek interest in science has resulted, over the centuries, in the growth of technology. While that technology has often had a negative impact on the environment in the past, it can also possibly prevent and correct the problems it has created. In this sense, the Greek philosophical tradition can contribute an essential element of an environmental ethic—scientifically sound environmentalism, the rationale for a secular environmental ethic.

Global Learning, Inc.

Islam Mohammad, the Prophet of Islam, regarded himself to be a prophet of the same God and in the same tradition as Jesus, Moses, and Abraham. Thus the Islamic religion has deep similarities to the Judeo-Christian and Greco-Roman cultures. During the European Dark Age, in fact, Greek science and mathematics would have been lost had they not been preserved and developed by Islamic scholars.

The *Koran* is more precise about the creation than is Genesis about the relationship of humans to nature. After Allah created Adam and his wife from clay or dust and breathed life into them, all other things were created by Allah for the sake of, the use of, and the benefit of humans. Adam and his offspring are made the viceroy of God on earth. Humans are at the center of creation and are the purpose of creation. As with the Genesis story, it is the right of humans to have power over and to subdue the Earth and all its animals, plants, rivers, seas, even the sun and moon. The subordination of nature to humans is spelled out in no uncertain terms.

The powerful role of humans, however, is not to be confused with tyranny. They should not be wantonly destructive. Humans are clearly told to be stewards of the Earth. Allah's creation was a divine work of art. The world and its parts are understood in Islam as signs to humanity that show the goodness, greatness, richness, and subtlety of the creator. To deface, defile, or destroy nature would be a blasphemous act. Although humans are given the temporary use of the Earth, they are not given the right to abuse it. Allah rewards and punishes deeds done on Earth in the next life, so persons who blaspheme God by destroying His creation will be punished in the next life.

Since humans are made of clay, they are at one with the Earth while they are living on it and there is to be a fellowship between humans and other creatures. Islam also values scientific knowledge of the natural world. As more is learned about the sciences, it becomes clear that the natural environment is a seamless whole. Thus the destruction of one part of nature will reverberate throughout the whole. Since humans are part of that whole, environmental destruction would be self-destruction.

Also according to Islam, all humans are descended from Adam and Eve, so all, regardless of race, color, or national origin, are equal members of one extended world family. No nation or race of people is privileged or chosen; none is better than another. Justice is one of the cornerstones of Islam. Since environmental abuse is often harmful to people, it is a form of injustice. To ruin or destroy the environment is the same as committing bodily injury or stealing. Furthermore, ignorance of the delayed effects of an act on the environment is no excuse, since Islam stresses the moral importance of knowledge as much as justice.

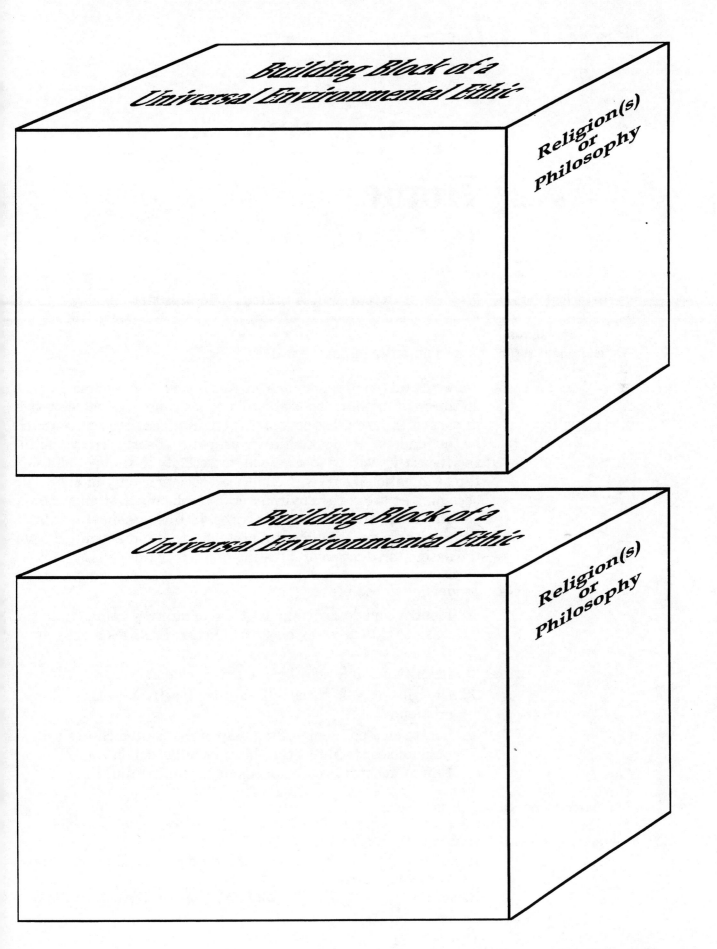

Building Block of a
Universal Environmental Ethic

Religion(s)
or
Philosophy

Building Block of a
Universal Environmental Ethic

Religion(s)
or
Philosophy

Global Learning, Inc.

Lesson 17

Nuclear Threat at Home
The Cold War's Lethal Leftovers

Historical Period   Postwar or Recent United States (1945-present)

Sustainable Development Topic   Environmental impact of war

Purpose   Warfare and the preparations for war have a tremendous impact on the environment, especially in modern times. All the negative impacts of industrial society on the environment are compounded by the tendency to cloak military preparations in secrecy and to sacrifice other values to the need for security in the face of a threat to national survival. American society is only lately becoming aware of the environmental problems that must now be faced as a result of these practices. In this lesson, students will explore the environmental problems that have resulted from the design, production and testing of nuclear weapons.

Objectives   Students will be able to:

1. Identify and describe the problem of military-related nuclear wastes that currently exists at nuclear facilities across the United States.
2. Identify possible solutions to this problem.
3. Describe at least three different perspectives on this problem.
4. Locate on a political outline map of the United States the nine nuclear facilities that have been placed on the U.S. Environmental Protection Agency's "Superfund" list.

Time Required   2 class periods

Materials Needed   Handout 1: *Nuclear Threats at Home*
Handout 2: *Nuclear Facilities Superfund Sites* and outline map (optional extension activity)
Background Reading 1: *The Well-being of the World Is at Stake* (optional)

Background Reading 2: *What Are Nuclear Wastes And Where Do They Come From?* (optional)
Atlas or map of the United States with local names.

Teacher Background
The student reading is taken from *The Defense Monitor* newsletter of the Center for Defense Information. The Center has three companion videos: *Nuclear Threat at Home, The Military and the Environment,* and *Protectors and Polluters,* VHS, $25 each or 3 for $65, (202) 862-0700. What follows is a summary of the article's main points:

- Decades of environmental, health, and safety abuses at U.S. Department of Energy nuclear weapons laboratory, production, and test facilities have left an estimated 4,500 contaminated sites covering tens of thousands of acres of land.

- Efforts to clean up contaminated sites and bring nuclear weapons facilities into compliance with the nation's environmental laws are expected to take at least 30 years and cost more than $200 billion.

- Nine nuclear weapons facilities have qualified for inclusion on the U.S. Environmental Protection Agency's "Superfund" National Priorities List of the worst contaminated sites in America.

- A number of nuclear weapons facility sites are contaminated so extensively that they may have to be sealed off forever from public access, becoming what some have referred to as "national sacrifice zones."

- Nuclear weapons facilities have generated more than 99 percent of all high-level radioactive waste in America. No suitable method yet exists for safely and permanently disposing of this waste.

- America's citizens are entitled to the full truth about the nation's nuclear dangers and to have a role in Department of Energy (DOE) cleanup decisions.

- Cleanup of U.S. nuclear weapons facilities needs to be accelerated.

- Additional federal money and resources for DOE cleanup are available in the billions of dollars the Pentagon still spends buying weapons designed for the Cold War.

- It is important that DOE and nuclear weapons facility contractors be held accountable for all future violations of the nation's environmental laws.

In order to provide a broader perspective on this issue, excerpts from an interview with Mikhail Gorbachev, former President of the former Soviet Union, published in *Parade Magazine*, 1/24/94, are included as Background Reading 1. This lesson could be adapted—and improved—by providing students with this second reading. In addition, Background Reading 2 is provided for use by either the teacher or students, entitled, "What are nuclear wastes and where do they come from?"

Additional sources of information on this topic include:

Coyle, Dana et al. *Deadly Defense: Military Radioactive Landfills*. New York: Radioactive Waste Campaign, 1988.

"Defending the Environment? The Record of the U.S. Military," *The Defense Monitor*. Center for Defense Information, Vol. XVIII, Number 6, 1989.

Del Tredici, Robert. *At Work in the Fields of the Bomb*. New York: Harper & Row, Publishers, 1987.

Procedure

1. Assign **Handout 1:** *Nuclear Threat at Home* as a reading and writing assignment for homework. You might want to note that some of the information in the reading could be discouraging, but encourage the students to complete the assignment.

2. If you want to assign an individual grade to the written assignment, collect it. This means the class activity will be delayed until you can return the papers to your students.

3. Form small groups of about 5 or 6 students per group and let them use their written assignments. Allowing the members of each small group to help one another, have each student re-write the problem statement, including its causes, so that each has a comprehensive statement of the problem. See Step 1: Defining the problem, in the Problem Solving Model: Contemporary Period, in Lesson 1.

4. Have half of the groups list on newsprint or the chalkboard their combined answers to question 4 and the other half list their combined answers to question 5.

5. Conduct a general discussion of the nature of this problem of nuclear wastes at weapons facilities in the United States and the possible solutions that have been identified.

6. *What other roles might citizens play in seeking solutions besides working on them at their jobs?*

7. To conclude, ask the class how they would describe the perspective from which the writer of this handout is writing. Have them identify and describe at least two other perspectives from which people might view this problem. Make sure the descriptions do not distort or stereotype these several perspectives.

Student Assessment   Students can be assessed on the basis of their written reaction paper and on the basis of class participation in both small group and large group discussions.

Lesson Extension

1. On the outline map of the United States in **Handout 2:**
   Nuclear Facilities Superfund Sites, locate by number each of
   the nuclear weapons facilities that have been placed on the
   U.S. Environmental Protection Agency's "Superfund"
   National Priorities List of the worst contaminated sites in
   America.

   Include the size of the facility and its stated mission.

   Using different colors, identify the kinds of contamination:

   > atmosphere
   > soil
   > groundwater
   > surface water
   > sediment (i.e., matter that has settled under water).

2. Have the class generate policy statements for the following
   scenario:

   *Suppose that in the next few years the United States perceives
   that another major country has become a serious threat to its
   national survival. Based on what we have learned from our
   nuclear waste problem, should our military leaders pay more
   attention to the environment than they have before? If yes,
   what, specifically, should they do? If no, why not?*

3. Have students rewrite the last two sections of Handout 1
   "Not All News Is *Bad* News!" and "Clean Up Now!" from one
   of the perspectives identified by the class in procedure #7.

Sources   Coyle, Dana et al. *Deadly Defense: Military Radioactive
Landfills.* New York: Radioactive Waste Campaign, 1988.

Greer, Colin. "The Well-Being of the World is at Stake," *Parade
Magazine,* New York, 1/24/94.

"Military Nuclear Wastes: The Hidden Burden of the Nuclear
Arms Race," *The Defense Monitor.* Center for Defense
Information, 1500 Massachusetts Avenue NW, Washington, DC
20005, 1981.

Murphy, Pamela. "Coming Clean: The Public's Evolving Role in
Nuclear Waste Cleanup," *National Voter.* League of Women
Voters, 1730 M Street NW, Washington DC 20036. March 1994.

"Nuclear Threat at Home," *The Defense Monitor.* Washington DC:
Center for Defense Information, 1994.

Nuclear Threat at Home: The Cold War's Lethal Leftovers

Write a brief reaction paper to the following article. Address the following questions:

1. What is *the problem* this reading addresses? Describe the problem in several sentences.

2. What are the *causes* of the problem mentioned in the article?

3. What does the writer suggest are *solutions* to this problem?

4. Can you think of *additional solutions* to this problem?

5. What kinds of *jobs or professions* will be required in the next 30 years to help solve this problem? List at least ten.

Nuclear Threat at Home: The Cold War's Lethal Leftovers

The Cold War may be over, but thanks to the huge mess that remains behind, it will not soon be forgotten. Lethal leftovers from the Cold War nuclear arms buildup have transformed vast tracts of land and water in the United States into radioactive and toxic chemical wastelands. The names of nuclear weapons facilities such as Fernald, Hanford, and Rocky Flats are to some as synonymous with environmental disaster as Chernobyl, Love Canal, and Three Mile Island.

For decades America's nationwide complex of facilities responsible for designing, building, and testing nuclear weapons has dumped, injected poured, spilled, and vented some of the most toxic substances known into the air, ground, and water. According to the U.S. Congress' Office of Technology Assessment, "There is evidence that air, groundwater, surface water, sediments, and soil, as well as vegetation and wildlife, have been contaminated at most, if not all, of the Department of Energy (DOE) nuclear weapons sites." Continued unsafe and impermanent storage of radioactive waste and other deadly by-products of nuclear weapons activities only promises to add to a long-term, tax-funded cleanup bill already estimated at more than $200 billion.

In preparing to fight a nuclear war with the former Soviet Union, America succeeded in "nuking" itself. With the Cold War now behind us, there is less reason to fear that we will die in a nuclear attack. However, communities in the shadows of nuclear weapons plants and the workers who made the bombs may have good cause to fear that they will be stricken with cancer or other ailments because of the nuclear threat at *home*. To the victor of war, it is said, belong the spoils. In the case of the Cold War, this is all too true.

4,500 Contaminated Sites

The U.S. nuclear weapons complex is a vast industrial enterprise that sprang from the secret Manhattan Project effort to develop the atomic bombs dropped on Japan in 1945. Its 15 major facilities collectively occupy some 3,350 square miles—an area larger than Delaware, Rhode Island, and the District of Columbia combined—in 13 states. They employ more than 100,000 workers. Although these facilities are owned by the federal government through the U.S. Department of Energy, they are managed and operated by private contractors such as Martin Marietta, Rockwell International, and Westinghouse.

In the half-century that it has existed, the nuclear weapons complex has manufactured nearly 70,000 nuclear warheads.[*] It has processed about 89 metric tons of plutonium and more than 500 metric tons of highly enriched uranium, the primary radioactive materials in nuclear weapons.[**] And it has carried out 1,056 nuclear explosions.[***] In the process, it has created a legacy of environmental contamination that, in the view of the Office of Technology Assessment (OTA), is "unprecedented in scope and complexity."

This happened because nuclear weapons facilities were permitted to operate behind a veil of secrecy, largely free from external oversight, public scrutiny, and environmental, health,

---

[*] According to DOE, more than 53,000 of these warheads have since been retired and disassembled. The United States has produces no new nuclear warheads since 1990.

[**] The United States has produced no new plutonium for nuclear weapons since 1988. It has produced no new highly enriched uranium for nuclear weapons since 1964.

[***] This number includes 24 British tests on U.S. soil and the nuclear explosions at Hiroshima and Nagasaki. The U.S. last tested a nuclear weapon in September 1992.

Global Learning, Inc.

and safety laws. The attitude was "bomb production, whatever the costs." Facilities treated, stored, and disposed of the vast quantities of waste materials they generated often in a careless and environmentally-harmful manner. Decades of environmental, health, and safety abuses at U.S. Department of Energy nuclear weapons facilities have left an estimated 4,500 contaminated sites covering tens of thousands of acres of land.[*]

Nine nuclear weapons facilities have qualified for inclusion on the U.S. Environmental Protection Agency's (EPA) "Superfund" National Priorities List of the worst contaminated sites in America. Much of this contamination was the result of accidents, spills, and leaks. In other cases, however, it resulted from planned and deliberate acts. In the past, disposal of liquid wastes at nuclear weapons facilities often meant pouring them directly into the ground. Wastes also have been injected or pumped into wells or holes deep underground, buried in landfills, stored in giant underground tanks, and vented into the atmosphere.

The 240,000-Year Threat

Contamination from nuclear weapons activities has posed a potential health and safety threat to some 600,000 past and present workers at nuclear bomb plants and millions of residents of surrounding communities. Radiation has been linked to higher rates of cancer, leukemia, brain tumors, thyroid disorders, birth defects, sterility, and miscarriages.

Plutonium is readily absorbed by the body and can remain there for decades. As little as .000000000001 gram of plutonium-239, the radioisotope of plutonium used in nuclear weapons, may be sufficient to cause lung cancer if inhaled in fine particles. With a *half- life* estimated at 24,000 years, half of the plutonium-239 in existence in 1994 will still exist in the year 25994. It will continue to emit radiation and remain a potential threat to life for about 10 half-lives—in other words, 240,000 years, or about 10,000 human generations!

The Cold War's Hidden Costs

"There is evidence that air, groundwater, surface water, sediments, and soil, as well as vegetation and wildlife, have been contaminated at most, if not all, of the Department of Energy nuclear weapons sites....Almost every facility has confirmed groundwater contamination with radionuclides or hazardous chemicals....Millions of cubic meters of radioactive and hazardous wastes have been buried throughout the complex....Contaminated soil and sediments of all categories are estimated to total billions of cubic meters....Available data can neither demonstrate nor rule out the possibility that adverse public health impacts have occurred or will occur as a result of weapons site pollution....Many sites may never be returned to a condition suitable for unrestricted public access." (Office of Technology Assessment, U.S. Congress, *Complex Cleanup: The Environmental Legacy of Nuclear Weapons Production,* February 1991)

Radiation Releases

While much information about past contamination releases is not yet publicly available, in the last year there have been some startling revelations. In 1993 the General Accounting Office, the investigative arm of Congress, reported that the U.S. military and DOE's

---

[*] DOE defines a contaminated site as "any location, ranging from very small to as large as a thousand acres, where *radioactive,* hazardous, or mixed waste has been released, or is suspected to have been released, to the environment." *Radioactive* waste contains atomic elements which emit radiation. *Hazardous* waste contains materials that are toxic, corrosive, flammable, or reactive. *Mixed* waste is radioactive and hazardous.

predecessor agency, the Atomic Energy Commission, purposely released large amounts of radiation into the atmosphere in the late 1940s and early 1950s as part of secret experiments to design a weapon that would kill enemy soldiers with radioactive fallout. Two such experiments took place at the Oak Ridge National Laboratory in Tennessee. Another six tests occurred at the U.S. Army's Dugway Proving Ground in Utah.

Waste Tank Explosions

A 1993 DOE report on the status of nuclear safety at weapons plants concluded that "the likelihood of a disaster is high." Foremost among DOE's concerns is the possibility of a chemical explosion or fire involving underground tanks that store high- level radioactive waste. The buildup in waste tanks of flammable hydrogen gas and potentially explosive ferrocyanide and organic nitrate compounds poses the risk of an accident similar to those that caused casualties and widespread radioactive contamination surrounding nuclear weapons facilities in Russia in 1957 and 1993.

Spent Fuel Leaks

According to Assistant Secretary of Energy for Environmental Restoration and Waste Management Thomas P. Grumbly, DOE's second-highest priority after waste tanks is its unsafe storage of "spent," or irradiated, nuclear fuel. Until 1988 the United States routinely *reprocessed* spent fuel in order to separate and recover plutonium for use in weapons. Since then millions of pounds of the highly radioactive fuel have been left to sit in aging and corroding storage facilities.

A 1993 DOE report identified more than 100 "vulnerabilities" associated with spent fuel storage, defined as "conditions or weaknesses that may lead to radiation exposure to the public, unnecessary or increased exposure to the workers, or release of radioactive materials to the environment." Some fuel has already leaked from rusting canisters. Other fuel "was buried without protective barriers or containers."

A $200 Billion Legacy

Efforts to clean up contaminated sites and bring DOE nuclear weapons facilities into compliance with the nation's environmental laws are expected to take at least 30 years and cost more than $200 billion. This cleanup and compliance bill amounts to more than $2.8 million for each nuclear warhead the nuclear weapons industry manufactured and almost $800 for every man, woman, and child living in the United States. It is more than twice what the country spent on the Apollo space program to put a man on the moon!

Since 1989 DOE has spent roughly $20 billion on environmental cleanup and waste management. For fiscal year 1994 Congress approved an additional $5.2 billion. At most facilities, however, permanent cleanup activities have not yet even begun because DOE is still defining the nature and extent of the contamination. Much of the technology and data needed to assess contamination problems and propose solutions simply do not yet exist. In a 1993 report on its cleanup program, DOE cautioned that "the full significance" of "the magnitude, scope, and eventual total cost" of cleaning up its weapons plants "has yet to be grasped."

A number of nuclear weapons facilities sites are contaminated so extensively that they may have to be sealed off forever from public access, becoming what some have referred to as "national sacrifice zones." According to a 1990 study by the Congressional Budget Office, in such cases "complete cleanup may be technically and economically unfeasible." Efforts instead may have to be limited to containing, rather than eliminating, problems.

Decontaminating groundwater, in particular, poses an enormous challenge. Groundwater beneath some nuclear weapons plants is believed to be contaminated at levels hundreds to thousands of times above drinking water standards.

In addition, DOE is faced with the necessity of decontaminating, decommissioning, and dismantling as many as 7,000 buildings, reactors, and other structures within the nuclear weapons complex that ultimately may be shut down during the next 30 years. Completing these tasks, DOE estimates, will take at least through the year 2050. Many of the structures are huge. The K-25 building at the Oak Ridge Reservation in Tennessee is about a mile long and covers 137 acres! The poor condition of many facilities poses ongoing dangers to individuals working in and around them.

Not All News Is *Bad* News!

Recent developments have reduced the likelihood that DOE will add to its contamination problems in the future. In 1992 Congress passed the "Federal Facility Compliance Act," waiving the principle of federal *sovereign immunity* which nuclear weapons facilities have invoked to exempt themselves from environmental laws. Now facilities committing environmental crimes or failing to meet agreed-upon cleanup and compliance goals can, like private industry, be subjected to fines and penalties.

Meanwhile, under the Clinton Administration, DOE is showing signs of much-needed new vision and direction. In December 1993 Energy Secretary Hazel O'Leary announced a new "openness initiative" and disclosed previously classified information about the U.S. stockpile of plutonium, unannounced nuclear test explosions, and secret radiation experiments on human "guinea pigs." DOE's new Office of Declassification, formerly the Office of *Classification,* is reviewing 32 million pages of documents for possible public release.

DOE is also working to improve its oversight of weapons facility contractors to make them more accountable for environmental performance.

Clean Up Now!

Cleanup of U.S. nuclear weapons facilities needs to take place in a manner that is as timely, effective, efficient, safe, and complete as possible. Additional federal money and resources for DOE cleanup are available in the billions of dollars the Pentagon wastes each year buying unneeded Cold War weapons. Plans by DOE to continue nuclear weapons activities far into the next century should be reevaluated. The scientists and engineers who perfected "the bomb" should now be working to perfect effective cleanup technologies. America's citizens are entitled to the full truth about the nation's nuclear dangers and to have a role in DOE cleanup program decisions.

Justice demands that people harmed by the "nuclear threat at home" be compensated for their suffering. For this, the private contractors who profited immensely from the nuclear arms race should be made to bear some responsibility. America may have won the Cold War, but it did so at a heavy price. We have not yet paid the full cost of victory in terms of cleaning up its lethal leftovers.

Source: *The Defense Monitor,* Vol. XXIII, Number 2, 1994; Center for Defense Information, 1500 Massachusetts Avenue NW, Washington, DC 20005

Nuclear Facilities Superfund Sites

1. Hanford Reservation, Washington

Location: Richland, Washington. Size: 570 square miles. Mission: Plutonium processing; uranium recycling. Placed on EPA's National Priorities List of America's worst contaminated waste sites in 1989.

The U.S. Department of Energy has called the cleanup of Hanford one of the "largest environmental restoration projects in history." Estimates of the cost range from $50 to $100 billion.

The production of 53 metric tons of plutonium for nuclear weapons from 1945 to 1987 created an estimated 68 million gallons of high-level radioactive waste, 65 percent by volume of all high-level waste stored within the nuclear weapons complex. About 61 million gallons of high-level waste are stored in 177 underground steel tanks, some of which have capacities of over a million gallons. According to DOE, 68 of these tanks are either known or assumed to have leaked as much as a million gallons of waste—with enough plutonium to build 50 bombs the size of the Nagasaki bomb—into the surrounding soil. At least 53 tanks may be at risk of fire or explosion due to a buildup of flammable hydrogen gas. Several workers have been injured or become ill when toxic vapors have escaped from tanks. The waste tanks themselves consist of 451,000 tons of metal that some day must be emptied out, decontaminated, and disposed of, as must nine shutdown plutonium-producing reactors.

Furthermore, enough liquid waste has been dumped into unlined pits and trenches at Hanford to form an 80-foot-deep lake the size of Manhattan. According to the General Accounting Office, the investigative arm of Congress, about 400 billion gallons of liquid waste has contaminated as much as 200 square miles of groundwater beneath the facility. Some wastes have been detected in the nearby Columbia River.

Documents made public in 1986 revealed that between 1944 and 1947 Hanford officials knowingly and without informing the public released to the atmosphere some 444,000 curies of radioactive iodine—several thousand times what was released by the 1979 accident at the Three Mile Island nuclear power plant. In 1990 DOE admitted that these emissions may be responsible for the high incidence of thyroid cancer and other illnesses in the region. An independent panel concluded that as many as 13,500 people living in the Hanford area at the time may have absorbed "significant" doses of radiation to their thyroid glands. Some infants may have received cumulative radiation from contaminated milk higher than those absorbed by victims of the 1986 accident at the Chernobyl nuclear power plant.

2. Lawrence Livermore National Laboratory, California

Location: Livermore, California. 50 miles east of San Francisco. Size: 12 square miles. Mission: Nuclear weapons research and development. Placed on EPA's National Priorities List in 1987.

Soil, groundwater, and sediment contamination.

3. Rocky Flats Plant, Colorado

Location: 16 miles northwest of Denver, Colorado. Size: 14 square miles. Mission: Plutonium processing; assembly of plutonium "triggers" for thermonuclear bombs. Placed on EPA's National Priorities List in 1989.

Soil, groundwater, surface water, and sediment contamination. Hundreds of fires have dispersed unknown quantities of plutonium into the air. Enough plutonium has accumulated in ventilation ducts to make seven nuclear bombs. Several workers are ill with berylliosis, a lung disease. In 1992 former plant operator Rockwell International pled guilty to 10 charges of violating hazardous waste and clean water laws and was fined $18.5 million. However, this was $3.8 million less than the government bonuses Rockwell received during the period in question. No individuals were prosecuted.

4. Idaho National Engineering Laboratory, Idaho

Location: 42 miles northwest of Idaho Falls, Idaho. Size: 893 square miles. Mission: Uranium recycling; research, design, and testing of naval propulsion reactors. Placed on EPA's National Priorities List in 1989.

Soil, groundwater, and sediment contamination. Wastes that were injected into the ground have polluted the Snake River Aquifer, a major source of water for much of the Northwest. Plutonium has been detected more than 100 feet underground. In 1992 the General Accounting Office reported that insufficient containment of wastes in underground pipes and tanks has resulted in at least 115 separate releases of radiation to the air. About 3 million gallons of high-level radioactive waste are stored in steel tanks and bins.

5. Fernald, Ohio

Location: 18 miles northwest of Cincinnati, Ohio. Size: 0.2 square miles. Mission: Processing of uranium metal. Placed on EPA's National Priorities List in 1989.

Soil, groundwater, surface water, and sediment contamination. Hundreds of tons of uranium dust were released into the air. Contaminated groundwater is threatening the Great Miami Aquifer, one of the largest sources of fresh water in the Midwest. In 1989 DOE paid $78 million to settle a class-action lawsuit by area residents claiming that radioactive releases have caused them emotional distress and reduced property values.

6. Oak Ridge Reservation, Tennessee

Location: Oak Ridge, Tennessee. Size: 58 square miles. Mission: Uranium enrichment; storage of uranium from retired nuclear warheads. Placed on EPA's National Priorities List in 1989.

Soil, groundwater, surface water, and sediment contamination. An estimated 750,000 pounds of toxic mercury have been released to the environment. Mercury and radioactive cesium have been found in the sediment of a reservoir used for recreation and fishing. Mercury-polluted soil from a nearby creek was used as fill in the construction of a local civic center. Radioactive wastewater was routinely pumped into the city sewer.

7. Savannah River Site, South Carolina

Location: 12 miles south of Aiken, South Carolina. Size 300 square miles. Mission: Plutonium and tritium processing. Placed on EPA's National Priorities List in 1989.

Soil, groundwater, surface water, and sediment contamination. The production of 36 metric tons of plutonium for nuclear weapons from 1953 to 1988 created 34 million gallons of high- level radioactive waste that are stored in 51 underground tanks. Solvents have polluted the Tuscaloosa Aquifer, a major source of water for much of the Southeast. The site was once described by DOE as a "Three Mile Island waiting to happen."

8. Mound Plant, Ohio

Location: Miamisburg, Ohio. Size: 0.3 square miles. Mission: Production of detonators for nuclear warheads; tritium recycling. Placed on EPA's National Priorities List in 1989.

Soil, groundwater, surface water, and sediment contamination. An accidental release of radioactive tritium in 1989 forced the evacuation of 200 workers.

9. Pantex Plant, Texas

Location: 17 miles northeast of Amarillo, Texas. Size: 14 square miles. Mission: Final assembly and disassembly of nuclear warheads; "interim" storage site for plutonium from retired warheads. Proposed for inclusion on EPA's National Priorities List in 1991.

Groundwater contamination. Possible contamination of Ogallala Aquifer. Open-air burning of explosives.

Source: *The Defense Monitor,* Vol. XXIII, Number 2, 1994; Center for Defense Information, 1500 Massachusetts Avenue NW, Washington, DC 20005

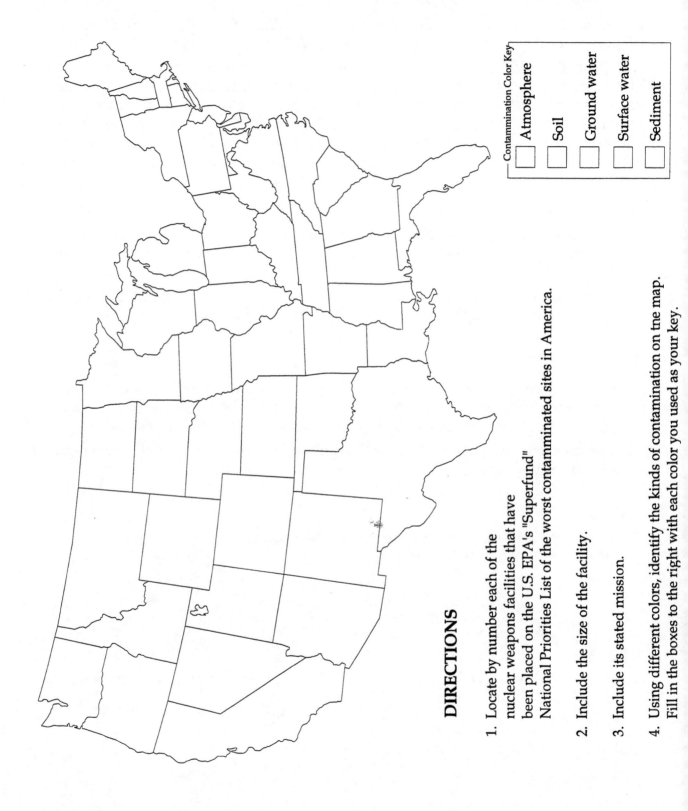

Contamination Color Key

☐ Atmosphere

☐ Soil

☐ Ground water

☐ Surface water

☐ Sediment

DIRECTIONS

1. Locate by number each of the nuclear weapons facilities that have been placed on the U.S. EPA's "Superfund" National Priorities List of the worst contamminated sites in America.

2. Include the size of the facility.

3. Include its stated mission.

4. Using different colors, identify the kinds of contamination on the map. Fill in the boxes to the right with each color you used as your key.

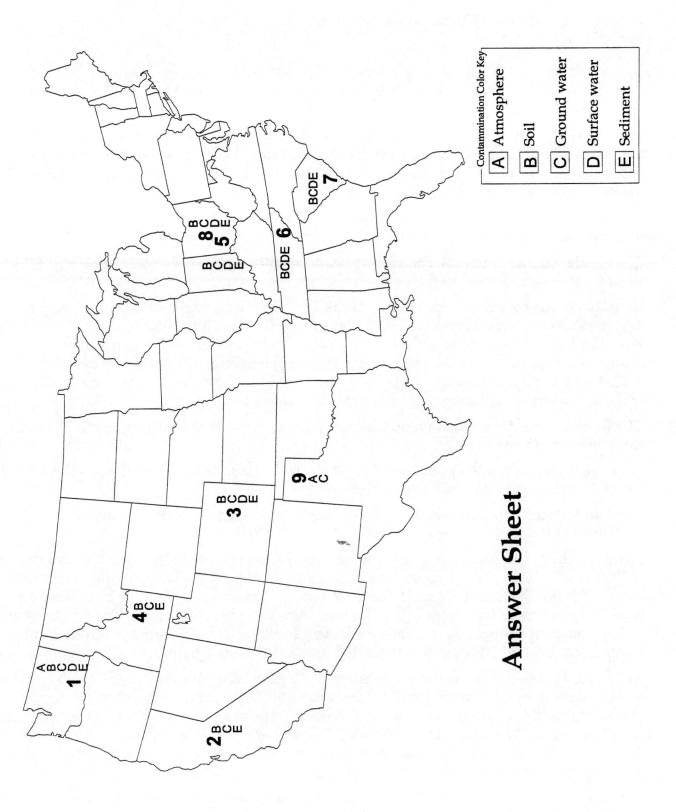

Answer Sheet

Contamination Color Key

A Atmosphere
B Soil
C Ground water
D Surface water
E Sediment

"The Well-Being of the World Is at Stake"

From an interview of Mikhail Gorbachev, former President of the Soviet Union
by Colin Greer

Colin Greer: I understand that you have become a strong environmentalist. Why have you chosen to join the Green Cross in its work?

Mikhail Gorbachev: We have to protect the environment. The Green Cross is in its infancy but is already drawing strong support. The organization began in several nations before becoming an international organization. We recognize the need for a new way to bring nations together on this question.

We need a global focus. We can't build an ecologically safe future unless nations work together.

CG: I understand that the Green Cross is making military toxins a major priority. Why is that?

MG: This is the ecological consequence of the Cold War. It is extremely severe. There are different types of toxic wastes stored and leaked worldwide which are the legacy of the Cold War. The U.S. and Russia hold first place as culprits in this. Several regions in both countries are second to none in the dangers they present from this kind of waste. What makes it even more alarming is that both countries have kept this all very secret. Citizens of these countries don't know enough to call for change.

CG: We face so many environmental hazards. How severe is the military toxic threat in the scheme of things?

MG: The toxic aftermath of the Cold War produced by its military priorities involves great dangers to us, from ozone safety to water safety.

CG: Can I assume you are speaking with unique knowledge based on your former position as leader of the Soviet Union?

MG: Yes, I have this knowledge, and I have a special responsibility to bring the world's attention to it. That's why I am making this commitment. Just a few examples can make you realize how big the problem is: Rocky Mountain Arsenal near Denver has stored 125 types of toxic waste. Nerve gas and pesticides were also processed there. The site has been called "the most polluted square mile on earth." In Dover, N.J., the groundwater in one location has over 5,000 times the permitted levels of trichlorethylene.

In Russia, there are even worse sites. Since 1952, near Lake Karichai in the Urals, liquid wastes were stored, eventually spilled, and traces of the wastes are found in the Arctic Ocean, thousands of miles away. By 1988, thermal energy produced by wastes resulted in the evaporation of an entire lake; 120 million curies of radioactive waste, 1 1/2 times that released in the Chernobyl accident, were released. Now the lake has been covered with a thick layer of concrete.

CG: In a recent speech at The Hague, you referred to humanity as members of the crew on Planet Earth. How do you see us all doing our part?

MG: We must work together as a crew. I spoke recently to *Fortune* magazine's annual conference and reported there the need to deal with the challenge of huge existing nuclear and chemical arsenals and the even bigger challenge of the conflict with nature that is fundamental to our weapons and chemical technologies. Political, military and business leaders and ordinary citizens must face the problem. We must all be involved. It won't work to ignore those making the political decisions or those making the profits—or the poor, who are most likely to live closest to the greatest toxic exposure.

CG: What needs to be done?

MG: We have to change our values. We have to educate people. We have to teach citizens and governments to be aware of the dangers to our children's future. I have looked at the geography of the post-Cold War toxic sites. The challenge is enormous. Educational systems all over the world must take up this task, international codes of law must be developed, and the practical work of environmental cleanup must be undertaken.

CG: What will it mean for values to change? Which values have to change?

MG: We have to begin with the question of secrecy. In both the U.S. and Russia, we face basically the same problem. The United States is in a somewhat better position than Russia and the former Soviet Union, because the environmental movement began in citizen groups in the U.S. in the 1970s, and some progress has been make. It was not until *perestroika* and even more recently that Russia and Russian citizens have become awakened. In Rio at the 1992 Earth Summit, the governments of the world showed themselves growing in awareness of the general environmental hazards before us. But they also showed themselves to be basically indifferent to the problem of military toxic waste. It wasn't on the agenda.

We also have to make new definitions of security. We have to recognize the impact of wars and the continuing danger of weapons proliferation. It's up to us to stop the denial. It's up to the citizens of each country to remove the secrecy and turn things around.

And we have to care about the impact on everyone. We have to care about the unique impact on the poor of the world, who live where toxic sites are most often placed. It's not always so obvious that if it hurts them, it hurts us all. The well-being of the world's poor must be an integral part of our global concerns. Without them, we cannot build a future. We must raise people out of poverty, so they have a stake in our civilization.

CG: How does this change happen?

MG: It is the task of education. Information has to be made available. Leaders in religion, politics, and science must speak out and point us in new directions, toward a new paradigm for our civilization. We have to remember that there are universal values. Perhaps it will be easier to care about each other's children if we also care more about the planet that they must live on.

CG: With new market forces opening up in many parts of the world, do you see new opportunities and new dangers for the environment?

MG: As I've said, we need to spawn a different intellectual and values climate and a different set of economic goals. No country actually believes the free market can be socially irresponsible. Nor can it be environmentally irresponsible. I want more socially oriented market economies in the world. The kind of safety net you have here and in Germany is indispensable.

At the same time, the business marketplace that is based on economic freedom, that can function with independent producers and owners, forms the material basis for democracies. I see no contradiction between the market and democracy.

If we're going to protect the planet's ecology, we're going to need to find alternatives to the consumerist dream that is attracting the world. Otherwise, how will we conserve our resources, and how will we avoid setting people against each other when resources are depleted?

CG: Will the increasing number of armed ethnic conflicts worldwide add new barriers to dealing with military toxins and other environmental questions?

MG: Yes. The conflict between man and man is as serious as the conflict between man and nature. It is important that we do not act too late in taking preventive actions. We have to draw attention to the relationship between environmental protection and weapons production on the global stage. Citizen organizations must provide governments and international authorities with analysis and studies to strengthen international law for peacekeeping and to prevent worsening environmental impact from the dismantling of old systems and weapons proliferation.

CG: How will the Green Cross be active in all of this?

MG: Our goal is to reach out to citizens all over the world to reform the toxic economy. Green Cross organizations will be formed in countries all over the world and will be affiliated with Green Cross International. There is now a Green Cross in Japan, and Green Cross organizations are being formed in Russia and the United States. We will have to call on the media to help spread the world throughout the world. We want to build an international communications network to shape a new consciousness based on environmental justice.

This must be a human as well as an electronic network. We need grassroots sources of information and monitors of the problem. This is crucial. It will not be enough to rely on governments and existing experts for our information. Ordinary citizens must become experts too. It will take public opinion on a wide scale to ensure that the world's leaders act.

The Green Cross does not plan extremist action. We recognize the gradualness of change, as we recognize the urgency of change. We need to make a sustainable citizens' movement against environmental poisoning. Governments have to become the allies of citizens in this. Citizens have to help bring governments to this position. We recognize that we will learn as we go. There is no clear answer, except that the old ideologies in our civilization must give way to the new challenges to our civilization. The growing environmental movement in the world must be a vehicle for that.

CG: Are you hopeful?

MG: Yes. I am optimistic.

For more information, write to: Global Green U.S.A., 665 Buena Vista Drive, Santa Barbara, CA 93108; or call (805) 565-3485.

Colin Greer, who is president of the New World Foundation, often writes for *Parade* on social issues.

Source: *Parade Magazine,* 1/24/94

What Are Nuclear Wastes And Where Do They Come From?

The Dangers of Radioactive Wastes.

Radioactive wastes emit gamma rays and atomic particles that can injure or kill living things. This radiation may kill cells or damage the genetic material essential to reproduction. Very high levels of exposure to radiation can make people sick and kill them very quickly. Lower levels of exposure can cause cancer, sterility, or birth defects. There is considerable controversy over just how little exposure to radiation can be harmful.

Nuclear wastes can be dangerous to human beings not only through direct contact, but also by getting into water supplies or the food chain of plants and animals that we eat. Some radioactive materials stay dangerously radioactive for thousands of years, so we have an obligation to future generations to permanently isolate those materials from the environment.

Uranium Mines and Mills.

Uranium is the ultimate source of nuclear energy for bombs and nuclear reactors. After being specially treated, uranium can be put directly in bombs to provide the nuclear fission energy for the explosions. Alternatively, the uranium can be used to fuel nuclear reactors which convert some of the uranium into another fissionable element, plutonium. Plutonium is also used in bombs. Both uranium and plutonium can be used as fuel for nuclear reactors that produce electricity.

The key element, uranium, is dug out of the earth as an ore, then milled to produce uranium oxide which can be turned into nuclear fuel or bomb material. The process of milling the uranium ore produces mountains of a sand-like-by-product, called tailings. These tailings are different from the residues of most mining and milling processes because they are still radioactive. The tailings look just like fine sand, but they give off a radioactive gas called radon. If people are exposed to this gas for a long time, for example by living in a house built with concrete using uranium mill tailings, their chances of getting lung cancer are increased. It is important, therefore, to keep the tailings away from people and people away from the tailings.

Out of a total of 140 million tons of U.S. uranium mill tailings that need to be isolated, about 79 million tons can be traced to military programs. It was only with the Uranium Mill Tailings Control Act of 1978 that the Congress and the Department of Energy finally acknowledged that the government has a responsibility for helping to isolate these tailings from contact with the public.

Uranium Enrichment.

The uranium oxide that comes from the mills is still not ready for use in nuclear reactors or nuclear weapons. Only a small percentage of the uranium atoms are the right isotope (kind of atomic nucleus) needed for nuclear fission reactions. Therefore the uranium must be brought up to the right level of concentration of the desired isotope, called U-235. This is done by first chemically converting the uranium oxide into a gas, uranium fluoride, and then passing that gas through a special process that increases the concentration of U-235 in the final product.

This process of uranium enrichment leaves behind low-level (relatively low radioactivity) nuclear wastes that must be securely buried to keep humans out of contact with its potential dangers.

Fuel Fabrication.

The enriched uranium fluoride gas has to be turned into a solid metal for use in nuclear weapons or nuclear reactors. Uranium metal to be used in weapons is called oralloy, and apparently U.S. stockpiles of that material are large enough that additional oralloy has not been manufactured since 1964.

Nuclear reactors on U.S. naval ships use uranium that is even more highly enriched than is necessary for weapons. Uranium fuel pellets for navy ships must be specially fabricated.

Less highly enriched uranium fluoride is converted into uranium oxide fuel pellets for other Department of Energy nuclear reactors.

The equipment and handling materials in the fuel fabrication plants become slightly radioactive because of their contact with the uranium. Worn out equipment and materials add to the sums of low-level nuclear waste that must be safely disposed of.

Nuclear Reactors.

The uranium in Department of Energy nuclear reactors enters a chain reaction of nuclear fission which is used to produce materials for nuclear weapons. One of those materials is plutonium, which comes out of the irradiation of uranium 238. The other major bomb material is tritium—a form of hydrogen—which results from the irradiation of lithium atoms.

To get the plutonium out of the materials in nuclear reactors, it has to be chemically separated from the uranium and other fission products.

As with other facilities handling radioactive material, nuclear reactor plants produce low level nuclear wastes. In addition, when any nuclear reactor is taken out of commission it must be scoured of radioactive residues (which then become nuclear wastes), and the equipment has to be disposed of where people will not be exposed to its radioactivity. Over the years the Department of Energy and its predecessors have operated many research and test nuclear reactors in addition to the production reactors. These test and research reactors also produce low-level radioactive wastes and spent fuels. Spent fuel is fuel that has been irradiated inside a reactor. It is highly radioactive. In the case of most U.S. nuclear power plants, the spent fuel will have to be treated as high-level nuclear waste.

Chemical Reprocessing.

Extracting the fissionable plutonium from spent nuclear fuel involves dissolving the fuel in acid. The liquid left over after the plutonium is chemically removed is highly radioactive.

Nuclear Weapons Manufacture.

Putting the plutonium into nuclear weapons requires shaping and machining the metal to fit into bomb mechanisms. This process, too, leaves radioactive wastes, mostly low level.

There is one more type of nuclear waste not mentioned so far, called transuranic waste. Transuranic elements are those beyond uranium in the scientists' periodic table of the elements. These elements are produced by nuclear reactions—plutonium is one such element. Most are radioactive. Equipment and handling materials at nuclear weapons manufacturing plants can be contaminated with transuranic elements. If the radioactivity of the contaminated objects is high enough, they are categorized as "transuranic wastes," or "TRU wastes" and must be disposed of in the same way that high-level wastes are.

Through the end of 1991, the Department of Energy was storing almost 395,000 cubic meters (100 million gallons) of *high-level radioactive waste;* 255,000 cubic meters of *transuranic (plutonium-contaminated) waste;* 2.8 million cubic meters of *low-level radioactive waste;* and 101,000 cubic meters of *mixed low-level waste.* The combined radioactivity of these wastes—about a billion curies*—is 20 times the radiation released by the 1986 Chernobyl nuclear power plant accident and 40 times the radioactivity of all high-level waste generated by America's civilian nuclear power industry.

Source: Center for Defense Information, *The Defense Monitor,* Vol. X, Number 1 .

---

* A unit of radioactivity, the amount of any nuclide that undergoes exactly 3.7×10^{10} radioactive disintegrations per second.

 Global Learning, Inc.

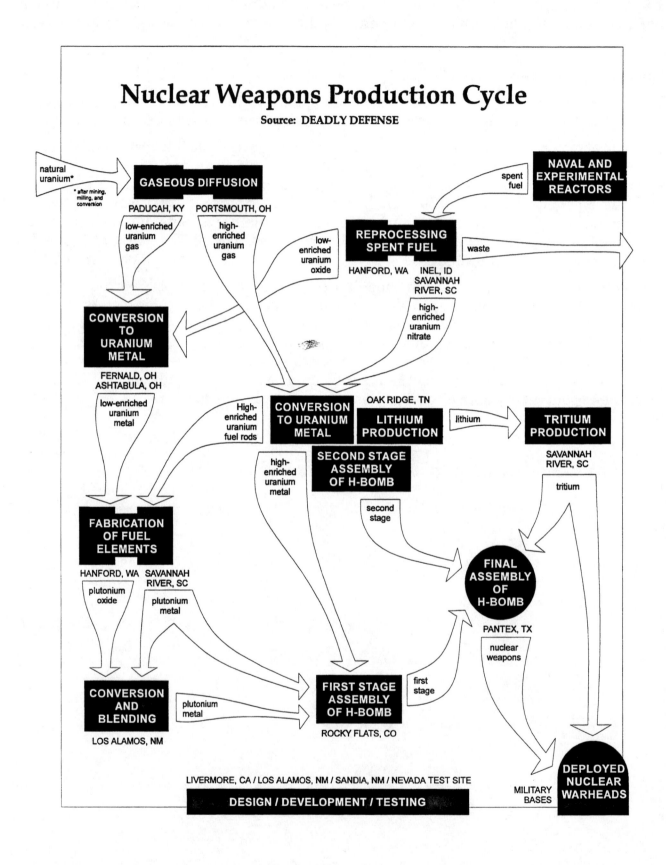

Nuclear Weapons Production Cycle
Source: DEADLY DEFENSE

Lesson 18

Business and the Environment

Historical Period	Recent U.S. (1975-Present)
Sustainable Development Topics	Economic development and environmental ethics
Purpose	To introduce students to how some businesses are taking the environment into account—literally, in their budgeting, and generally by moving toward procedures that will lead to more sustainable growth.
Objectives	Students will be able to:

1. Explain how some businesses are changing their relationships to the natural environment.
2. Give 3 examples of specific business practices which have changed.
3. Apply the CERES Principles as a way of analyzing the environmental ethics of a business practice; and
4. Research the environmental concerns of businesses in their locality as an action follow-up to the lesson.

Time Required	1-2 class periods
Materials Needed	Handout 1: *The CERES Principals* Handout 2: *Ten Trends in Corporate Environmentalism*
Teacher Background	Students can become overwhelmed with all the "bad news" about the state of the planet. It is thus important for students to hear that issues are being addressed and that some workable solutions can be found for our seemingly intractable problems. This lesson on business and the environment provides a number of "success stories" for problems the global community is facing today.

Procedure

1. Distribute **Handout 1:** *The CERES Principles* the day before the lesson. Explain that the CERES Principles were originally called the Valdez Principles. (If students are not familiar with the 11 million gallon Exxon Valdez oil spill in Prince William Sound, Alaska, review the incident briefly in general terms to establish the reason for developing a set of environmental ethics for businesses.) Tell students to read the Principles as background for an activity in the next class period. Ask that each student prepare a written question for discussion.

2. Begin by asking for comments and reactions to the reading. List on the board the issues raised in the discussion. If answers are not readily available for the questions the students raise, flag them as research questions.

3. Divide the class into ten groups (2-3 students per group). Give each group 1 of the 10 trends from **Handout 2:** *Ten Trends in Corporate Environmentalism*.

4. Ask each group to:
   a. List the positive things that they learned about in their handout.
   b. List the things that seem negative—any why they seem negative.

5. After sufficient time for reading and small group discussion, groups report back by telling the rest of the class at least:
   a. 2 positive stories from their reading, explaining, when necessary, what makes the story positive (e.g., in reading 9, why would German and Dutch cities stop buying tropical timber?).
   b. 1 story about something that looks like a problem still to be solved.

   Ask them if there were any "surprises" in the reading.

6. Debriefing:
   Tell the groups to refer to their copies of the CERES Principles. How would they evaluate the practices they read about in their "trends" in terms of the ethical guidelines put forth by CERES?

7. Follow-up activity:
   Ask students to identify businesses in the area. These could be banks, corporations, manufacturers, etc. After brainstorming a list of businesses, each group selects one to research to find out:
   a. Their main environmental concerns related to their business;

b. Any innovations they were making in how they conducted their operations in relation to the environment;

c. If they were familiar with the CERES Principles—and if yes—what comments they would have.

Lesson Extension   If students find some innovative environmentalism in their surveys, they might consider asking a spokesperson for the business to address the class.

Source   "Putting it All Together: Ten Trends in Corporate Environmentalism," *Tomorrow: The Global Environment Magazine.* (Kungsgatan 27, S-111 56 Stockholm, Sweden) Vol. 2 No. 2, 1992.

Global Learning, Inc.

The CERES Principles

Introduction

By adopting these Principles, we publicly affirm our belief that corporations have a responsibility for the environment, and must conduct all aspects of their business as responsible stewards of the environment by operating in a manner that protects the Earth. We believe that corporations must not compromise the ability of future generations to sustain themselves.

We will update our practices continually in light of advances in technology and new understandings in health and environmental science. In collaboration with CERES, the Coalition for Environmentally Responsible Economies of the Social Investment Forum, we will promote a dynamic process to ensure that the Principles are interpreted in a way that accommodates changing technologies and environmental realities. We intend to make consistent, measurable progress in implementing these Principles and to apply them in all aspects of our operations throughout the world.

1. Protection of the Biosphere

We will reduce and make continual progress toward eliminating the release of any substance that may cause environmental damage to the air, water, or the earth or its inhabitants. We will safeguard all habitats affected by our operations and will protect open spaces and wilderness, while preserving biodiversity.

2. Sustainable Use of Natural Resources

We will make sustainable use of renewable natural resources such as water, soils and forests. We will conserve nonrenewable natural resources through efficient use and careful planning.

3. Reduction and Disposal of Wastes

We will reduce and where possible eliminate waste through source reduction and recycling. All waste will be handled and disposed of through safe and responsible methods.

4. Energy Conservation

We will conserve energy and improve the energy efficiency of our internal operations and of the goods and services we sell. We will make every effort to use environmentally safe and sustainable energy sources.

5. Risk Reduction

We will strive to minimize the environmental, health and safety risks to our employees and the communities in which we operate through safe technologies, facilities and operating procedures, and by being prepared for emergencies.

6. Safe Products and Services

We will reduce and where possible eliminate the use, manufacture, or sale of products and services that cause environmental damage or health or safety hazards. We will inform our customers of the environmental impacts of our products or services and try to correct unsafe use.

7. Environmental Restoration

We will promptly and responsibly correct conditions we have caused that endanger health, safety or the environment. To the extent feasible, we will redress injuries we have caused to persons or damage we have caused to the environment and will restore the environment.

8. Informing the Public

We will inform in a timely manner everyone who may be affected by conditions caused by our company that might endanger health, safety or the environment. We will regularly seek advice and counsel through dialogue with persons in communities near our facilities. We will not take any action against employees for reporting dangerous incidents or conditions to management or to appropriate authorities.

9. Management Commitment

We will implement these Principles and sustain a process that ensures that the Board of Directors and Chief Executive Officer are fully informed about pertinent environmental issues and are fully responsible for environmental policy. In selecting our Board of Directors, we will consider demonstrated environmental commitment as a factor.

10. Audits and Reports

We will conduct an annual self-evaluation of our progress in implementing these Principles. We will support the timely creation of generally accepted environmental audit procedures. We will annually complete the CERES Report, which will be made available to the public.

Disclaimer

These Principles establish an environmental ethic with criteria by which investors and others can assess the environmental performance of companies. Companies that sign these Principles pledge to go voluntarily beyond the requirements of the law. The Principles are not intended to create new legal liabilities, expand existing rights or obligations, waive legal defenses, or otherwise affect the legal position of any signatory company, and are not intended to be used against a signatory in any legal proceeding for any purpose.

For further information on these Principles, contact CERES, 717 Atlantic Avenue, Boston, MA 02111, (617) 451-0927.

1. Change of Mind, Change of Heart

The single greatest influence on the greening of corporations has been the recognition that durable poisons, like chlorinated compounds and heavy metals, are accumulating in the biosphere and pose a serious risk to human and planetary health. Out of that recognition has evolved a more environmentally sensitive way of looking at materials and technologies.

In industry, this new awareness has led to some revolutionary concepts: the prevention of pollution through process change rather than its control through end-of-pipe solutions; toxics reduction strategies; waste elimination; "clean" technologies; and what is being called the "precautionary principle," which holds that the use of any potentially toxic substance should be curtailed because it might cause biological damage. In the energy business the new awareness has spawned the minor miracle of demand-side management and large-scale conservation programs. "New forestry" is beginning to emerge. In the automobile industry manufacturers are ""designing for disassembly." And in agriculture it's "alternative agriculture," the slow move away from chemical-intensive farming. The need for appropriate technologies has also bred an acceptance of the low-tech solution. Duckweed and marsh grass are being used commercially to filter wastewater; high temperatures are being used to kill termites.

Corporate success stories about the benefits of waste and toxics reduction are getting too numerous to tell. 3M Company remains legendary. At last count it had saved, since 1975, more than US $500 million through more than 2,500 process changes and another $650 million through energy conservation measures. Everywhere you look there are inspiring examples. Reynolds Metals replaced solvent-based inks with water-based inks in its packaging plants and saved $30 million it would have had to spend on pollution- control equipment. Carrier Corp, part of United Technologies Corp., changed the way it makes air conditioners and in doing so eliminated a solvent-based de-greasing line, saved $1.2 million a year, and began turning out better air conditioners. AT&T saves more than $1 million in disposal fees by recycling all its waste paper. Quaker Oats of Canada saves nearly $100,000 a year by visually inspecting granola bars at the end of the production line when their wrapping machine goes down temporarily, then putting the good ones back in the machine rather than throwing them out.

As for low-tech, examples also abound: ICI, the giant English chemical company has installed seven large reed beds at its Billingham, U.K. plant to filter 3,000 tons per day of amine-contaminated effluent that used to be flushed into a river; British Petroleum has eliminated fish plant odors in Ireland by pumping them through a multi-million dollar peat bog; and IBM now cleans the flux from circuit boards at its disk drive factory in San Jose, California, with soapy water and a blow drier, thereby eliminating 95 percent of the CFCs formerly emitted by the factory.

A model for us all is the J.R. Simplot Co., a $1.2 billion company that supplies more than half the French fries sold by McDonald's each year. Jack Richard Simplot, the chief executive of the firm, has turned waste into money with a system that's so inventive its almost comical. Because French fries are a quality-controlled product, over 50 percent of Simplot's potatoes normally ended up as waste—until the company learned the residues could be mixed with grain to feed cattle. The peelings now feed more than 150,000 animals. But that's only the beginning. Waste water from potato processing is used for irrigation. Cattle manure is anaerobically digested to create methane for power plants. Power is also derived from ethanol made from potatoes. The sludge from the ethanol process is converted to low-cost fish food for a commercial fish-breeding operation. The water from the fish tanks is filtered through tubs filled with water hyacinths. The flowers process nitrogen from the fish waste so the water can be reused. The hyacinths are fed to the cattle. And after the fish are harvested, their offal is mixed back into food for more fish.

All of these examples are as much changes of mind as changes of process; a willingness to rethink long-held notions of disposability, risk, responsibility, and the right to pollute. In the electricity supply business in the United States, demand-side management and conservation are the new heroes. Through the installation of more efficient lighting, motors, appliances and insulation, the recovery of waste heat, and direct computer control of peak and off-peak power usage, utilities are improving efficiency and radically easing demand. A report from the Electric Power Research Institute, an industry-funded center in Palo Alto, California, shows that energy-saving technologies that exist today could reduce the total U.S. demand for electricity by 24 to 44 percent by the year 2000—enough to satisfy the power needs of the 11 eastern states. This avoided outlays of tens of billions of dollars, representing both a competitive advantage for American industry and a major stabilization of carbon dioxide, sulfur dioxide, and nitrogen oxide emissions.

Global Learning, Inc.

2. The Spread of Full-Cost Analysis

To accommodate the environment, companies are being forced to look past a traditional narrowly focused cost-benefit analysis of their operations (i.e. what are the costs and benefits to us?) to holistic full-cost analysis (i.e. what are the costs and benefits to society and the environment and us?) This emerging holistic approach to production and consumption has given us: the environmental audit, cradle-to-grave product design and management, life-cycle analysis and full-cost accounting—all powerful concepts now being tested in major corporations and many governments.

Under the "Responsible Care" code of operational ethics adopted by the world's largest chemical companies, cradle-to-grave product stewardship is now being built into operations. Dow Chemical, for example, has decided, because of concerns about proper handling, that it will not sell small quantities of certain hazardous chemicals. As one manager at Britain's ICI Chlor-Chemicals says, "we want to be in the position of 'lending' the solvent to the customer." Chemical firms, like other manufacturers, are also designing their products with their disposability in mind. Engineers and chemists are now asking questions like: who is likely to use it? How will they use it? Whom will it affect? Where will it end up?

At the root of all these questions is the emerging notion of "true-cost" or "real-cost" accounting. It is making old Keynesian concepts of consumption, investment, savings and government expenditure obsolete because they do not take into account depletion of the earth's natural resources. As economist Robert Repetto of the Wold Resources Institute reminds us, the whole idea of Gross National Product is dangerously out of step with the times because it ignores ecology. As long as a country's GNP is up, it is considered economically healthy, even if it is exhausting the fertility of its soils, cutting down its forests and polluting its fresh water. The consequences, says Repetto, "are illusory gains in income and permanent loss in wealth." The illusion applies to corporations as readily as countries.

Germany is taking the bold step of developing what is being called "a new model of wealth." Over the next decade it will attempt to quantify its "Gross Ecological Product," employing 40 statisticians and economists at the Federal Statistical Office to merge the country's natural resource accounts with its national income accounts and come up with a methodology for determining ecological costs. One government economist predicts hidden, external environmental costs will add roughly 66 percent to prices. Under full-cost accounting, corporations—and consumers—will eventually have to absorb these costs.

3. Accidents Force Accountability

Two important events have convinced North American companies they must be more accountable to the public. The first was the lethal gas leak at Union Carbide's Bhopal, India plant. "Bhopal," says Monsanto chairman Richard Mahoney, "galvanized my thinking in terms of reducing risk and communicating with the public." In fact, it galvanized the entire chemical industry. The other key event was the passage through the U.S. Congress, in 1986, of changes to the Superfund Amendments and Reauthorization Act (SARA) that required companies to report their emissions levels of 300 hazardous chemicals under Title III (the Emergency Planning and Right-To-Know provision). An unprecedented degree of environmental disclosure was suddenly mandated by law.

Mandatory emissions reporting has coincided with the voluntary public accountability called for under the chemical industry's "Responsible Care" code. Public accountability is now being seen as an important means for the chemical business to recover from what Mahoney calls "being at near-zero in the public mind." Secrecy doesn't work anymore. As Union Carbide found out, those who are secretive are more culpable in the case of disaster. Accordingly, Monsanto and Dow have opened their plants to the public, and begun issuing "report cards" showing environmental progress (or lack of it). A similar public report was first issued in 1989 by Norsk Hydro, Norway's largest industrial group. A conglomerate with a number of environmentally unfriendly operations like the production of nitrogen-based fertilizers, PVC, aluminum fittings and fish farming, Norsk moved voluntary corporate disclosure upward a notch by hiring an independent auditor to assess six of its plants. Deficiencies were duly noted in the report.

Although disclosure is certainly a trend, 'full disclosure" is still a rhetorical term. According to Friends of the Earth, big chemical companies may have opened their plants, but they still resist sharing the detailed hazard studies they have done on those plants—the worst-case scenarios that predict what will happen if a tank full of poison explodes or a spill occurs. Full disclosure also implies no hidden agendas, yet many large manufacturers, including big chemical firms, quietly lobby the U.S. Congress through industry associations to dilute and defeat laws that would require the very ecological improvements they claim to stand for.

Global Learning, Inc.

4. Opposites Attract

Business and the environmental community are talking to each other more than ever before. Practically unthinkable just two or thee years ago, it is now acknowledged within environmentally aware companies and governments that well-informed environmentalists bring valuable opinions to the table. In fact, their involvement may well become a necessity. "The answers are not going to be credible unless you have campaigning environmentalists built into the process from the outset," says John Elkington, managing director of the English consultancy SustainAbility. "It is only a matter of time before companies will pull environmentalists into their operations."

Some already have: the Environmental Defense Fund helped McDonald's Corp. through the wrenching decision to abandon polystyrene burger boxes. EDF continues to advise McDonald's on its ambitious green plan that includes the diversion of as much as 80 percent of its solid waste. Two other environmental groups—the Natural Resources Defense Council and the Conservation Law Foundation—were instrumental in working with big electrical utilities to convince regulators in California and new England that electric utilities should profit from saving energy rather than selling it, and thanks to recent rate structure changes, utilities in those regions are now investing billions in energy conservation and demand-side management. In 1991, Safeway became the first supermarket chain in the U.S. to adopt a dolphin-safe policy—worked out with the environmental group Earth Island Institute. There was also news last year of Fuji Photo Film consulting with the Audubon Society before converting from plastic film canisters to paperboard ones. And in 1990, Nissan asked a group of science writers, ecologists, energy experts and anthropologists to brainstorm via a computer conference on how an ecologically responsible car maker might act.

In Canada, environment-and-economy "round tables" were formed in 1989 in each province and at the federal level, bringing together representatives from government, business, the environmental community and native groups to try to influence environmental policy. While these high-level gatherings of opposites have generally bogged down in rhetoric and process, they have at least brought industrialists and environmentalists together as colleagues—an important gate to open—and they have inspired round tables in a growing number of Canadian municipalities.

5. Purchasing Driven By Policy

Business likes to formalize its goals in "mission statements." Most major companies express their financial and strategic objectives in a mission statement. Many are now stating their environmental goals the same way.

Once again, the chemical industry has jumped out ahead with its "Responsible Care Principles." While some corporate environmental statements are badly watered down with caveats like "if achievable" and "where feasible," the "Responsible Care" code is written in fairly direct language. Two examples of the ten principles:

- To develop and produce chemicals that can be manufactured, transported, used and disposed of safely.
- To report promptly to officials, employees, customers and the public, information on chemical-related health or environmental hazards and recommend protective measures.

In some global companies, the principles are being applied throughout worldwide operations in spite of competitive concerns. Monsanto, Dow and ICI are among multinational chemical and other industrial companies that have vowed to bring the health, safety and environmental standards of all worldwide operations up to the standard of their domestic plants (or to higher standard if the host country requires it). Had such a policy been in effect in 1984, the Bhopal disaster would have been avoided.

Profiting from waste is another strategy becoming policy. 3 M calls its waste- reduction program "Pollution Prevention Pays." At Dow it's "Waste Reduction Always Pays." At Westinghouse it's "Achievements In Clean Technologies." Of course, money is far more influential than slogans. The purchasing policies of a growing number of corporations and many municipal, state and federal government agencies in the United States now favor recycled goods such as paper, re-treaded tires, plastic lumber and re-refined motor oil. In 1990, 39 states and the District of Columbia had policies in place.) The state of Nebraska spends its entire office paper budget on recycled paper. The U.S. Conference of Mayors has a "Buy Recycled" program to encourage its members to revise their municipal recycling policies. And any U.S. federal agency that buys more than $10,000 worth of these products in a year must buy items that meet Environmental Protection Agency recycled-content standards. Bell Canada (Canada's most profitable company in 1990), another big buyer of recycled products, requires a written environmental policy from all its suppliers. The ripple effect of such policies can be seen at General Motors, which has refused to accept disposable packaging components from its suppliers since 1989. The result has been the development of durable steel and plastic containers and racks that make dozens of round trips before being dismantled for recycling.

 Global Learning, Inc.

6. Pressure from the Top

If environmental policy is to have significant and rapid impact on a big company, it must emanate from the top. Thus, in a now-famous line, Du Pont's chairman Edgar Woolard, Jr. called himself Du Pont's "chief environmental officer." In 1990, Sir Denys Henderson, the chairman of ICI, wrote a personal letter to all 134,000 ICI employees worldwide emphasizing the company's environmental commitment and informing them that environmental spending would double. Monsanto chairman Mahoney says: "I think you will find that the CEOs of most major companies—and certainly the major chemical companies—are fully involved in environmentalism.

"That involvement implies progress: decision making that can circumvent the corporate bureaucracy, cut across divisions and penetrate protected territory; major allocations of capital from budgets not traditionally tapped for environmental improvement; an increase of senior-level environmental executives with greater authority; and a greater willingness to make environmental experts board members. Indeed, these are all trends today."

As a breed, chief executives should become even more committed in the coming decade because, with a few exceptions, environmental enthusiasm appears to be a symptom of age—the younger you are, the more you care. A 45-year-old with growing children is more likely to worry about the environment and the value of his beach property than a 70- year-old whose outlook was forged in a chemical-happy world hooked on disposability and conspicuous consumption. Hence, progress within corporations will gain momentum as older CEOs are replaced by younger ones.

"Whatever your opinion of the sixties culture," says Mark Plotkin, vice president of the environmental group Conservation International, "the one sentiment that endures is a respect for nature. It doesn't matter that these people get older and get married, have kids and start moving to the right politically. They care for the environment in a way that many of their parents and grandparents did not."

7. Pressure from the Inside

Executives run companies but common people make them work. And common people are showing less and less tolerance for environmentally irresponsible companies. People don't leave their convictions with the receptionist when they come to work in the morning. This explains the enthusiasm most employees show for corporate recycling initiatives, and the fact that jobs related to environmental R&D are so popular in major firms.

Employees, like everyone else, have a deepening awareness of the effects of pollution and where it's coming from. "[These are not] card-carrying environmentalists," said former Texas commissioner of agriculture, Jim Hightower, in a 1990 speech. "I am talking about people who take their kids down to the Jersey shore and the Gulf beaches but when they get there can't let their kids go into the water because of what's in the water. I am talking about the lower-middle income family that's got a $60,000 suburban home up against a cotton field noticing that their roses died after the third cotton spraying this year, remembering that their neighbor's cat was found dead under the bush about this time last year, and beginning to wonder if the rash their kids have might be connected to some of this."

Labor is also adding to the growing rumble from within corporations. Organized labor is beginning to state, in an important change of mind, that environmental improvement is an imperative, that jobs should not be the cost of cleanup, and that hazardous working conditions are often related to environmental pollution. The United Steelworkers of America have adopted a much tougher stand on the environment and wrote this line into a report at their convention in the summer of 1990: "In the old days, we thought smoke meant jobs. Today, we know better...We believe that the greatest threat to our children's future may lie in the destruction of their environment. For that reason alone, the environment must be an issue for our union." And labor unions and environmentalists are starting to work together. Loggers and conservationists hammered out important forestry accords in Montana in 1990 and British Columbia in 1991. Environmentalists have also been working with construction workers in California and oil workers in Louisiana.

Inside pressure extends to those who are almost inside, or will be inside soon: students. A growing number of North American business schools are making environmental courses part of their curricula. But more to the point, talented and environmentally aware students emerging from colleges and universities over the next five or ten years will be both sought after—as the pool of qualified graduates shrinks with the aging of post-war baby boom—and discerning about whom they join. Companies that pollute will be regarded as second rate choices.

8. Pressure from the Outside

Environmental regulations are one of the strongest outside influences on corporate behavior and it's safe to say they will continue to tighten. But market forces will be even stronger and less controllable. Markets are shifting to accommodate the environment and will continue to make companies move on the issues.

Some examples:

- Japanese food-buying co-operatives are among the largest offshore customers of U.S. agribusiness. One of the key concerns of these giant groups is food purity. They don't want pesticide residues in their food. This requirement may well push American agribiz into "organic" farming.

- The Japanese have recently announced significant improvements in the gasoline mileage of their cars. At the same time, U.S. automakers are fighting laws that would improve the average mileage of the American-made car. Yet consumers want efficient cars and some cities and states are insisting on them through air-quality legislation.

- In 1991, for the first time, German pulp and paper buyers began refusing products from Canada that are bleached with chlorine. Canada's pulp exports to Europe are worth billions.

- States like California, Wisconsin, Minnesota, Massachusetts, New Jersey, Florida, and the New England states are moving well ahead of the U.S. federal government on environmental issues such as solid waste planning, packaging restrictions and consumer product labeling. Legal requirements in two or three large state markets can force big national manufacturers to change their processes and products across the country.

- In spite of concerns about environmental standards impeding free trade, the European Community appears to be moving toward the high-end standards now being set by Germany, Switzerland and Denmark. Global firms will eventually have to follow.

9. Maverick Leaders

Competition dictates that companies must follow rivals who jump out in front, and there are a growing number of companies that have decided to turn environmental improvement to their competitive advantage. Their competitors will have little choice but to follow. In the public sector, progressive governments force less progressive governments into action by example.

It has already happened in the paper business with recycled papers. In pulp- making, manufacturers are starting to build chlorine-free and "closed loop" mills that have zero effluent. Louisiana-Pacific is talking about getting more of its pulp from cultivated tree plantations and less from old-growth forests. In the automobile business, the maverick leaders will develop new battery technologies and cars that run on alternatives to gasoline. In the energy business, California utilities have demonstrated the enormous gains to be made through demand-side management. The world is now following. In agriculture, it is farmers like Eric Schroeder, owner of a 230-acre chemical- free dairy farm in Minnesota. In a 1988 interview about sustainable farming, he said, "If I had known in 1981 what I know today, by 1983, I could have been where I am today—with a lot more money in the bank."

Cities and states are showing the same leadership. Irvine, California, has passed a comprehensive law controlling the use of ozone-depleting chemicals. Other U.S. cities— Berkeley, California, St. Paul, Minnesota and Portland, Oregon—have banned polystyrene foam. Toronto has pledged to reduce its carbon dioxide emissions by 20 percent by the year 2005. More than 200 German cities and 60 in the Netherlands have stopped purchasing tropical timber.

Global Learning, Inc.

10. Legal Liability

Environmental liability is already a serious issue for those holding contaminated real estate. Exxon and Union Carbide have paid large fines for Valdez and Bhopal. And in Texas, where the courts are allowing foreign plaintiffs to sue American corporations, liability for hazardous substances shipped offshore is now coming home to roost.

But these legal costs may one day appear trifling if Patrick McCully, an editor of Britain's *The Ecologist,* is correct in his prediction. In the May/June 1991 issue of *The Ecologist,* McCully wrote an editorial titled "A Message to the Executives and Shareholders of E.I. Du Pont de Nemours and Co. and Imperial Chemical Industries, Ltd." He contends that the thinning of the earth's ozone layer, which is occurring far more rapidly than was expected, is primarily the responsibility of the two chemical giants. Du Pont supplies 15 to 25 percent of the world's CFCs and is the biggest producer of halons. ICI provides some 40 percent less CFCs than Du Pont but approximately half the global production of ozone-destroying carbon tetrachloride. Both firms intend to make and sell HCFCs, another ozone-damaging solvent, for the next half century.

As McCully says, chemical companies have known about ozone destruction from chlorine- and bromine-based chemicals since the mid-1970s, yet they fought regulations to control these substances, worked on alternatives only when the political climate dictated and aggressively promote the sale of HCFCs, which are not yet as tightly regulated as CFCs.

In the meantime, the ozone layer continues to thin. And the U.S. EPA and the United Nations continue to revise upward the estimated millions of deaths from skin cancer due to increased exposure to UV rays—to say nothing of incalculable losses to world agriculture and tourism.

In the short term, says McCully, Du Pont and ICI will face mounting consumer boycotts of all their products. In the long term, he predicts withering civil suits that could well ruin both companies—a prospect of great interest to shareholders and other citizens of the world.

To my mind, he's right. The thinning of the earth's protective ozone—a measurable catastrophe with an undeniable industrial source—changes the rules. It has rendered absurd the whole notion of business talking to itself about the environment, setting its own deadlines and selectively choosing its sources of information. So far, trends like those above can be attributed to a gradual pull on the part of good corporate citizens, or at least smart corporate citizens, and a growing push from common people and regulators. My bet is that push will most certainly come to shove without a greater acknowledgement of the seriousness of the problems caused by industry—and a commitment to solve them once and for all.

Lesson 19

Save the Earth II!
Organizations' Approaches

Historical Period   Recent U.S. (1975-present)

Sustainable Development Topics   Human environment interaction, views of the environment, problem solving

Purpose   To identify and evaluate alternative approaches and solutions to environmental problems.

Objectives   Students will be able to:

1. Research, evaluate, and synthesize diverse views about environmental problems.
2. Evaluate, select, and implement solutions to environmental problems.
3. Anticipate consequences that may grow out of problem solving decisions.

Time Required   One day for preparation and two days for class meetings

Materials Needed   Handout 1: *Environmental Issue Research Project*
Handout 2: *Grading the Speeches*
Problem Solving Model: Contemporary Period (from the beginning of this book)

Teacher Background   This lesson can be used as a contemporary follow-up to *Save the Earth! But How?* or on its own. **The lesson involves preliminary research. Therefore it must be introduced approximately two months prior to the actual class meeting when student research will be discussed.**

You will note on Handout 1 that there are four steps in the research phase of the lesson. Students are required to:

1. write a business letter to an environmental organization requesting specific information;
2. read and outline three articles about their assigned environmental topic;
3. prepare a one page position paper; and

    Global Learning, Inc.

4. write a two to three minute speech.

All of these assignments are part of the portfolio they will bring to the class meeting.

You will need to decide due dates for each phase of the process once you have chosen a date for the class meeting. You will also notice that each step of the research process has a point value which totals 100 points. You may want to alter or eliminate the point values. On the day of the lesson meeting, students will present their speeches to their issue group and work through the *Problem Solving Model: Contemporary Period* found in this publication. There is a final essay assignment which allows students to comment on their personal views about environmental problems and their solutions.

Procedure Preparation for Research Phase (approximately 2 months prior to class meeting date):

1. Ask students to name contemporary national environmental issues. You might want to prompt students with the Forest Conference of April '93; ancient forest preservation; protection of endangered species; Alaskan wilderness preservation; logging, grazing, and mining in federal land, etc. Record their suggestions on the board.

2. Ask students to select an issue from the list which they would like to learn more about. Ideally you will have five issues and approximately five students to investigate each issue.

3. Within each group, assign students to the following environmental or public policy groups for the purpose of research and role play during the class meeting. The groups have been selected to represent a range of perspectives and approaches; you may want to substitute or add others to the list:

Cato Institute
214 Massachusetts Avenue, NE
Washington, DC 20002
(202) 546-0200

Environmental Defense Fund
257 Park South
New York, NY 10010
(212) 505-2100

Friends of the Earth
218 D Street, SE
Washington, DC 20003
(202) 544-2600

Greenpeace, USA, Inc.
1436 U Street, NW
Washington, DC 20009
(202) 462-1177

The Heritage Foundation
214 Massachusetts Avenue, NE
Washington, DC 20002
(202) 546-4400

Sierra Club
730 Polk Street
San Francisco, CA 94109
(415) 776-2211

4. Review the assignments and your due dates on **Handout 1** and be sure that students understand the goal of each part of the process and the purpose of the class meeting. Also advise students that they should share information that they receive from their organization with other students who were assigned to that organization.

Procedure Day 1 (class meeting)

1. Group meetings should be scheduled for approximately eight weeks from the day the project was assigned. All parts of the portfolio should be complete and brought to this meeting. You may want to evaluate the parts of the portfolio as they are due so that students are able to make changes or additions to it prior to this day.

2. Students will be separated into their issue groups for speech presentations. Students should use the grading criteria when fellow group members deliver their speeches. To simplify the process, copy the grading sheet on **Handout 2** and have enough copies available so that students can evaluate each other directly on the form.

3. At the conclusion of speeches, collect the evaluation sheets and give each group a copy of the *Problem Solving Model: Contemporary Period* from the beginning of this book.

4. Ask students to assume one of the following roles as they work through problem solving:
   a. Group Leader—runs discussion and keeps group on task;
   b. Scribe—takes notes from discussion;
   c. Secretary—responsible for working with the scribe in drafting the final copy of the plan of action;
   d. Representative—will present the plan to the full class meeting;
   e. Representative II—will assist Representative I in presentation and answering questions during the class meeting.

5. Remind students that they are to work together to find their preferred solution, but they should stay in character and represent the view of the organization they researched rather than their personal opinion. Take time to review the problem solving model with them before they begin. They should complete steps 1 (Define the Problem) through 5 (Implementation). Step 6 (Evaluation) will be completed the following day after presentations are made.

Procedure Days 2 and 3

1. This is a plenary session during which students will present their group plans for action on their issue to the members of the class. Ask students to respond to the questions posed in

Global Learning, Inc.

step 6 of the model after each plan is presented. Encourage open discussion whenever appropriate. You may want to ask students to vote on each plan once the questioning phase has concluded.

2. To conclude the lesson, ask students to reflect back to earlier lessons when the clash of views about problems resulted in debate about alternative solutions. This clash of views was illustrated in the lesson *Save the Earth! But How?* when *conservationists, preservationists, ecologists,* and *laissez faire* believers debated Theodore Roosevelt era policies about the environment.

   The following questions might help to spark some connections:

   - What were the basic *differences* among the environmental and public policy organizations' policies?
   - How did each organization view the *environment / human relationship?* How did this basic philosophical difference affect consensus about your action plan?
   - What should the *role of government* be in resolving environmental issues according to each organization? How did each organization interpret government policy?
   - How did organizations differ about *how to achieve their goal?*
   - What were the differing ideas about *their highest priorities?*
   - Who *funded* the organizations represented? How did funding influence policy?
   - Which organizations seemed to be the most *effective?* What characteristics made them effective?
   - Which problems seemed to be more easily resolved? What characteristics of those problems made them so? What made the solutions more effective?

3. As a culminating activity, ask students to respond to the following essay topic for homework:

   If you had a million dollars to give, to which environmental or public policy organization would you give it, and for which environmental problems would you like it earmarked?

"I'm really starting to lose patience with all these special-interest groups."

Global Learning, Inc.

Environmental Issue Research Project

Step 1   *Write to an environmental or public policy organization* requesting specific information on the assigned issue, their mission statement, annual report and funding sources. A copy of this letter to be submitted
for **15 points. Due**_____

Step 2   *Research at least three recent articles* regarding the issue assigned. Bibliography information and outline for each article to be submitted
for **30 points. Due**_____

Step 3   *Prepare a one page Position Paper* about the environmental group's view of the issue using your background information of the issue and the information you receive from the organization to which you wrote. Paper to be submitted in the following format
for **40 points. Due**_____

>   *One Page Position Paper*
>   Paragraph One—statement of the problem
>   Paragraph Two—arguments for the position presented
>   Paragraph Three—arguments against the position and their
>   weaknesses
>   Paragraph Four—proposed resolution to the problem

Step 4   *Write a two to three minute speech* presenting your organization's position on the issue. Present the speech to your issue group during group meeting. The speech will be evaluated by other group members using the following criteria
for **15 points. Due**_____

>   *Grading the Speeches*
>   *1=poor 2=good 3=excellent*
>   a. The problem is stated, described and backed by facts.
>   b. The impact of the problem on the country is explained.
>   c. The position of the environmental group is presented in an organized way.
>   d. The weaknesses of opposing views are presented.
>   e. The speech was very effective overall.

Grading the Speeches

Name of Speaker:_____ Name of Evaluator:_____

1=poor 2=good 3=excellent

_____ 1. The problem is stated, described and backed by facts.

_____ 2. The impact of the problem on the country is explained.

_____ 3. The position of the environmental group is presented in an organized way.

_____ 4. The weaknesses of opposing views are presented.

_____ 5. The speech was very effective overall.

_____ **Total**

Comments:

Name of Speaker:_____ Name of Evaluator:_____

1=poor 2=good 3=excellent

_____ 1. The problem is stated, described and backed by facts.

_____ 2. The impact of the problem on the country is explained.

_____ 3. The position of the environmental group is presented in an organized way.

_____ 4. The weaknesses of opposing views are presented.

_____ 5. The speech was very effective overall.

_____ **Total**

Comments:

Global Learning, Inc.

Lesson 20

Model Senate Hearing on the Environment

Historical Period Recent U.S. (1975-present)

Sustainable Development Topics Environment, economy, governmental policies

Objectives Students will be able to:

1. Utilize standard research resources.
2. Draft legislation according to the format of the United States Senate.
3. Identify, and propose solutions regarding, sustainability issues of the environment and the economy.

Time Required 9 class periods, with four to six weeks for letter writing and responses between days 3 and 4

Materials Needed Handout 1: *Witness Roles: Environmental Organizations/ Agencies*
Handout 2: *Witness Roles: Business*
Handout 3: *Witness Roles: Senator Roles*
Handout 4: *Directions for Writing a Bill*
Handout 5: *Position Paper Format*

Teacher Background This lesson is intended as a culminating activity for a United States History course which has included the environment as an important topic for consideration. Students will assume roles as senators or witnesses as they prepare for and present the simulation. Preparation for the simulation should begin approximately six weeks in advance of the actual activity. Students will begin by writing a business letter requesting information and researching their particular role.

Procedure Day 1

1. Divide the class into three groups: environmental organizations/agencies, businesses, senators. Each group will

have a different assignment, so reproduce as many copies of **Handouts 1, 2, and 3** as needed.

2. Students should select their roles and return a copy of the completed handout to you (step 1 on handouts).

3. Provide students with a format for writing a business letter.

4. Borrow copies of the *Environmental Almanac, The World Almanac,* and *The Almanac of American Politics* from your library so that each group member can use these resources to find the address of the organization, company, or senator they will represent. The addresses are also provided at the end of the lesson plan in case students have difficulty locating any of them.

5. Assign a due date for the business letter. Allow students to write rough drafts of their letters for the remainder of the period. Ask them to peer edit their letters (step 2 on handouts).

Procedure   Days 2 and 3

1. Bring students to the library to begin their initial research (step 3 on handouts).

2. Students will research the specific information described in step 3 on the Handouts.

3. Students will take notes from at least three sources, including one recent periodical. If students are not familiar with the *Readers Guide to Periodical Literature* or the computer index available in your school, you should arrange for a demonstration and presentation by the librarian. Students should also be provided with a format for bibliographic information (MLA form). Notes should be taken on note cards for easy reference, and bibliographic information should be recorded on the top of the cards.

4. Assign a due date for collection of these cards. It should be approximately four weeks later in order to allow for a reply to their letter. This information can be included as part of their notes.

Procedure   Day 4 (four to six weeks later)

On the day you collect the note cards, assign an essay for each group. This essay can be done as a homework assignment, or as an in-class essay. The topics for each group are:

Senators: What are the major environmental concerns in your state or region? What are your senator's views regarding environmental protection? Which environmental problem do you think the Senate Committee on Environment should address? Explain your choice.

Businesses: On which environmental concern does this industry have the greatest impact? How is this impact felt?

What is this company's policy regarding the environment? Is there anything this company can do to lessen its impact on the environment? (You may want to refer this group to some of the readings in the lesson *Business and the Environment*.)

Environmental Organizations: What are the particular concerns of the organization you represent? How are they working to improve this problem? What is their policy regarding the balance between economics and the environment?

Procedure Days 5 and 6

1. Once you have reviewed the essays and note cards, identify three to four areas of concern (e.g., clean air, clean water, toxic waste, acid rain, forest preservation, mining, waste disposal, protection of species, use of pesticides).

2. Proceed with group work during days 5 and 6.

   Senators: Divide the senate group into sub-committees in order to write bills that will address each of the areas you have identified. Senators will share their concerns and the concerns of their state on the particular topic their committee is assigned. They will spend the remainder of the period drafting a bill that will address this topic (bill format enclosed as **Handout 4**). The completed bills should be returned at the end of Day 6.

   Witnesses: Divide the witnesses into small groups to prepare a position paper on each topic to be addressed. The small groups will brainstorm their concerns and priorities in considering the particular topic their group is assigned. They will spend the remainder of the period drafting a position paper and group poster (position paper format and poster requirements enclosed as **Handout 5**). The completed position papers and signs should be submitted at the end of Day 6.

Procedure Day 7

1. Distribute position papers and bills to all members of the class.

   Witnesses should review these documents in their groups and prepare questions and testimony for the Committee Session. It is recommended that witnesses be responsible for testifying for or against at least one bill. You might ask students to sign up for a speakers' list so that each bill is given consideration.

   Senators should review each document and prepare introductory speeches for the bills they have written. It is recommended that each student be responsible for speaking for or against at least one bill. Senators should also write

questions for witnesses who will testify during the
Committee Session and senators who are sponsoring bills.

Procedure   Days 8 and 9—Committee Session Procedure

1. The senator who is sponsoring the bill should read it aloud and deliver a brief speech explaining the bill's main points.
2. Questions from other senators and witnesses will be directed to the sub-committee responsible for the bill.
3. The Chair (teacher) will recognize witnesses who wish to testify for or against the bill.
4. Chair will recognize senators to speak for or against the bill.
5. Vote is taken. Only senators may vote. Majority passes the bill. Repeat the process for each remaining bill.

Final Essay   For the future development of the United States, which interests should come first—business or the environment? Can both interests be addressed simultaneously? Explain your answer.

Addresses   Environmental Organizations/Agencies

American Freedom Coalition
800 K Street, NW
Washington, DC 20006
(202) 371-0303

Keep America Beautiful
9 West Broad Street
Stamford, CT 06902
(203) 323-8987

Audubon Society
8940 Jones Mill Road
Chevy Chase, MD 20815
(301) 652-9188

Sierra Club
730 Polk Street
San Francisco, CA 94109
(415) 776-2211

Greenpeace USA, Inc.
1436 U Street, NW
Washington, DC 20009
(202) 462-1177

U.S. Department of the Interior
1849 C Street, NW
Washington, DC 20240
(202) 208-3100

The Heritage Foundation
214 Massachusetts Avenue, NE
Washington, DC 20002
(202) 546-4400

U.S. Environmental Protection
Agency
401 M Street, SW
Washington, DC 20460
(202) 260-2090

Global Learning, Inc.

Addresses   Businesses

Dow Chemical Co.
2030 Dow Center
Midland, MI 48674
(517) 636-1000

Occidental Petroleum Corp.
10889 Wilshire Boulevard
Los Angeles, CA 90024
(213) 879-1700

E.I. Du Pont de Nemours & Co.
1007 Market Street
Wilmington, DE 19898
(302) 774-1000

Scott Paper Co.
Scott Plaza
Philadelphia, PA 19113
(215) 522-5000

Exxon Corp.
225 E. John W. Carpenter
Freeway
Irving, TX 75062-2298
(214) 444-1000

United Mine Workers of America
900 15th Street, NW
Washington, DC 20005
(202) 842-7200

Minnesota Mining and
Manufacturing Co.
3M Center
St. Paul, MN 55144-1000
(612) 733-1110

Weyerhauser Co.
Tacoma, WA 98477
(206) 924-2345

Addresses   Senators

The general address and telephone number for U.S. Senators is
United States Senate, Washington, DC 20510; (202) 224-3121.

Witness Roles
Environmental Organizations/Agencies

Step 1: Each member of the group should choose one of the following roles. Fill-in the names of group members next to the role they have chosen.

Role	Student's Name
U.S. Environmental Protection Agency	
Greenpeace	
Sierra Club	
Audubon Society	
U.S. Department of the Interior	
The Heritage Foundation	
Keep America Beautiful	
American Freedom Coalition	

Step 2: Write a business letter to the organization/agency you have chosen. Addresses for environmental organizations can be found in *The Environmental Almanac*. In the body of the letter, you should request information about their policies regarding environmental and economic issues and their particular areas of concern. Request a profile of the organization/agency including their funding sources and any literature that would acquaint you with their environmental policies.

A copy of this letter is due on _____.

Step 3: Begin to research your organization/agency in the library through periodicals and other reference sources. Once you have received the information you requested through the mail, you may use it to supplement your library research. You must use a minimum of three sources and take careful notes from each on note cards. Be sure to keep bibliographic information at the top of each card. Your research should address the following points: history of the organization/agency, the focus of their mission, and their actions on at least two current environmental issues.

Note cards are due on _____.

Witness Roles
Business

Step 1: Each member of the group should choose one of the following roles. Fill-in the names of group members next to the role they have chosen.

Role	Student's Name
Du Pont	
Minnesota Mining and Manufacturing (3M)	
Weyerhauser	
Scott Paper	
United Mine Workers Union	
Exxon	
Dow Chemical	
Occidental Petroleum	

Step 2: Write a business letter to the business you will be representing. The addresses for these businesses can be found in the World Almanac under the topic "Business Directory." In the body of your letter, you should request information about the location of the company and its production facilities, the nature of the company's business, the number of employees, and specific concerns and policies regarding protection of the environment.

A copy of this letter is due on: _____.

Step 3: Begin to research the industry your company represents. Library periodicals and other reference sources will provide information for this initial research. Once you have received the information you requested through the mail, you may use it to supplement your library research. You must use a minimum of three sources and take careful notes from each on note cards. Be sure to keep bibliographic information at the top of each card. Your research should address the following points: a general description of the industry, the products provided by the industry, natural resources used, and the impact of the industry on the environment.

Note cards are due on: _____.

Senator Roles

Step 1: Each member of the group should choose one senator representing one of the following states. Fill-in the names of group members next to the role they have chosen.

Senator Role	Student's Name
New Jersey	
Pennsylvania	
Louisiana	
Florida	
Washington	
Alaska	
Montana	
Texas	
Minnesota	

Step 2: Write a business letter to the senator you will be representing. The addresses for their home state office and Washington D.C. office can be found in *The Almanac of American Politics*. In the body of your letter, you should request information about major environmental concerns of their home state, their position and recent votes on federal environmental legislation, and their judgment about how to balance economic opportunity and environmental protection.

A copy of this letter is due on: _____.

Step 3: Begin to research environmental concerns of the state your senator represents. Focus on the following areas as it applies to your state: clean air, clean water, toxic waste, acid rain, forest preservation, mining, waste disposal, protection of species, use of pesticides. Use periodicals and other reference sources for this initial research. Once you have received the information you requested through the mail, you may use it to supplement your library research. You must use a minimum of three sources and take careful notes from each on note cards. Be sure to keep bibliographic information at the top of each card. Your research should address the following points: the particular environmental problems of the state, the senator's position on environmental issues, and conflicts between environmental concerns and economic development.

Note cards are due on: _____.

Global Learning, Inc.

Directions for Writing a Bill

Title of Bill
(Must state the purpose of the bill in 5-15 words.)
(Capitalize and underline.)

example:

A Bill to Limit Clear Cutting on Federal Lands

Preamble or Perambulatory Clauses (These are statements that begin with "Whereas." They should state why the bill is necessary. Notice the punctuation in the examples!)

example:

Whereas: Deforestation of federal lands has grown 20% in the past 2 years;

Whereas: Clear cut areas are not replanted with the variety of trees that were cut;

Introduction (This is a standard clause that introduces the body of the bill. Notice punctuation and capitalization.)

example:

BE IT ENACTED by the Senate and the House of Representatives of the United States of America in Congress assembled, that:

Body or Provisions (These sections should state the specific actions called for to address the problems presented in the perambulatory clauses.)

example:

Section 1.   _Clear cutting on federal lands is prohibited effective one month after the passage of this bill._

Section 2.   _Companies wishing to harvest wood from federal lands must submit a written proposal for selective cutting and a list of the varieties of trees that will be replanted._

Section 3.   _Companies who fail to comply with this required proposal or violate the provisions of an approved proposal shall be fined 1 million dollars per acre._

Position Paper Format

Introductory Paragraph: Three to five sentences introducing the group's position on the assigned topic.

Body: One to three paragraphs on the priorities from their point of view that the Senate Committee on the Environment should act on through legislation.

Conclusion: One paragraph on legislation or regulations the group would not agree with.

Group Poster

Brainstorm a slogan that best represents your group's policies and views about the environment.

Draw a poster for your group using the slogan and appropriate symbols and other visuals to explain your point of view.

 Global Learning, Inc.

Student Assessment

If students experience several of the activities in this book, what will they know about sustainable development?

The project that created these resources wanted the answer to this question and thus created an evaluation design consistent with current concerns for alternative assessment. Readers who want to know more about alternative assessment can see *Assessing Student Performance* by Grant P. Wiggins (San Francisco: Jossey-Bass Publishers, 1993).

Dr. Michael Knight, Director of Assessment of Student Learning and Development at Kean College of New Jersey, served as external evaluator and directed the process of creating and administering the student assessment. Step one was to have the teachers who field tested the activities and members of the project team identify *five major objectives* for students studying about sustainable development. The teachers then identified *four performance indicators* for each objective, ranging from level 1, students' needing opportunity for further development, to level 4, outstanding performance. Thirdly, *five student tasks* were identified as the vehicles for identifying the performance indicators. These materials were then submitted to several "experts in the field" for their critique and feedback as to both the sustainable development content and the process for assessing student mastery of the content. The original materials were then modified.

The design was administered to approximately 500 students in the Freehold Regional High School District in central New Jersey in the 1994-95 school year. The rangefinding process recommended by Educational Testing Service was used to initiate the sessions when student work was read. Each student performance was assessed by at least two examiners, and an inter-rater reliability was determined to be .826, indicating that the reviewers were consistent in their expectations of student performance and the application of the scoring rubric. The results of the post test were not available prior to the publication date, but the pre-test indicated quite clearly that most high school students do not have an understanding of sustainable development to any depth or breadth. What follows are the elements of that assessment design for the reader to adapt for your own use.

Sustainable Development Objectives

As a result of experiencing these sustainable development activities, students will be able to:

1. Define sustainable development and all related terms.
2. Apply the process goals of acquiring, processing and presenting information.
3. Within the problem solving context, describe and analyze the consequences of past decisions about sustainability at the local, national, and international levels and the possible effects of current decisions.
4. Determine the role of cultural and individual values and moral reasoning in environmental decision making and problem solving.
5. Analyze the role of self-interest and the relationship to sustainable development and implications for the environment.

Performance Indicators

Students' performance of the assessment tasks were scored on one of four performance levels. A level one performance means students need opportunity for further development. Level two is minimal competency, level three is average competency, and level four is outstanding competency.

Global Learning, Inc.

OBJECTIVE 1.	Define sustainable development and all related terms.
LEVEL FOUR Outstanding competency	Given several different examples of environmental problems, the student will be able to develop a definition of sustainable development, as well as to critique the "official" definition of sustainable development.
LEVEL THREE Average competency	Given a problem in sustainable development, the student will be able to provide examples of both sustainable and non- sustainable development.
LEVEL TWO Minimal competency	Given a problem in sustainable development, the student will be able to give examples of sustainable development.
LEVEL ONE Needs opportunity for further development	The student is able to provide a pre-defined example of sustainable development.

OBJECTIVE 2.	Apply the process goals of acquiring, processing and presenting information.
LEVEL FOUR Outstanding competency	Mastery of research mechanics; exhaustive use of resources, critical analysis, cross referencing, testing for truth, accurate presentation, creative, and enlightening.
LEVEL THREE Average competency	Proficient mechanics; use of all available resources, restructuring information, clear and informative presentation.
LEVEL TWO Minimal competency	Proficient use of basic mechanics; some primary and secondary sources as provided, combining information, accurate presentation.
LEVEL ONE Needs opportunity for further development	Needs direction to sources, especially primary sources; off topic, unclear, inaccurate.

OBJECTIVE 3.	Within the problem solving context, describe and analyze the consequences of past decisions about sustainability at the local, national, and international levels and the possible effects of current decisions.
LEVEL FOUR Outstanding competency	Student proposes and defends a creative or unique solution other than those presented.
LEVEL THREE Average competency	Student proposes logical alternatives and dependable solutions; provides more alternatives, clearer understanding of short and long term, positive and negative consequences.
LEVEL TWO Minimal competency	Student can work within the problem solving model and demonstrate minimal proficiency.
LEVEL ONE Needs opportunity for further development	Student is unable to apply the problem solving model.

OBJECTIVE 4.	Determine the role of cultural and individual values and moral reasoning in environmental decision making and problem solving.
LEVEL FOUR Outstanding competency	Student is able to argue and persuade from another cultural viewpoint with reasons for acceptance and rejection of other viewpoints; is able to withhold judgement.
LEVEL THREE Average competency	Student is aware of their[*] own cultural/ moral values, as well as alternative cultural perspectives; is able to support their own perspective.
LEVEL TWO Minimal competency	Student is aware of their own cultural and moral framework along with some alternate perspectives.
LEVEL ONE Needs opportunity for further development	Student is aware of their own cultural moral values or framework, but cannot accept individual responsibility necessary to work within the problem solving model.

* The plural form was chosen to avoid sexist or awkward language use.

Global Learning, Inc.

OBJECTIVE 5.	Analyze the role of self-interest and the relationship to sustainable development and implications for the environment.
LEVEL FOUR Outstanding competency	Student can evaluate a contemporary situation in terms of the impact of self-interest on sustainability.
LEVEL THREE Average competency	Student can compare and contrast differing self-interests to determine if they are compatible or conflicting.
LEVEL TWO Minimal competency	Student can list and describe various self-interests.
LEVEL ONE Needs opportunity for further development	Student cannot identify the self-interests of each group represented.

Assessment Tasks   The pretest for the project consisted of task number one. Each of the five items corresponds to the five sustainable development objectives. For a post test, teachers selected one of the five tasks to use with their students. In order to make sure that all five objectives were addressed, students were instructed to include the following items in their responses to whichever task was assigned:

1. A requirement for a definition of sustainable development.
2. Use of a problem solving approach.
3. Demonstration of the effects of past and current decisions regarding sustainable development.
4. Addressing the perspectives of varying cultures and roles.
5. Identifying the involvement of self-interest in decision-making.

Task 1

1. Define the term "sustainable development." Give some examples of both sustainable and non-sustainable development. What are the strengths of the sustainable development concept? What are some problems with it?
2. List and describe the steps you would take in identifying and solving an environmental problem.
3. Identify a governmental policy relating to a particular environmental issue. Describe the positive and negative consequences of this policy.

4. Consider the roles of cultural and individual values in making decisions about environmental issues. Choose an historical or current environmental conflict and identify at least three conflicting values expressed in this problem.

5. How did self-interest contribute to creating the problem identified in either question 3 or 4 and how might self-interest contribute to the solution?

Task 2 Assign, or have students select, a new economic/environmental problem with local implications. Have the students accumulate information on the problem, e.g., by reading news articles, research, or a visit from a local "expert." Assign several different roles for students to take on the issue, assuming different views of sustainable development. Assign writing an editorial or a speech or a letter to a local board or agency regarding this issue from a particular role.

Task 3 Conduct a United Nations Forum to propose an international protocol dealing with the disposal of nuclear waste. Divide the class into five groups to be experts in the following five perspectives of the problem: 1) local, 2) national, 3) international, 4) economic, or 5) technological. Students will develop a research report describing the current situations and alternatives to contribute to sustainable development.

Task 4 Select a pressing sustainable development issue or problem that occurs both locally and globally, e.g., water quality, toxic waste, air pollution etc. Prepare an extended response to the following questions:

1. What are the primary threats to the quality of the natural resources?

2. What is being done to preserve these resources for the future?

3. Describe several alternative approaches to preserving these resources.

Task 5 Using the electronic informational system in the media centers, students will research environmental disasters and/or individuals instrumental in contributing to environmental degradation, or individuals successful in bringing about a solution to such disasters. Students will complete any of the following tasks: 1) write biographies, 2) organize and present a research report, or 3) evaluate actions of individuals researched.

Conclusion A frequent observation made by those comparing standardized tests and alternative assessment is that the tests ask the student to "identify" the correct answer while the alternative approach requires the student to "create" the answer. This comparison clearly represents different levels and types of thinking. It might best be described by a quote from Wiggins:

> There is an inescapable tension between the challenges presented by contextualized performance and conventional bar scale generic testing....Understanding is not cued knowledge, performance is never the sum of drills, problems are not exercises, mastery is not achieved by the unthinking use of algorithms. We cannot be said to understand something, in other words, unless we can employ it wisely, fluently, flexibly and aptly in particular and diverse contexts. (p.207)

It is our hope that, as a result of participating in a number of learning activities from this book, students will thus "understand" *sustainable development*.

Acknowledgements

American Association of Retired Persons. *Modern Maturity.* Lakewood, CA, 1993.

Catton, Bruce. *The American Heritage Picture History of the Civil War.* New York: American Heritage Publishing Co., 1960.

Clearinghouse Bulletin, Carrying Capacity Network, 1325 G Street, NW, Washington, DC 20005.

Cleaveland, Alice Ann et al. *Universals of Culture.* New York: Global Perspectives in Education, 1979.

"Conversations With Oprah: Maya Angelou," *The Oprah Winfrey Show.* Chicago: Harpo Productions, Inc., July 13, 1993.

Coyle, Dana et al. *Deadly Defense: Military Radioactive Landfills.* New York: Radioactive Waste Campaign, 1988.

Douglas, George H. *All Aboard! The Railroad in American Life.* New York: Paragon House, 1992.

Dubois, Cara. *Wintu Ethnography.* Berkeley, CA: University of California Press, 1935.

Encyclopedia Americana, Vols. 15 and 23. Danbury, CT: Grolier Inc., 1994.

Esper, George, "Former Foes," New York: Associated Press, 9/12/94.

Finkelstein, Milton et al. *Minorities: USA.* New York: Globe Books, 1971.

Frank, Al. "OPEN ROAD." Newark, NJ: *The Star Ledger.* 11/20/93.

Greer, Colin. "The Well-Being of the World Is at Stake," New York: *Parade Magazine,* 1/24/94.

Heady, Earl O. "The Agriculture of the U.S.," *Scientific American.* September 1976.

Heiman, Michael. "Production confronts consumption," *Environment & Planning D: Society & Space,* Pion Limited, London, 1989, pp. 165-178.

The History of Picatinny Arsenal. Rockaway, NJ: Picatinny Arsenal, March 31, 1931.

History of Water Pollution Problems—Arsenal Streams. Rockaway, NJ: Picatinny Arsenal, 1944.

Holbrook, Stewart H. *The Story of American Railroads.* New York: Crown Publishers, 1947.

Global Learning, Inc.

Interstate Route 287 from U.S. Route 202, Montville, NJ to the New York Thruway, Suffern, NY, FINAL Environmental Impact Statement and Section 4(f) Evaluation, U.S. Department of Transportation Federal Highway Administration and New Jersey Department of Transportation. September 1982.

Johnson, James and J. Rosamond. *The Book of American Negro Spirituals.* New York: Viking Press, 1969.

Kaye, Seymour M. *Encyclopedia of Explosives and Related Items.* Patr 2700, Volume 8, Dover, NJ: US Army Armament Research and Development Command, 1978.

Knapp, George L. *North American Review,* 191 (1910).

Krehbiel, Henry Edward. *A Study in Racial and National Music: Afro-American Folk-Songs.* New York: Fredrick Ungar Publishing Co., 1962.

Lanier-Graham, Susan D. *The Ecology of War: Environmental Impacts of Weaponry and Warfare.* New York: Walker and Co., 1993.

Leighton, Tony. "Putting it All Together: Ten Trends in Corporate Environmentalism," *Tomorrow: The Global Environment Magazine.* Stockholm, Sweden: Vol. 2 No. 2, 1992.

Letto, Jay, "1872 Mining Law Meets 1993 Reform," reprinted with permission from *E: The Environmental Magazine,* September/October 1993. Subscriptions are $20/year from: E Magazine Subscriptions, P.O. Box 899, Mount Morris, IL 61054-7589 (800) 967-6572.

Lovell, John, Jr. *Black Song: The Forge and the Flame.* New York: Macmillan, 1972.

Marsh, George Perkins. *Man and Nature.* New York: Charles Scribners Sons, 1864.

"Military Nuclear Wastes: The Hidden Burden of the Nuclear Arms Race," *The Defense Monitor.* Washington, DC: Center for Defense Information, 1981.

Moneyhon, Carl H. "The Environmental Crisis and American Politics, 1860-1920," in Lester J. Bilsky, ed. *Historical Ecology: Essays on Environmental and Social Change,* Port Washington, NY: Kennikat Press, 1980.

Muir, John. *The Yosemite.* New York: Century, 1912.

"Nuclear Threat at Home," *The Defense Monitor.* Washington, DC: Center for Defense Information, 1994.

Opie, John (ed.). "Patterns of Environmentalism: The Reflective Environmentalist," *Environmental History Review.* Spring, 1992, vol. 16, pp.83-98.

Osby, Liv. "Bad Water Stirs Fears in Rockaway Township," Parsippany, NJ: *The Daily Record,* 2/13/91.

Roosevelt, Theodore. *Proceedings of a Conference of Governors in the White House.* Washington, D.C. Government Printing Office, 1909.

Segal, Charles M. et al. *Puritans, Indians and Manifest Destiny.* New York: G.P. Putnam's Sons, 1977.

Starr, Jerold M., ed. *The Lessons of the Vietnam War.* Center for Social Studies Education, 3857 Willow Avenue, Pittsburgh, PA 15234, 1991.

Stein, R. Conrad. *The Story of the Erie Canal.* Chicago: Childrens Press, 1985.

Steinbeck, John. *The Grapes of Wrath.* Copyright 1939, renewed (c) 1967 by John Steinbeck. Used by permission of Viking Penguin, a division of Penguin Books USA Inc., New York.

Straubing, Harold Elk, ed. *Civil War: Eyewitness Reports.* Hamden, CT: Archon Books, 1985.

Todd, John, *The Sunset Land.* Boston: Lee and Shepard, 1870.

"A Universal Environmental Ethic—The Ultimate Goal of Environmental Education, *Connect—the UNESCO-UNEP Environmental Education Newsletter.* 7 place de Fontenoy, 75352 Paris 07 SP, France; Vol. XVI, No. 2, June 1991.

US Environmental Protection Agency. "Fact Sheet, Picatinny Arsenal," New York: September 1993.

US Environmental Protection Agency. "Picatinny Arsenal, New Jersey, EPA ID# NJ3210020704," New York: February 1994.

Vallentyne, J.R. & A.M. Beeton.*The Ecosystem Approach to Managing Human Uses and Abuses of Natural Resources in the Great Lake Basin.* Great Lakes Laboratory for Fisheries and Aquatic Sciences, Department of Fisheries and Oceans, 1986. Reprinted with permission from E.D.I.T. File 10, *Environment First: The Idea of Sustainable Development.* Common Heritage Programme, 200 Isabella Street, Suite 300, Ottawa, Ontario, Canada K1S 1V7.

Wilson, George F. *European Settlers: Saints and Strangers.* New York: Raynel & Hitchcock, 1945.

Withuhn, William L., ed. *Rails Across America: A History of Railroads in North America.* New York: SMITHMARK Publishers, Inc. 1993.

Woyach, Robert B. et al., *Bringing a Global Perspective to American History.* Columbus, OH: Mershon Center, The Ohio State University, 1983.

Global Learning, Inc.